PANAMA CANAL DAY

PANAMA CANAL DAY

An Illustrated Guide to Cruising The Panama Canal

Richard Detrich

My special thanks to Bill Benny for reading the manuscript, offering suggestions, making corrections, and sharing the perspective of someone who lived in the U. S. Canal Zone and worked for the Panama Canal. Thanks to Ric Winstead who shared his experiences growing up in the U. S. Canal Zone. My thanks to Lorelei Gilmore for her assistance in preparing this manuscript.

Joining the World Together for Over 100 Years

Charcoal sketch by William B. Van Ingen creator of murals in the rotunda of the Panama Canal Headquarters building

Contents

Foreword

What astounds me every time I go through the Canal is that here is something that was built a hundred years ago, and it still works exactly the same way it was designed to work. We live in a throw-away society. How long does a toaster last? If you're lucky it may last one or two years. Every few years you dump your old computer and monitor. Your printer is broken? It's cheaper to throw it away and buy a new one, than try to fix it. But here is this engineering marvel, still working after a hundred years ... working twenty-four hours a day, 365 days a year.

When we owned travel agencies, we always gave clients who booked Panama Canal cruises a copy of David McCullough's definitive Panama Canal book, *The Path Between The Seas: The Creation of the Panama Canal 1870-1914*. It took me a while to realize that, although it is the definitive story of the Canal, it is also a long and heavily footnoted historical tome, so in many cases folks just stuck it on their book shelf. I had a captain once tell me, "Richard, I'm trying to read it, but I keep falling asleep." I told him to stick with it and once he got through the first 150 pages, he'd be hooked … and he was.

But since 1914, over a million ships have passed through the Canal, the Canal Zone has ceased to exist, and the Canal has been returned to the people of Panama. The Canal is being massively expanded, and even while the expansion is being completed, engineers of the Canal de Panamá are beginning plans for yet another expansion that will be able to accommodate the newest and largest class of container ships yet, ships that carry over 18 thousand containers.

I've always been amazed at how many cruise ships continue to play McCullough's video about the Canal … which was filmed on a Royal Viking ship. A lot has happened with the Panama Canal since Royal Viking went out of business in 1998.

Nothing against McCullough, who is one of my favorite historical writers, and who has written what is, unquestionably, the authoritative history of the United States building the Panama Canal, but Panama, the Canal, and the world have changed since 1914.

While lecturing on ships transiting the Canal, I realized that there was a need for a simpler and more current book, a book written for cruise passengers that included information about Panama as well as information about the Canal. I wanted to write a book that would be helpful to folks planning a Panama Canal trip, as well as serve as a guide during the voyage.

Unlike McCullough, who is a fantastic historian, I'm not a historian. My challenge is to take this enormous story and distill it down to an interesting tale, which will be a "page turner" for you, and will give you information that will make your day in the Canal more meaningful and memorable.

Panama Canal cruises offer a variety of itineraries, including a wide variety of ports, but the Canal is the centerpiece and the reason why people book a Panama Canal cruise. This book is about what is known on board ship as "Canal Day."

I had just completed a lecture in the show lounge on a ship scheduled to transit the Canal. After the talk, as I walked out of the lounge, I was behind two ladies, both in their early 60s, and I overhead one say to the other, "I didn't know the Canal was man made." Here these gals were, taking the "bucket list," trip-of-a-lifetime through one of the great wonders of the world, and they didn't have a clue!

The Q&A sessions on board ships are great fun ... except when I get questions like, "Is Panama like a territory of the United States?" The more you know about Panama and its unique place in the world, its complicated relationship with the United States, and the history of the Canal, the more you will enjoy your cruise between the oceans.

A good trip has three memorable parts: anticipating and planning, taking the trip, and reliving the experience when you get home. Reading this book will help you understand the history of Panama and its Canal, let you know what to expect, and, if you have a port call in Panama, know what there is to see and do. The Panama Canal is special, and I want you to fully enjoy and appreciate your voyage. And I hope the pictures help you anticipate the excitement of your "Canal Day!"

Canal Day with my daughter, Rebecca.

Out and about on deck in the Canal.

1. It's 4:30 a.m.

Since 4:00 a.m. people have been out on deck to capture the "best" spot for viewing the Panama Canal, almost as if lining up for tickets to a hot concert or the day-after-Thanksgiving sale at Walmart. The reality: there is no one "best" spot on the ship for Canal Day but folks will figure that out eventually.

Our ship arrived "on station" at about 4:00 a.m., just to be certain to be on time for the arrival of the Panama Canal authorities and pilot, scheduled to arrive at 5:00 a.m.

A junior officer on the bridge writes in the ship's log ...

4:18 a.m. contacted the pilot station to confirm an ETA of 5:00 a.m.

The cruise line reserved this slot to go through the Panama Canal years ago when it developed this year's itineraries. To reserve our "slot" the cruise line paid a preferential booking fee of $25,000, plus a daylight transit reservation fee of $30,000.

If we don't show up on the designated day, the Canal de Panamá, formerly know as Autoridad de Canal de Panamá or "ACP," just like the shore excursion office onboard, doesn't give any refunds, so we lose our money, pay all over again, and there goes the captain's bonus. If we show up late we pay a fifty to a hundred percent penalty. So we are on time.

Excitement is running high. Folks turned in early last night, leaving the nightclub almost deserted. Everyone set early morning wake up calls, determined not to miss a single moment of our passage between the oceans. Even on the bridge excitement is high. No matter how many times you have been through the Canal, it's hard to sleep the night before. Generally, I sense when the ship's engines shift and wake up almost automatically about 4:00 a.m.

It's 4:45 a.m. and, after a quick shower, I head to the bridge.

The bridge, like the engine room and communications center, is a secure area of the ship. There are reinforced doors, security protocols, and panic buttons with which to notify authorities in case of attack. Although cruising is all about fun and relaxation, behind the scenes it is all work in order to protect the fun and relaxation. In today's world a high level of security is essential.

The bridge has two "zones": "green" and "red." When the bridge is in "green zone," non-essential people and crew are allowed to phone and visit the bridge. Sometimes special VIP passengers or royal suite guests, are invited to the bridge, or crew members, and sometimes their family members, are allowed to visit. But when the bridge is in "red zone" only essential people and emergency phone calls are allowed.

As one, somewhat over-the-top, captain explained to me, "When the bridge is in 'red' it is like landing a fighter plane on an aircraft carrier: everyone needs to be totally focused." True and, yes, his bridge felt very focused … also quite uptight and super tense. It may have just been military training, seamanship, or potty training … who knows. But on most ships, being on the bridge is like being in a hospital operating theater where a group of skilled professionals are focused on doing what they do best. Folks are cool, confident, doing the job they do well, without any drama.

I've been through the Canal on ships where the captain was doing what everyone else on the ship was doing … taking pictures. Lest you worry, the ship was in the capable hands of the first officer, as is usually the case. But the Panama Canal requires that the captain be physically present on the bridge during the transit. I've also been on ships where the captain had ordered rock salt … just like you use for winter ice on the driveway … thrown all around the bridge. Apparently, this old Italian seafarer tradition was to guarantee good luck. And we needed good luck! On our world cruise the ship had been dead in the water three times, a fact which, conveniently, no one bothered to mention to the Canal authorities. It would not do to have a cruise ship dead in the water in the middle of the locks. So luck was with us and we made our transit with no problems. Thanks to the rock salt? Who knows?

I push the security button for access, hear the click, and step into an anteroom bathed in red light. Bridges are dark and the red-light anteroom keeps a bright swath of light from messing up the night vision of the guys and gals driving the ship. Most passengers don't realize it, but if you have a nighttime watch, known amongst crew as the "anti-social" watch, you show up on the bridge at least twenty minutes before your watch begins to allow your eyes to adjust to the darkness. I walk into the darkness of the bridge where, not having time to for my eyes to adjust, all I can make out are shadows of people, lots of people. It seems like the entire deck team are on the bridge this morning. This is one day everyone wants to experience, especially junior officers and deck cadets for whom this might be their first Canal transit.

"Morning Captain!"

Today will be an interesting day for the captain since he won't be the one calling the shots.

Usually pilots give the captains suggestions but not in the Panama Canal. The Panama Canal is the only place in the world where, if you want to use the Canal, the ship must be signed over to the Canal de Panamá and the Canal pilot is calling the shots. It's not easy for a captain to turn over control of a $350 million dollar ship, when, even although he's not calling the shots, if something goes wrong it's his reputation on the line.

"Good morning folks!" At this point, my eyes only just adjusting to the darkness, they are all just shadowy figures.

I scrounge around in the darkness for a flashlight and some spare batteries for the wireless microphone. It will be a long day. I feel around for a chair without accidentally feeling up a deck officer, and pull the chair up to the bridge window. Already I see the shadowy shapes of guests lining the foredecks.

My eyes now accustomed to the darkness, I walk out onto the open wing bridge to get a feel for the weather … and to inhale the muggy morning air of home. It already feels and smells like Panama. Although my home, up in the Chiriqui mountains near to the Costa Rican Border, is over six hours away, it is still good to be home in my adopted land.

Early morning on Canal Day is a magical time.

On southbound ships the clock is usually turned back the night before the Canal, so you end up with an extra hour of sleep to make up for the early morning wake up. A plus, I guess, for going south! Because Panama is about nine degrees north of the equator, there is very little variance, not only in temperature, but also in the time of sunrise and sunset. Generally in Panama the sun comes up around 6:30 a.m. and by 6:00 a.m. it's starting to get light.

Some ships make a big deal out of Panama Canal morning … setting out coffee and tea and even, on Holland America, serving a special treat called "Panama Canal Rolls." I've tried, without success, to find the claimed historical association of these treats, but they are "Dam[1]" good! To be out on the forward deck in the darkness, watching the ships from the nighttime convoy sail by, and experiencing all the activity as the sun comes up… is just plain magical!

It's 5:00 a.m. and Canal Day!

"Good morning! *Bienvenidos a Panamá* and welcome to the Panama Canal! And it's going to be a beautiful day as we make our way across what has been called 'the path between the seas.'

"Since I now live in Panama, for me to be able to guide you through the Canal is a great pleasure. I still get excited every time I do this, which is why I didn't sleep very well last night.

"You'll notice all of the ships anchored out here. Generally there are twenty to thirty ships waiting to get through the Canal. The number of ships waiting is a good indication of the state of the world's economy. A few years ago some ships were sitting out here waiting for up to five weeks to get through the Canal. Now, with the world's financial crises, Canal traffic is off a bit, although the profits are up due to increased tolls.

"If you want to go through the Canal, you don't just show up. The Canal works on a slotting system. The Canal can handle forty ships a day, and there are usually more ships wanting to pass through the Canal than the Canal can accommodate.

"In good economic times there are usually about sixty ships waiting, thirty ships on each side. If there is maintenance going on in one of the lock chambers the line can be longer."

For much of the day, I will be on the bridge, microphone in hand, explaining what is happening, and pointing out various features of the Canal. Since I've already been lecturing on this cruise, most of our guests have a pretty good idea of the history of Panama, how the Canal works, and its significance as the crossroad of world trade.

A ship sailing from New York to San Francisco via the Canal travels 6,000 miles [9,656 kilometers], well under half the

The last of the nighttime convoy of ships.

Control Central – Marine Traffic Control.

distance of the 14,000 miles [22,531 kilometers] around Cape Horn, if the ship didn't use the Canal.

A ship sailing from New York to San Francisco via the Canal travels 6,000 miles [9,656 kilometers], well under half the distance of the 14,000 miles [22,531 kilometers] around Cape Horn, if the ship didn't use the Canal.

Assume you're a toy manufacturer in China and have a container of toys going to Walmart, toys you need to get to Houston or New York, to have on the shelves by some upcoming holiday. Losing a few days waiting to get through the Canal is a long time! But the alternatives are traveling around the tip of South America or trying to get your container into Los Angeles harbor, where there is an enormous bottleneck. Once in Los Angeles, your container would need to be trucked or shipped by rail across the United States. So it's worth a little wait to get through the Canal.

Over a million ships have transited the Canal since it was opened in 1914.

One hundred years ago when the Canal was built, the demands were far different than they are today. There are only three locks, each with two "lanes" ... and the process takes as long as it takes. Although there has been continuing improvement and widening of the Canal, there are now many ships that are just too large to fit through the Canal. All of this has led to the "amplification" or expansion of the Canal, in order to widen the choke-point areas and install a "third lane" of new locks. As you make your way through the Canal you will see a lot of work going on for the Canal expansion, originally scheduled to be completed in 2014 for the 100th Anniversary of the Panama Canal. The enormity of the expansion project has created some delay, and, if all goes well, the new locks are now scheduled to be opened in 2016.

With all these ships waiting, how do we go to the front? First, we reserved our spot for a daylight transit paying $55,000 for the privilege. This works well for cruise ships since we know exactly when we are going to be at the entrance to the Canal. It doesn't work for many other ships that may be delayed along the way, or have to pick up, or drop off cargo. For them it's often not only cheaper, but also more efficient, to wait a few days in order to get a slot to pass through the Canal. During that wait … you just sit there and wait. No shore leave for the crew.

Second, the Canal gives preference to passenger ships with fifty or more passengers. Every ship entering the Canal is given an identification code "N" for northbound or "S" for southbound. Following the directional letter is a schedule number, odd numbers for northbound transits and even numbers for southbound transits. Passenger ships are given the "zulu" preferential identification.

If the ship were making a southbound transit, the identification would be something like "Zulu Eight," meaning it is a passenger ship, a preferential vessel, and the eighth ship of the day making the southbound transit. If it were a northbound transit, it would have an odd number, like "Zulu Seven."

Flags Flying

If you look at the flags flying on our ship you will see the cruise line's house flag, the flag of the country where the ship is registered, which in our case just happens to be the flag of Panama because, like many of the world's ships, our ship is registered in Panama. There is also a red and white flag called "hotel," the flag for the letter "H" but also the maritime signal for, "I have a pilot on board." If it is a southbound transit below the hotel flag will be flags giving the identification number, or, if it is a northbound transit the numbers will be above the hotel flag. Since our ship is a passenger vessel and preferential ship, the "zulu" flag, or flag for the letter "Z', will fly along with the identification number.

Waiting for the pilot to climb on board.

First officer, pilot, captain, Canal official on the Bridge

A ship flying a red pendant or "bravo" flag means the vessel is carrying flammable or explosive material. In the Canal a ship flying the "tango" flag, with vertical red, white, and blue stripes, means it carries toxic or radioactive material. A ship awaiting a pilot will fly the "golf" flag, with vertical blue and yellow stripes.

How much?

The Panama Canal takes cash only. No credit. No credit cards. And the check must have cleared, with the cash in the Canal de Panamá account, before you get in the line … so, no toll booth. The ship's agent handles the transaction and wires the cash into the Panama Canal's account.

Tolls for the Canal are decided by the Panama Canal Authority, now known as the Canal de Panamá, and are based on vessel type, size, and the cargo carried. Large passenger vessels are charged per passenger berth. The current rate is $134 per berth, so with a 3,070 berths, our toll is $411,380.[2] That's our toll. If you think of an airline ticket, the toll is like the cost of the ticket. But then you have ... all the fees. In addition to the toll, somewhat like going into an a la carte restaurant, you pay extra for each tug boat, each mule, each inspection, etc.

Tug boats, $11,445, line handlers $4,745, a fee for this, fee for that … so it adds up quickly.

My estimate for our hypothetical ship …

Toll $411,380
Fees around $76,802
The total? Somewhere around $488,182 … give or take a few thousand.

But what's money among friends? With fees, we're paying around $159 per berth. With 2,120 paying passengers, it's about $230 per guest.

Cha-ching! The Canal makes a direct contribution to Panama, not just an economic contribution, but a direct check to the government each year, of about $981 million per year. In a country of 3.7 million people that's significant. So thank you for your business! But in all fairness, cruise ships account for only about 8.9 percent of Canal revenue.

We are a Panamax[3] ship or one of the largest ships that can transit the Canal. Ships that are too large to pass through the current Canal are called Post-Panamax ships.

A Panamax vessel, such as our ship, usually requires up to 22 line handlers, 6 to 8 locomotives, half at the bow and half at the stern, and 2 tugs to assist the vessel. One pilot will remain on the bridge at all times, moving between the wheel room and to either wing bridge to call out instructions, "full ahead," "ahead one-third," "amidships," etc. The other pilot will move about the vessel from bow to stern, port to starboard, keeping watch on the ship's progress. Generally a ship like ours will use 2 pilots, but some ships may have 3 pilots.

The pilot who takes a Panamax ship through the Canal is a senior pilot, generally with about ten years experience. A Panama Canal pilot has one of the highest paying jobs in Panama.

The lowest toll ever paid was thirty-six cents, paid by Richard Halliburton for swimming the Canal in 1928. Richard Halliburton was an adventurer and author who in the '30s made headlines with his adventures.

The bridge has ordered one of the shell doors on the hull to be opened, and a ladder dropped alongside. A number of small boats will approach the ship and the officials will board, including Canal officials, immigration officials, inspection officers, the ship's agent, and the Canal pilots. All will have to climb up the ladder to board the ship.

In the Panama Canal the pilot is in charge.

My neighbor in Panama is a woman by the name of Sarah Terry, who was the first U. S. woman to get her master's license and the first woman Panama Canal pilot. Sarah says that at the beginning a woman pilot was often a surprise. The most important thing, according to Sarah, was to establish your "command presence." Not every captain is eager to relinquish control ... and in those early days, certainly not to a woman. The pilot is a licensed captain, with a master's license. During the Canal transit, although the captain must physically be on the bridge, the Canal pilot will be in charge. "The pilot assigned to a vessel shall have control of the navigation and movement of such a vessel." But if something goes wrong ... it's the captain who has to explain to the home office.

The pilot gives the instruction to the captain who, preserving the chain of command, relays the pilot's instructions to his crew members, who then perform the proper maneuver. To make sure everyone understands the instruction, the instruction is repeated. When I am narrating a voyage through the Canal from the bridge, there is often a lot of background "chatter" as orders are given, and repeated for confirmation.

If the captain doesn't like taking orders from the pilot, there is always the long way around the southern tip of South America.

The pilot climbs aboard carrying what traditionally known as the "orange box," a computer hookup to Marine Traffic Control. Marine Traffic Control is a heavily secured, small building away from the shores of the Canal, and controls the movement of all ships in Canal waters. Marine Traffic Control slots ships for passage, assigns Canal pilots, and monitors all ships in Canal waters. Marine Traffic Control has television screens that show movement in the Canal and in the locks. The public can view Web cams of ships in the locks at PanCanal.com.

INTERNATIONAL FLAGS AND PENNANTS

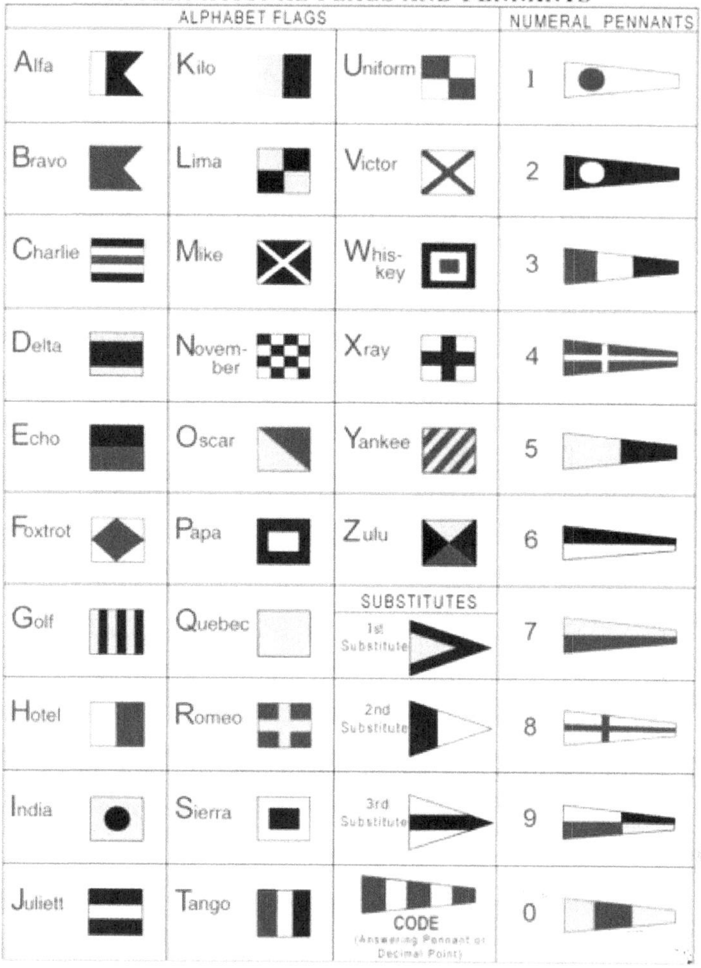

ALPHABET FLAGS			NUMERAL PENNANTS
Alfa	Kilo	Uniform	1
Bravo	Lima	Victor	2
Charlie	Mike	Whis-key	3
Delta	Novem-ber	Xray	4
Echo	Oscar	Yankee	5
Foxtrot	Papa	Zulu	6
		SUBSTITUTES	
Golf	Quebec	1st Substitute	7
Hotel	Romeo	2nd Substitute	8
India	Sierra	3rd Substitute	9
Juliett	Tango	CODE (Answering Pennant or Decimal Point)	0

The pilot climbs aboard carrying what traditionally known as the "orange box," a computer hookup to Marine Traffic Control. Marine Traffic Control is a heavily secured, small building away from the shores of the Canal, and controls the movement of all ships in Canal waters. Marine Traffic Control slots ships for passage, assigns Canal pilots, and monitors all ships in Canal waters. Marine Traffic Control has television screens that show movement in the Canal and in the locks. The public can view Web cams of ships in the locks at PanCanal.com.

Sarah Terry retired about the time of the Canal turnover. She began her Canal career as captain of one of the tugs, became a Canal pilot, a senior pilot and finally a port captain. There are two port captains on duty who control the Canal, one in Panama City and the other in Colon.

A ship cadet writes in the logbook ...

5:04 a.m. -- The first set of pilots were boarded.

"Pilot on board."

"Pilot on board" is automatically repeated, to acknowledge the order or information.

The pilot is escorted to the bridge by ship security along with the Canal inspection officers and a Canal computer technician.

"Morning Captain!"

There are introductions and offers of coffee. The Canal computers are set up and connections with Marine Traffic Control are established. A Canal inspection officer is quickly running through a checklist.

Since this is a regular run for our ship at this time of year, the Canal folks already know the ship. If it was our first time in the Panama Canal, or if the ship had any modifications since the last time it was in the Canal, the inspection officer may

The "orange box" amongst other things gives the distance to the lock.

First shot of the day.

have some questions or may even want to see the plans. He gets an update on the status of the engines and bow thrusters, any problems the ship may be having: all is in order. He may want to flash some lights, or toot the horn as a perfunctory check, but we are good to go.

Down in the purser's office, the "PRACTICA," or port paper officer ["PPO"], is with the ship's agent, Panama immigration and inspection officers along with other officials who are sitting around drinking coffee, munching breakfast pastries, reviewing, stamping, and signing a three-inch high stack of papers, declarations, and documents. There are lists of passengers and crew, all of which has been previously conveyed to Panamanian authorities in advance via computer. This being Panama, there is a lot of rubber stamping going on.

The authorities want to know if anyone is in quarantine, or if there are any medical emergencies to be offloaded. This morning two of our crew members are quarantined to their cabins for thirty-six hours for suspected norovirus and four guests are quarantined for the same reason, below one percent, and well below any cause for concern.

One guest is scheduled to be disembarked with a ship's agent due to the concerns about an arrhythmia, which the senior doctor feels needs to be evaluated ashore, and frankly, because it is the cruise line's policy is to get people with questionable medical conditions off the ship as soon as possible.

Also, having completed my pre-Canal lectures, and after giving my Canal transit commentary, I am all packed, ready to climb down the ladder, and leave with the pilot at the other end of the Canal. It's a unique and different experience as your luggage is heaved to a tiny boat and you climb down the ladder!

I go back home to my wife, dogs, and coffee farm high in the Chiriqui mountains of Panama, just outside the little town of Boquete. The Canal pilots always find this interesting since

Boquete is a favorite vacation destination of folks living in Panama City. In fact we sell the coffee we raise on our farm to one of the Panama Canal pilots who has a farm and coffee processing facility down the road.[4]

The Isthmus of Panama, home to the Republic of Panama, is a little squiggle that joins the continents of North and South America. At 28,702 square miles [74,338 square kilometers], the Republic of Panama is little smaller than South Carolina. Panama has 1,547 miles [2,490 kilometers] of coastline on both the Atlantic Ocean [Caribbean Sea] and Pacific Ocean. The highest point is Volcán Baru, 11,398 feet [3,474 meters], the mountain where I live.

Panama runs east to west, with the western border being with Costa Rica, and the eastern border with Colombia. Because the Isthmus joins North and South America many people wrongly assume the country runs north to south. The Panama Canal, although facilitating transits between east and west, actually runs north to south.

Since the introduction of lighting in 1963, the Canal operates twenty-four hours a day, 365 days a year and is bi-directional, that is with ships moving in both directions, with a maximum of 14,600 ships a year. The Canal has carefully worked out scenarios to get the maximum traffic through the Canal, and so during the night they usually run a north and south convoy of ships, entering opposite ends at roughly the same time, passing one another in the middle, and exiting in the early morning. So the ships we see slowly passing in the early morning hours are part of the convoy that went through the Canal during the night.

From beginning to end the Canal is 50 miles [80.5 kilometers]. It is going to be a long day. Usually, even with priority status, it takes ten to twelve hours for a cruise ship to make the transit, assuming no major delays en route.

Captain and pilot on bridge. Panama Canal requires that the captain be present on the bridge at all times.

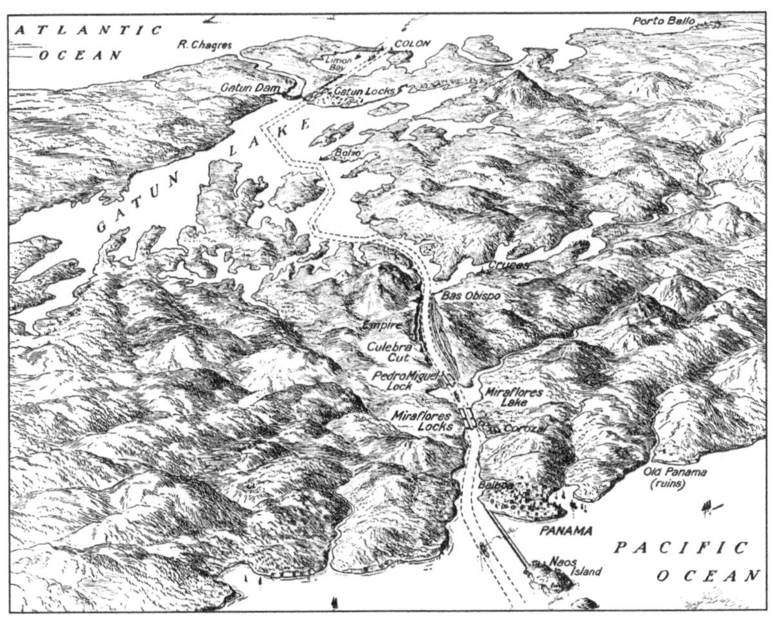

2. The Bridge of Life

The more you know about the unique place of Panama, its context in the history of the New World, and the history and role of the Canal, the better you will enjoy your voyage through the Canal.

Twenty million years ago there was no Panama.

The oceans covered what today is Panama and the gap between the continents allowed waters of the Atlantic and Pacific oceans to flow freely. There was no connection between the North and South American continents. But beneath the surface of these oceans two tectonic plates of the Earth's crust were slowly colliding into one another, forcing the Pacific Plate to slide slowly under the Caribbean Plate. The pressure and heat caused by this collision led to the formation of underwater volcanoes.

These underwater or submarine volcanoes continued to erupt as the tectonic plates moved until somewhere around fifteen million years ago, the volcanoes pushed through the surface and islands began to emerge. Over millions more years, ocean sediment, sand, mud, and soil, began building up around the volcanic islands and eventually filled in the space between the islands. If you've ever visited a mangrove forest along the ocean shore you've seen a similar process at work, as shells, mud, and sediment is trapped by the mangrove forest's extensive root system and additional frontage is slowly created.

By about three million years ago, an isthmus had formed between North and South America. Scientists believe the formation of the Isthmus of Panama is one of the most important geologic events to happen on Earth in the last sixty million years.

The Isthmus of Panama became the great bridge of life, linking the continents together, and playing a major role in the biodiversity of our world.

The bridge made it easier for animals and plants to migrate between the continents. So in North America the opossum, armadillo, and porcupine all trace back to ancestors that came across the land bridge *from* South America, and ancestors of bears, cats, dogs, horses, llamas, and raccoons all made the trek *to* South America across the Isthmus

Panama City's new museum, "Panama: Bridge of Life," is a celebration of this biodiversity and the important role of the Isthmus of Panama in creating the world as we know it. The museum was designed by Frank Gehry who also designed the Experience Music project in Seattle and the Walt Disney Concert Hall in Los Angeles. How did Panama get this world-renowned architect? Simple, his wife is Panamanian.

Scientists have different theories about how the migration of people occurred from Asia to the Americas, but the general consensus is that the Indigenous people inhabiting the Americas made their way from Asia, either via land bridges or by sea along the coast. Regardless, the great bridge of life formed by the Isthmus of Panama allowed people to migrate between the continents. By the time the Europeans and Columbus "discovered" the Americas, there were highly developed civilizations in the Americas, particularly in Central and South America.

A Changing World and the Age of European Discovery

During the "Late Middle Ages" in Europe, a period of history roughly from the 14th to the 16th century, Europe was undergoing major changes. People were gravitating to cities and with the growth of cities a new merchant or middle class was emerging. As cities grew, and grew without basic sanitation, Europe was ripe for the bubonic plague that swept across Europe. The plague epidemic has been described as the worst human disaster in European history.

Prior to the plague the focus of life was religion, evidenced by the fact that European towns and cities arose around great cathedrals. But during the plague everyone died. It made no difference if you were the worst sinner in town or the priest, everyone died. After the plague Europeans began looking beyond the constrictions of faith and the promise of the hereafter.

People developed an interest in the world around them, an interest which would ultimately flower in both the Renaissance and the European Age of Discovery.

A growing merchant and middle class created demand for luxuries and the finer things in life, things like spices, silks, ivory, and other luxury goods, most of which came from the Far East. The "Silk Road" developed, not a well-marked Interstate, but a loose trail of villages and oases along the way between the Far East and the Mediterranean. Many of these treasures arrived in the thriving Republic of Venice, from which goods were shipped across Europe. One of the most famous Venetians was Marco Polo, an explorer, exporter, importer, and first travel writer. When Polo returned from seventeen years in Mongolia, he electrified Europe with the tales of his adventures.

Turkish conquests along the Eastern Mediterranean eventually disrupted the flow of goods from the Far East to Europe and spurred European exploration, as the primary powers of the day, Spain, Portugal, Italy, Holland, and Britain, all sought alternate routes to the Far East.

Henry the Navigator pushed Portuguese exploration along the Western coast of Africa. He was followed by Bartolomeu Dias who managed to push all the way to what is today the Cape of Good Hope.

The idea that the world was round had been around since the Greeks, and by the Late Middle Ages, most of Europe accepted the idea of a spherical Earth. So logic dictated that there should be a way to the riches of the Far East by sailing west. Christopher Columbus was an Italian who managed to sell the Spanish crown on supporting his expeditions to find a path to the riches of the East by sailing west.

Columbus would make four voyages to the "New World" over a ten year period. On his first and most famous voyage, in 1492, he reached the Bahamian island of San Salvador, and then explored along the coasts of Cuba and Hispaniola. Columbus returned to Spain believing that he had discovered the outer islands of India, a belief he held throughout his life. Believing he was in India, Columbus called the islands the "West Indies" and the Indigenous people he met, "Indians."

On his fourth and final voyage, 1502 to 1504, Columbus sailed along the Caribbean coast of Central America visiting what are today Honduras, Nicaragua, and Costa Rica, before dropping anchor in October 1502 in Almirante Bay, located in the archipelago of Bocas del Toro, Panama.

Now convinced he was actually in the Far East, Columbus sailed through a channel between the islands thinking it was the channel he would need to reach China and India. Columbus and his accompanying caravels sailed into what is today known as the Chiriqui Lagoon.

Columbus went ashore meeting the Guaymí or Ngöbe Indigenous people and trading for more gold objects. Columbus remained for ten days gathering as much information as possible. He heard the Indians speak of a great sea on the other side of the cordillera, and another land called

Columbus takes possession of the New World for Spain.

Columbus trading with the Indigenous of Panama

Chiriqui, which Columbus assumed was India.

Setting out to explore the area, Columbus came upon natives wearing large gold medallions. Columbus was able to trade small bells to the natives in return for the gold medallions. Examining the medallions, Columbus realized that, unlike gold items from previous landings, these were not made of a gold alloy but of pure, solid gold.

Columbus continued sailing Eastward following the coast of Panama along the Mosquito Gulf, stopping along the way looking for areas the Indians in Bocas had said were rich in gold. Columbus managed to trade more bells for gold, but increasingly found natives who were openly hostile. He sailed on intending to return to explore further and find the gold mines. Along the way they were hit by a storm and forced past Limon Bay, and put into a natural harbor which Columbus named Puerto Bello. They stayed for a week and then set sail, pushing around Manzanillo Point and anchored near Nombre de Dios, where Columbus remained for twelve days making repairs to his ships.

In mid December 1502, Columbus explored a harbor area on a river he called The River of the Alligators. He named the harbor Puerto Gordo, now Limon Bay and the Atlantic entrance to the Panama Canal. Columbus noted in his charts that the bay was large enough to accommodate all the ships in the world.

He succeeded in exploring the area around Veragua. His men reached the area where the natives obtained their gold, and were able to extract gold using only their knives. Columbus decided to build a settlement at the mine and return to Spain for reinforcements. He sent his younger brother, Bartholomew Colón, and fifty-four men, to build a settlement, called Santa María de Belén. The Indians, who had previously been hospitable, noting that the Spaniards weren't just visiting, but planning to stay, became hostile, and Columbus was forced to abandon the settlement and retreat.

Mid-April, with only three of his five ships remaining, and those badly leaking from shipworm, Columbus headed for

Cuba. Columbus' primary purpose was not to trade or collect gold, but to demonstrate the potential of the region. He succeeded in demonstrating that, China or no China, here was a source of wealth beyond imagination. Under orders to deal peacefully with the local inhabitants, Columbus for the most part succeeded.

Of the Indigenous peoples who lived in Panama when Columbus arrived, several of those groups still exist. One of the most powerful and numerous today are the Guaymí or Ngäbe-Buglé, the only Indigenous never subjugated by the Spanish.

The Spaniard who would most influence the future of Panama hardly looked the part initially. Born of a noble family and inspired by the discoveries of Columbus, Vasco Núñez de Balboa joined an expedition to the New World led by Rodrigo de Bastidas. After three years Balboa elected to remain on the island of Hispaniola and became a planter and pig farmer.

By the age of 34, he had failed as a farmer, was deeply in debt, and to escape his creditors he stowed away on a ship bound for Panama, hiding inside a barrel together with his dog. He was eventually found out, but befriended by the crew and eventually came to the attention of the leader of the expedition, Francisco Pizarro. Because Balboa had explored part of Panama earlier with Bastidas and knew something of the area, he gained the trust of Pizzaro. Pizzaro left Balboa in Panama to found the first permanent settlement on the mainland American soil in September 1510, named Santa María la Antigua del Darién.

Balboa went on to become Governor of Veraguas and with the governorship gained absolute authority. Balboa acquired new territory and lots of gold, most of it taken by force. The Spanish conquistadores had a reputation for brutality, but even amongst them, Balboa was unbelievably cruel.

Friar Bartolomé de las Casas was a conquistador who later repented of his actions and became a priest. He was so

"Balboa Setting Dogs on The Practitioners of Male Love", 1594

Balboa was caught up in a power struggle with his father-in-law who had replaced Balboa as governor. Arrested by Pizarro and hastily tried and convicted, Balboa was decapitated in 1519. It took the executioner three swings to sever Balboa's head.

appalled by the abuse he saw heaped upon the Indians in the Americas that he wrote "A Short Account of the Destruction of the Indies" and sent it to Phillip II of Spain in 1552. Forty years after his death, it was published in part as *"Apologética Historia,"* but never published in full until 1909. Friar de las Casas viewed Indians as "noble savages" and thought that the answer to enslaving the Indigenous in the Americas, would be to import black Africans as slaves.

Hearing the same Indian tales of a southern sea that piqued the interest of Columbus, and eager to expand his territory and obtain additional gold, Balboa set out to slog across the Isthmus in search of a southern sea. On September 1, 1513, along with 190 Spaniards, all dressed in woolen underwear, leather britches, and steel armor, accompanied by a few native guides and a pack of dogs, Balboa set forth. On September 29, Balboa stepped into what is today the Pacific Ocean, named it the South Sea and claimed it for Spain.

Balboa is viewed as somewhat of a heroic figure in Panama, with the official name of Panamanian currency being the "Balboa," although it is in fact the U. S. dollar. Not only did he establish the first permanent settlement on the mainland of the Americas, which didn't last long, but Balboa was the first European to see what he called the "South Sea," later renamed the Pacific by Magellan.

The Spanish conquest and occupation of the New World was ostensibly to increase trade and spread the Catholic faith, but perhaps just as importantly, to rape, plunder and pillage.

The wealth that Spain took home from the Americas far exceeded anything they could have obtained had Columbus found a secret passage to the Far East

For almost four centuries Spain controlled most of the Americas, with the exception of Canada and the Northeastern portion of what is today the United States, which went to England, and Brazil, which went to Portugal.

Eventually Spain would rule its New World colonial empire through three Viceroyalties. The Viceroys ruled as direct representatives of the Spanish crown.

The administration was divided into:

- The Viceroyalty of New Spain 1535 which originally included everything north of the Southern border of Costa Rica, including most of what are today the Western U. S. states, Cuba, Hispaniola, Puerto Rico, Jamaica, the Philippines, originally Venezuela and even parts of British Columbia and Alaska [Mexico City];
- The Viceroyalty of Peru 1542 which originally included most of Spanish-ruled South America[Lima];
- Viceroyalty of New Granada 1717 which included modern Colombia, Ecuador, Panama, Venezuela, Guyana, and parts of Suriname, Brazil, Costa Rica and Nicaragua [Bogota].

Royal Audience of Panama [1538] was a supreme court of appeals for Panama and all of northern South America. It was closed and reinstated several times before it was closed in 1751 and responsibilities shifted to Bogota.

Balboa, at his most heroic, claiming and naming the "South Sea" for Spain.

3. New Granada

To fully appreciate Panama and the Canal it is necessary to understand a little about Panama and its history, first as a colony of Spain, later as part of Gran Colombia, and eventually in the mid 18th as a part of New Granada.

The first European to visit Panama was not Christopher Columbus, but Rodrigo de Bastidas, a Spaniard, who mapped the Atlantic coast of Panama in 1501. But the first European to explore Panama was Christopher Columbus, who visited Panama on his fourth voyage. Columbus wasn't big on naming everything he saw, instead giving a lot of areas general names. But sometimes, as was the case with two stops in Panama, he did give names. In 1502 to escape a storm he sailed into what he called "a beautiful port" which became Portobelo. Sailing on he arrived tired and discouraged in a natural harbor further east on the Isthmus and reportedly said to his crew, "in the name of God we will go no further," hence the name Nombre De Dios.

The Richest City in the World

Other Spanish conquistadores would follow including Vasco Núñez de Balboa and Francisco Pizzaro. Panama was the base for Pizzaro's explorations of the western coast of South America and the European discovery, exploitation, and development of Peru.

Nobody is quite sure how the name "Panama" came about. There are theories the name came from an Indigenous word for "abundance." Some say it referred to the abundant of species of trees, or abundant butterflies, or the abundance of fish. The Ministry of Education in Panama takes a safe stance claiming that it means "abundance of fish, trees and butterflies." But "abundance" of natural resources and beauty seems a common, and appropriate, theme for Panama.

The Isthmus of Panama, although tiny in comparison to other New World territories, became one of the crown jewels in the Spanish New World empire.

Over the years Panama City, Portobelo, and Nombre de Dios became strategic centers to collecting and transporting tons of gold, silver, hides, tropical woods, and precious stones from the New World to Spain. The amount of treasure brought back from the New World to Spain dwarfed anything that Spain would have gained had Columbus been successful in finding a path to India and the riches of the Far East.

Panama City was founded in 1519. By 1670 it had ten thousand inhabitants and was the richest city in the world, because all of the gold and silver from Peru had to pass through Panama City. From there it was carried by mule train across the Isthmus of Panama and stored in the Treasure House at Portobelo, awaiting the arrival of the Spanish Treasure Fleet that would take all the loot back to Spain.

In 1538 the Royal Audiencia of Panama was established in Panama City. The Audiencia functioned as a kind of royal court, with jurisdiction from Nicaragua to the tip of South America. With Panama as a center of Spanish Royal administration, as well as the storage and transfer point of New World treasure back to Spain, Panama gained strategic and political importance within the Spanish Empire.

By the 18th century power was shifting. Spain's power was dwindling in Europe and Panama's influence was lessening. It was possible to navigate around Cape Horn to reach the Pacific and while the route across Panama was shorter, it was also labor intensive and risky. When the Spanish attempted to colonize Panama, many of the Indigenous simply fled into the impenetrable jungle, so it was necessary for Spain to import slaves from Africa to do the work, many of whom just escaped into the jungles. African slaves who escaped into the jungle, known as *cimarrones,* would attack the mule trains laden down with treasure as they made their way through the jungles. And on the both coasts there was always the fear of attack by pirates and British and Dutch privateers like Henry Morgan, Francis Drake, and Piet Hein.

Other European powers attempted to take advantage of Spain's dwindling power by trying to seize Spanish territory in the New World. Although the Spanish had various small settlements along the northern coast of what is today Colombia, the first settlement at Santa Marta was not established until 1525, six years after Panama City.

In 1713 the Viceroyalty of New Granada was established in Bogota and given responsibility for most Spanish territory in northern South America. In 1751 the Audencia in Panama was finally closed and responsibilities shifted to the Viceroyalty of New Granada. Panama took offence at this change creating a long-lasting tension between Panama and Bogota.

The End of the Spanish Empire

The 19th century brought major changes, including the collapse of the Spanish empire. In Europe Spain briefly aligned with the French in the Napoleonic Wars, causing Britain to blockade Spain. Defeated at Trafalgar in 1805, Napoleon tried to attack Britain economically with an alliance of European nations known as the Continental System or Continental Blockade in which members embargoed trade with Britain.

The embargo was largely a failure because Britain retained control of the seas and smuggling was rife. Portugal not only refused to join the Continental Blockade, but openly aligned with Britain. Frustrated, Napoleon decided to invade

Simón Bolivar, liberator of Latin America and President of Gran Colombia.

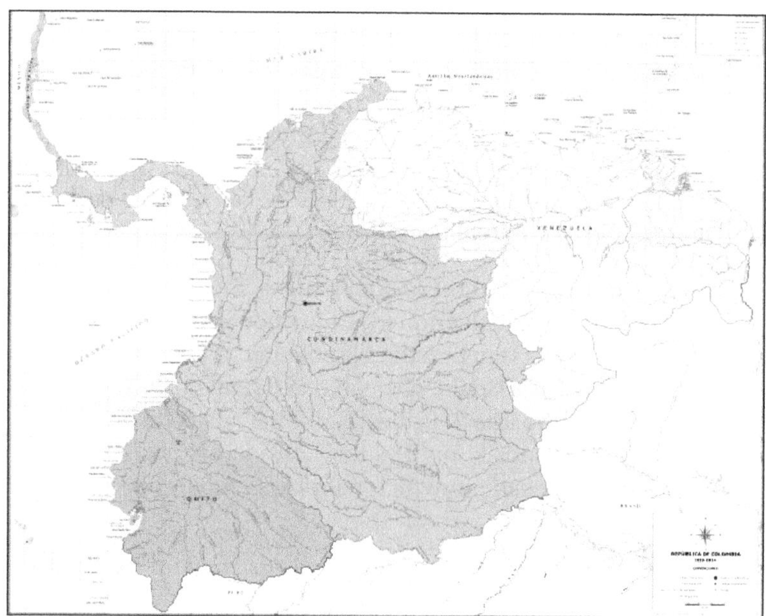

Gran Colombia 1820.[5]

Portugal and, along the way, take Spain as well. In 1808 Napoleon deposed Ferdinand VII, installing in his place his eldest brother, Joseph Bonaparte, as King of Spain. Almost immediately Spain was in rebellion with insurrection against the French with guerrilla warfare across Spain.

Aided by the British and Portuguese and led by the Duke of Wellington, who would later go on to decisively defeat Napoleon at the Battle of Waterloo, largely Spanish guerrilla forces fought the forces of Napoleon and King Bonaparte in the Peninsula War [1807-1814]. Some historians have given that brutal war the dubious distinction of being the first national war and the first guerrilla war.

Between 1806 and 1807, taking advantage of Spanish preoccupation in Europe, the British attempted unsuccessfully to invade and seize control of Spanish colonies in and around what is today Argentina and Uruguay.

All of this had far reaching consequences for the Spanish possessions in the Americas, already chafing under Spain's heavy-handed rule and yearning for independence. The defeat of Napoleon at Waterloo provided striking evidence that traditional armies, no matter how large and sophisticated, could be defeated. Guerilla warfare was shown to be an effective way to attack even the most powerful armies.

Eventually the French were forced out of Spain and the Constitution of 1812 was drafted. Amongst other liberal provisions, the Constitution of 1812 eliminated all discrimination in the American colonies between Spaniards who were born in Spain and those Spanish citizens that happened to be born in the colonies of New Spain.

Ferdinand VII, living in exile, believed the Constitution of 1812 too liberal for Spain, and when he returned to Spain in 1814, he refused to swear to uphold the new Constitution, continuing to rule in the autocratic tradition of the Kings of Spain. Spaniards on the mainland reluctantly accepted the King's decision, but those in the New World did not, and revolution broke out in Spanish colonies in 1820.

Near bankruptcy as a result of the war with France, Spain was forced to sell Florida to the United States for five million dollars. In 1820 an expedition intended to show Spanish sovereignty in the colonies, revolted in Cadiz, and armies across Spain acting in sympathy, forced the King to relent and accept the Constitution of 1812, and eventually placed the King under house arrest.

The Great Liberator

A new heroic leader emerged in Venezuela. Simón Bolivar was an unlikely candidate to become the Great Liberator of Latin America. He was born with a silver, or perhaps in his case, a copper, spoon in his mouth. He came from a wealthy family with extensive land holdings, silver and gold mines, and most importantly, extensive copper mines. It was the wealth of the Bolivar family that financed Bolivar's revolutionary activities.

The family entrusted the care of baby Simón to a household slave, Hipolita, who Bolivar would eventually describe as "the only father I have known." Bolivar's father died before he was three years old, and his mother died before he was nine. The extremely wealthy boy bounced around a number of tutors but eventually came under the tutelage of Don Simón Rodríguez. Don Simón, who later became Bolivar's friend and mentor, was somewhat of a revolutionary, and he introduced the wealthy young man to ideas of liberty, enlightenment, and freedom.

When Bolivar was fourteen, Don Rodriguez was accused of being involved in a conspiracy against the Spanish government in Caracas and had to flee Venezuela. Bolivar entered the military academy and began his military career becoming a great tactician.

There were periodic rebellions against Spanish rule, but none successful, until Bolivar led the charge against Spanish domination, taking advantage of a now weakened Spain. Bolívar led the rebellious Spanish colonies to form the first union of independent nations called Gran Colombia, which eventually included today's countries of Venezuela, Colombia, Panama, Ecuador, Peru, and Bolivia.

In 1819 Panama, realizing its comparatively small size and fearing a reemergence of Spanish power, looked at options of aligning with other participants in Bolivar's Gran Colombia. Panama declared its independence in 1821 and, like most of Latin America, was in awe of Simón Bolivar, so decided to join Bolivar's Gran Colombia by aligning with Colombia.

Bolivar responded to Panama, "It is not possible to me to express the feeling of joy and admiration that I have experienced in the knowledge that Panama, the center of the Universe, is segregated by itself and freed by its own virtue. The act of independence of Panama is the most glorious monument that any American province can give. Everything there is addressed; justice, generosity, policy, and national interest."

Bolivar convened his Congress of Latin American Presidents in Panama City, fully recognizing, even then, Panama's position at the crossroads of the world, and believing that, "If the world ever had a capital, it would be Panama."

Bolivar predicted that Panama, with its "magnificent position between the two great oceans, could with time become the emporium of the universe. Its canals will shorten the distances of the world: they will narrow commercial ties between Europe, America and Asia; and bring to such fortunate region the tributes of the four parts of the globe."

Eventually Bolivar's plans for a Latin American union were undone by squabbling between the participants and Bolivar retired. By 1831 Panama had aligned itself with Colombia as the Republic of New Granada. After New Granada dissolved, Panama remained with Colombia until the relationship was severed in 1904, when Panama separated from Colombia with the backing of the United States.

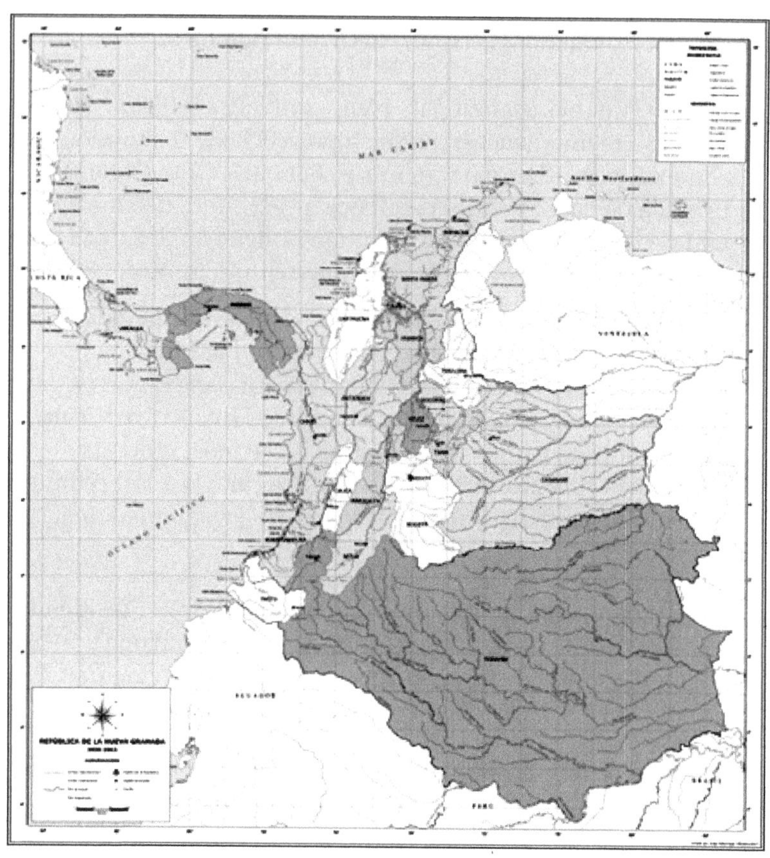

The Republic of New Granada 1830-1843[6]

4. The Dream

When the first European explorers came to this region, they were looking for a path between east and west. When you make a Canal voyage between the seas, you are making the voyage that was the dream of those early explorers.

Christopher Columbus, on his fourth voyage in 1502, embittered and sickly, sailed along the eastern coast of the Isthmus of Panama, searching for the "hidden straight" Columbus believed would get him to the Far East. In 1502 Columbus anchored near the very spot in the Caribbean where ships now wait to enter the Canal. Columbus believed that the Isthmus of Panama and the islands today known as Bocas del Torro were the outer islands of India, and so he called them the West Indies and called the Indigenous people he met, Indians.

Due east of the Atlantic entrance to the Canal is a cove in the Darien first reached by Europeans in 1501 and spied by Columbus on his last voyage.

In 1510 the first successful European settlement on the mainland of the Americas was established on the western side of the Gulf of Urabá and named Santa María de la Antigua del Darién. The settlement was short lived and abandoned in 1524 after being attacked and burned by the Indigenous people.

So ... the dream began!

Unable to find a natural passage across the Isthmus, people began dreaming of a canal. In 1534 King Charles V of Spain ordered that the Chagres River be mapped and cleared, all the way to what by then was already Panama City. He ordered land studies with a view toward excavating a canal. At the same time he was also looking at the San Juan River that runs from Lake Nicaragua to the Caribbean, creating what would eventually become a rivalry between Nicaragua and Panama.

The discovery of the Pacific and further conquests of the Spanish Conquistadors, produced a flood of gold and silver from the New World that dwarfed any treasure the Spanish might have gotten from the Indies, had Columbus been successful in finding a path to the East by going west. Panama became the crossroads of Spain's empire in the New World. Gold and silver were brought by ship from across the Americas to Panama City.

Without the canal Charles V had dreamed about, King Phillip II devised a system of convoys in the 1560s that would not only get the riches of Spain's vast empire back home, but also ward off attacks of privateers and pirates.

The "*Flota de Indias*" fleet left Spain each year in two convoys bound for the treasure cities of Veracruz, Portobelo, Nombre de Dios, and Cartagena, where treasure was stored in warehouses awaiting the fleet's arrival. All of these ships would rendezvous in Havana, before sailing for Spain as one mighty naval force. Additional treasures were brought from the Philippines to Acapulco, then across Mexico to Veracruz where they were loaded onto the Caribbean treasure fleet.

To get the gold and silver from Panama City back to Spain it had to first be transported across the Isthmus of Panama by mule train. A single mule train could include hundreds of mules all loaded down with gold and silver.

"The Road of the Crosses"

The route across the Isthmus became known as the Camino Real, or the Royal Road, although it was more commonly called the *"Camino de Cruces"* ["Road of the Crosses"], because of the abundance of gravesites along the way. Don't let the name fool you: it was really nothing more than a jungle trail, often knee deep with mud and frequently washed out by landslides. After the trek across the jungle of Panama, the gold and silver ended up in the custom house in Portobelo to await the arrival of the treasure fleet. Sometimes mules laden with silver fell off the path, tumbled down ravines, and, being Panama even back then, sometimes a mule and with its load of treasure would just disappear with the loot hidden in the jungle to be recovered later. Some claim there still may be lodes of lost silver and gold still buried in the mud and jungle overgrowth along the route of the Royal Road.

Portobelo is about a half hour east of Colon. There are tours that will take you to Portobelo where you can still see the old Spanish Forts that guarded the town, and the restored Custom House, where the treasure was stored to await the Spanish Fleet. Today the Spanish fortifications from Portobelo to San Lorenzo, just west of the Atlantic entrance to the Canal, are UNESCO World Heritage sites.

Panama: Too Good to Pass Up!

Portobelo was too good for pirates and privateers to pass up!

In 1572 Sir Francis Drake carried an enormous pile of silver back to England, silver he had looted in Panama from the Spanish. Working as a privateer for the Queen of England, Drake seized Spanish ships off the coast of Panama, captured and looted Number de Dios, and ambushed a mule train carrying Peruvian silver across the Isthmus.

Drake returned twenty years later in an attempt to capture the entire Isthmus for England, only to die of dysentery and be buried in a lead coffin somewhere east of the Bay of Limon.

The pirate most associated with Panama is Henry Morgan. Morgan operated as a privateer under a letter of marque from the British Crown, authorizing him to attack Spanish ships and possessions. (The difference between pirates and privateers: pirates were thieves and privateers were sanctioned thieves.) Morgan attacked and captured Portobelo, the third richest city in the world in 1668. He went on to attack the Spanish stronghold of Maracaibo in Venezuela in 1669. Emboldened by his victories in Venezuela, Morgan set his sights on the richest city in the world, Panama City.

In our imaginations we often think of pirates in terms of a single ship, like Disney's "Black Pearl," lurking for prey. But frequently the well-known and powerful pirates and privateers travelled with a fleet of ships, many of which had been captured in prior encounters. So it was with Morgan.

January 6, 1671, Morgan came back to Panama and captured Fort San Lorenzo on the Atlantic side. Leaving 300 men to guard the fort, on January 19, Morgan set out for Panama City, sailing up the Chagres River with 7 small ships and 36 boats and canoes. As Morgan moved across Panama, the Spanish generally fled rather than fight. January 28th, Morgan arrived at the gates of the city of Panama with around 1,500 men. The Spanish defense force of around 1,200 infantry and 400 cavalry fell apart and by mid-afternoon Morgan's men were following fleeing Spanish soldiers into the city. The fighting that ensued left much of the city in flames.

Looting The Pirate

The privateers tried to put out the fires as they searched for the city's gold, but much of the wealth had been loaded onto ships that managed to sail in the confusion of the attack, or was hidden in the Bay of Panama. Morgan's men stayed four weeks poking through the smoldering remains of the city, looking for treasure. In the end they managed to plunder so much that it took 175 mules to carry the loot back across the Isthmus.

What Morgan missed was the greatest treasure of all, for in Panama City was an altar of solid gold. Hearing that Morgan had sacked Portobelo and was headed for Panama City, residents of the city began dismantling the golden altar. Any part of the altar that could be removed was taken and hidden beneath the Bay of Panama. The problem was that the gold base of the altar was just too heavy to move and too big to hide. A priest in the church had a brilliant idea: he simply whitewashed the solid gold base of the altar.

When Morgan arrived to loot the church, the priests readily gave up their gold crosses and gem-encrusted chalices. Just before Morgan left, the priest asked Morgan to come with him into the sanctuary. The priest pointed at the altar, now whitewashed, and said to Morgan, "Sir, you can see that we are a poor, humble church, with nothing but this poor altar. We would be very grateful to you, sir, if you would make us a donation to help us build something better."

Morgan coughed up a donation saying, "This is the first time the pirate has ever been looted," without ever realizing the whitewashed altar was actually solid gold.

In the looting and fighting the city caught fire and much of it was destroyed. The original city had been built in a low-lying area that was the cause of much disease and didn't take advantage of the sea breeze, so the residents decided to build a new city on a point sticking out into the Bay of Panama. The new location had better drainage, took advantage of the sea breezes, and was easier to defend against attack.

The remains of that original city are known today as Panama Viejo or "Old Panama" and today it is a UNESCO World Heritage Site. You can walk across what remains of bridge that's five hundred years old or climb to the top of the iconic tower that has been restored and today is the symbol of Panama City.

The famous golden altar was moved, reassembled and today can be seen in all of its glory in the Church of St. Joseph in the colonial area of Panama City known as Casco Viejo.

What Morgan didn't know is that during his voyage, England had signed a treaty with Spain and his attack on Panama City violated that treaty. Morgan was taken back to England, tried, and during the trial he managed to prove that he didn't get the "email" about the peace treaty, so was knighted and made Lieutenant Governor of Jamaica.

Morgan settled down in retirement with his buddies in Jamaica, was a heavy drinker, and died in 1688 in his early 50s, quite possibly of liver failure. So why would you name a popular and delicious brand of spiced rum "Captain Morgan?"

From King Charles V of Spain [1534] onward, many people have looked longingly at the idea of a canal across Central America. Benjamin Franklin was entranced by the idea of a canal. When Thomas Jefferson became U. S. ambassador to France, he was interested in seeing a canal in Panama.

The "Great Liberator" Simón Bolivar was captivated by Panama. Bolivar chose Panama City as the site for his Latin American Congress, claiming that if the world would have a capital, it would be Panama. Bolivar was passionately in favor of a canal. Plagued by internal squabbling Gran Colombia dissolved and Panama ended up part of Colombia with whom it had little in common. Panama became a largely neglected region of Colombia except when Colombia needed to conscript troops, but the dream of a "path between the seas" remained.

"Captain Morgan Interrogating Panamanians."

Gold storage: the restored Custom House in Portobelo.

5. A Century of Expansion

The 19th century was a century of exploration, discovery and expansion.

The son of a Scottish farm worker and his wife in Yorkshire became the darling of the British Admiralty and the Royal Society. Captain James Cook set out on an expedition presumably to observe the Transit of Venus from Tahiti and then went on to explore and discover territory for England, specifically New Zealand and Australia

The Age of Exploration

Cook made three voyages of discovery concentrating heavily on the South Pacific and New Zealand. The adventures of Cook comprise one of the most compelling sagas of exploration and discovery. Although killed in Hawaii, Cook created the pattern for exploration, discovery, expansion, and, at times, exploitation, which came to full bloom in the 19th century. From 1804-1844 Britain sent voyages to almost every corner of the globe intent to expand British influence and empire, as well as advance scientific knowledge.

Cook was followed by John Ross, who, at the beginning of the 19th century, made three expeditions to the Arctic looking for the fabled Northwest Passage which had eluded Cook.

The geopolitical world changed dramatically in the 19th century with the collapse of the Spanish, Portuguese, French, Chinese, Holy Roman, and Mughal empires.

After defeating France and Spain, the British Empire expanded to control one quarter of the world's population and one fifth of the total land area. It was a century of colonialism and empire building. Increasing understanding of anatomy, disease and prevention, combined with urbanization, led to exploding populations. In Europe the population doubled during the 19th century.

The 19th century was also an age of invention. In 1800 Alessandro Volta invented the first chemical battery. The Industrial Revolution was underway and practical applications of steam power were emerging. In 1803 William Symington demonstrated what he called the "first practical steamboat." The steam locomotive was under development at the end of the 18th century, but the first full-scale working railway steam locomotive was built by Richard Trevithick. Initially, steam railways were used to move coal in Wales, but by 1812 there was a steam powered public railway known as the Stockton and Darlington railway in north-east England.

As the century marched forward, the Erie Canal was opened and aluminum was isolated [1825], the electric motor was invented [1828], and the first police force was established in London [1829]. Slavery was abolished in the British Empire [1833], anesthesia was developed [1842], the first public telegraph line was established [1844], and the safety pin and gas mask were invented [1849].

A Growing Nation

At the turn of the century the United States was still an infant nation. In 1801 it wasn't a case of "hanging chad," but a flaw in the Constitution that enabled Thomas Jefferson to become third President of the United States. After a bitter campaign that featured slander and personal attacks between the sitting President, John Adams and Thomas Jefferson, even without benefit of political action committees running wild, the flaw in the U. S. Constitution resulted in the House of Representatives needing to elect a President, and Jefferson was chosen after thirty-six ballots. [The Twelfth Amendment in 1804 resolved the Constitutional flaw.]

In 1803 the United States massively enlarged its territory with the Louisiana Purchase, gaining 828,000 square miles [2.1 million square kilometers] of France's claim to the territory of Louisiana for something like today's equivalent of 42 cents per acre. Far more than what is today Louisiana, the land purchased contained all or part of 14 present-day U. S. states as well as portions of what are today the Canadian provinces of Alberta and Saskatchewan.

In 1803 U. S. President Thomas Jefferson commissioned the Corps of Discovery, and named a 27-year-old U. S. Army Captain Meriwether Lewis as its leader. Lewis was accompanied by a 33-year-old former Army officer named William Clark. Their goals were to explore the Louisiana Purchase, establish United States sovereignty along the way, and preempt the Europeans from establishing a claim to the Pacific Northwest and Oregon territories.

Long before 24-hour news coverage, the Corps of Discovery Expedition, which became known as the Lewis and Clark Expedition, did not receive much public attention at the time. But, it was the first transcontinental expedition to the Pacific Coast, and it did establish a U. S. claim to the Pacific Northwest.

The Lewis and Clark Expedition marked the beginning of U. S. exploration. As the century progressed, ironically it was a half-cocked, crazy theory that pushed the United States into exploration and discovery.

In 1825 John Quincy Adams saw the need to get the country involved in exploration and proposed a National Observatory and a National University, as well as a Voyage of Discovery to explore the Pacific Northwest. But Congress refused to fund any of his proposals.

Then along came a retired Army Captain, John Cleve Symmes, who went on the lecture circuit to propose his theory that the world was hollow. Land masses at the poles gave the earth "balance," but there were "holes in the poles" through which you could sail down into the center of the earth to a miraculous land. Even without the Internet, Symmes' wacky ideas created a stir. Meanwhile New England maritime communities, anxious for new shipbuilding contracts, launched a campaign urging Congress to send a maritime expedition to the South Pacific.

This led to what was known as the U. S. Exploring Expedition, also called the Wilkes Expedition, from 1838 to 1842. In May, 1828, the U. S. Congress, after prodding by President John Quincy Adams, voted to send an expedition around the world with the understanding that the country would derive great benefit. And of course it gave those shipbuilders in New England business as well as offered protection to the heavy investment in the whaling and seal hunting industries, particularly in the Pacific. Since the only ships capable of circumnavigation were those of the Navy, Congress authorized a Naval Expedition.

The expedition explored 280 islands, mostly in the Pacific, and over eight hundred miles of Oregon were mapped. Of no less importance, over 60,000 plant and bird specimens were collected. The Wilkes Expedition played a major role in development of 19th-century science, particularly in the growth of the American scientific establishment. A collection of artifacts from the expedition also went to the National Institute for the Promotion of Science, a precursor of the Smithsonian Institution. These joined artifacts from American history as the first artifacts in the Smithsonian collection.

Between 1840 and 1860 the United States would spend between one quarter and one third of the National budget financing expeditions and scientific publications.

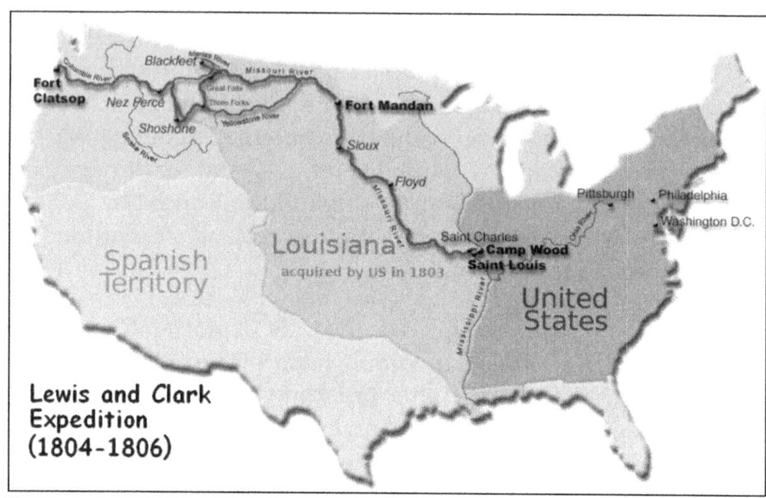

7

"Manifest Destiny" an Allegorical Painting by John Gast 1872.

In 1844 a French promoter by the name of Ferdinand de Lesseps, pitched a plan to build a Canal across the Suez to Sa'id Pasha, with whom de Lesseps had some diplomatic contact. There had been smaller ancient canals across the desert, but this was a stunning proposal. Excavation took eleven years using the forced labor of some thirty thousand Egyptian workers. The British felt threatened, so officially condemned forced work, and sent armed Bedouins to provoke revolt but despite their efforts, the Suez Canal opened and the first transit occurred in 1869. In that day the creation of the Suez Canal was the equivalent of the first landing of a man on the moon.

The world was quickly shrinking! There was an amazing confidence in the ability to achieve, to explore, to discover, and to exploit. It was a time of great optimism.

Religion was booming in the United States and the Second Great Awakening was in full swing with churches growing and the founding of new denominations. There were many reform movements designed to correct perceived evils, such as slavery and the lack of rights for women, and movements like temperance, all in anticipation of a new millennial age and the Second Coming of Christ. Methodism took off featuring revivals and camp meetings with itinerant preachers riding the circuit of a rapidly expanding U. S. frontier.

Manifest Destiny

The frontier offered opportunity. The United States was developing an optimistic, can-do attitude where every person had the opportunity to achieve and find freedom. Unlike Europe, where the class of society into which a person was born determined in large part their future, in the United States there was a developing belief that anything was possible. In Europe, land was controlled by families who had owned the land and wealth for generations. By moving westward in the United States it was possible to have your own land, albeit in many cases simply appropriated from the Indigenous. You could build your own log cabin, farm, and find freedom and upward mobility. For many who came to the United States from Europe it was the opportunity of a lifetime.

By 1840, nearly seven million Americans, forty percent of the nation's population, had moved west of the Appalachians. John O'Sullivan was a first-generation American journalist who founded a magazine called *"Democratic Review,"* meant to champion Andrew Jackson's democratic ideals. In 1845, writing in support of the westward movement, O'Sullivan argued that it was the "manifest destiny" of the United States to carry the "great experiment of liberty" across the continent, and to "overspread and to possess the whole of the [land] which Providence has given us." O'Sullivan declared that the very survival of the United States and democracy depended on fulfilling this "manifest destiny."

The concept of manifest destiny wasn't new to the Americas. When Columbus and the other conquistadores came to claim the Americas for the Spanish Crown, convert the Indigenous to Catholicism, loot, and plunder, they were exercising what they believed was their God-given right or manifest destiny. So, too, when the Pilgrims left England and landed on Plymouth Rock, or the Dutch when they settled South Africa, or the British when they colonized India ... all believed they were exercising their manifest destinies.

In 1810 a Missouri banker was granted a large tract of land in Texas, then Spanish territory part of the Viceroy of New Spain, but already struggling to throw off the Spanish yoke. Moses Austin planned to recruit U. S. settlers but died before he could implement his plan. His son, Stephen F. Austin, managed to recruit over three hundred families to migrate and colonize in Texas. The Mexicans originally saw these U. S. colonists as a buffer between Mexicans and the Comanche Indians, but the settlers preferred the richer land and to be far from the Indians. The numbers grew and by 1829 Mexico, now having thrown off Spanish rule and known as the United Mexican States, attempted to re-establish control and taxation. The settlers objected, which led to Mexico closing Texas to additional immigration.

Area of Southwest in White represents Mexican territory acquired by the United States following the U. S-.Mexican War. The dark area to the south of Arizona and New Mexico is the Gadsden Purchase.

"The Plains Across"

In 1834 General Antonio Lopez de Santa Anna decided to settle the matter by force, but led by Stephen F. Austin, the Texans declared independence and called Texans to arms. After defeat at the Alamo, the Texan Army commanded by General Sam Houston, defeated Santa Anna and forced him to sign a treaty recognizing the independence of Texas. Texas was recognized as an independent republic by Britain, France, and the United States. After Congressional wrangling Texas became the twenty-ninth state of the United States at the close of 1845.

Despite the recognition of Texas as an independent republic, Mexico continued to consider Texas as part of its territory leading to the U. S. -Mexican War between 1846 and 1848. U. S. forces took New Mexico, upper and lower California and even managed to capture Mexico City.

Following the U. S. victory both the United States and Mexico signed the Treaty of Guadalupe Hidalgo in which Mexico gave up claims to the territories of Upper California, New Mexico, and Texas and recognized the Rio Grande as its border with the United States.

A few years later, in 1853, the United States would purchase a 29,670 square mile [76,845 square kilometer] section of present day southern Arizona and New Mexico for $10 million U. S., about $393 million today, known as the Gadsden Purchase, named after the American ambassador to Mexico at the time.

During the first half of the 19th century ships from Boston began calling at Spanish towns and missions along the California coasts seeking otter and beaver pelts, and so trappers and hunters from the Eastern states began migrating to continent's west coast. Yankee traders visited San Diego, Los Angeles, Buena Ventura, Santa Barbara, Monterey and Yerba Buena. These were small settlements with Yerba Buena, later to become San Francisco, only having about five hundred residents in 1847. That same year the first printing press arrived and a four-page weekly newspaper, called *"The California Star,"* was published.

After the Spanish War of Independence, Alta California came under the control of the Mexico government in Santa Barbara, and shifted to civilian control with the first city council forming in 1826. Santa Barbara developed a lively trade with the United States in tallow and hides, which were carried to Boston by the California clipper ships. By 1845 the population of Santa Barbara was around twenty-five hundred, Los Angeles around fifteen-hundred, and San Diego around a thousand. These were not yet thriving cities or metropolitan areas, yet they were attractive ports for people seeking new lives and prosperity in the West.

Further up the coast, by 1843 the Oregon Country had already established an autonomous government, and in 1848 became the Oregon Territory. The rich Columbia and Snake rivers were attractive to traders, explorers and settlers. The rich Willamette Valley began attracting settlers arriving by wagon train. The steamboat COLUMBIA began to call regularly at the newly established port of Portland, which at the time had fewer than eight hundred people.

There were only three ways by which people could reach the Western coast.

- "The Plains Across" - the long, exhausting, and at times dangerous journey by wagon train across the American continent. Far from being a Route 66, there were various trails to California and Oregon. The most famous became known as the California Trail. There wasn't a reliable map of California until 1848, and trails weren't marked, so it was easy to get lost en route, particularly as the trail snaked through mountains. The most famous party to get lost and perish was the Donner party, who arrived in California in 1846. An early snowfall caused the party to be stranded in the Sierras and the result was starvation, cannibalism, and death.

- "The Horn Around" - the long, arduous voyage by boat around the Southern tip of South America often changing ships en route.

- "The Isthmus Over" – by boat to Chagres, Panama, then slog across the Isthmus and board a boat in Panama City bound for the tiny western port towns.

Not only settlers, but equipment, goods, mail, and even news had to travel by one of these routes. Without CNN, news came only when a clipper ship arrived. It wasn't until 1849 that it was possible to send news and correspondence nineteen hundred miles across the continent in about nine days using the Central Overland California & Pike's Peak Express Company, parent company of The Pony Express.

Europe had been experimenting with short-run telegraphs, but it wasn't until 1844 that the first practical telegram in the United States was sent by Samuel F. B. Morse: "*what hath God wrought.*" In 1843 the U. S. Congress funded an experimental telegraph line from Washington, D.C. to Baltimore. It was not until 1861 that the first transcontinental telegraph system was established in the United States.

The U. S. Congress recognized the need for communication and supply of the rapidly expanding westward region of the still relatively young country. With a transcontinental telegraph and railroad still years away, Congress began to look at other options.

6. The Panama Railroad

Bolivar had envisioned Panama as the crossroads of the world, and it was a vision that took hold on the Isthmus. New Granada had long sought partnership with other nations in opening up the Isthmus as a pathway for world trade. England studied the idea, but backed down due to the magnitude of the project. France surveyed the Isthmus and actually contracted for a railroad, but backed down at the price tag.

As the United States expanded westward there was an increasing need for communication and transport between the coasts. In 1832 the United States sent Colonel Charles Biddle to look for a possible railway route as well as negotiate a concession for U. S. construction of a railroad. Biddle died shortly after returning to the United States, but the United States continued to pursue a railroad concession. In 1846 Congress signed the Midlack-Mallarino Treaty with New Granada that granted the United States the right to build railroads through Panama.

Additionally, and significantly, the Midlack-Mallarino Treaty gave the United States the right to intervene militarily against what was, even then, a brewing revolutionary fever in Panama against Colombia, then still known as Gran Colombia.

Panama had joined Bolivar's Gran Colombia because it believed in Bolivar and his vision of a united Latin America which loosely followed the concept of the United States of America. Bolivar was a great admirer of George Washington and hoped to create a similar union in Latin America. When Bolivar's vision dissolved due to internal squabbling and conflict amongst the member countries, Panama had every intention of eventually withdrawing from Colombia to once again be independent. The effect of the Midlack-Mallarino Treaty was to promise a developing U. S. Navy and military the right to keep the Isthmus bound to Bogota.

The Midlack-Mallarino Treaty would set the stage for continued United States meddling in Panama's affairs for almost a century and a half. From 1850 until 1903 U. S. troops were used in Panama to put down separatist uprisings and demonstrations, fueling animosity against the United States and resentment against Bogota, with whom the United States was aligned.

It was not until 1999 when the United States finally withdrew from Panama and turned the Canal Zone and the Canal back to Panama that the United States would stop interfering in Panamanian affairs. Free of U. S. interference, but without all the jobs and income generated by the U. S. Canal Zone, the first few years were difficult for Panama, but after a few years of struggle, Panama was able to operate the Canal at a profit and took off economically, becoming what is today a booming economy in the face of worldwide financial turmoil.

The Little Railroad That Could

With the right to build a railroad in place, in 1848 Congress authorized contracts for two mail lines of steamships, one to go from New York and New Orleans to Chagres, Panama, and the other to go from Panama City to California and Oregon. A New York businessman, George Law, seized the Atlantic contract, but finding someone to undertake the risk involved in the Pacific contract proved more difficult.

A New York businessman and entrepreneur by the name of William H Aspinwall, along with his uncle Gardiner Green Howland, Henry Chauncey, and Edwin Bartlett, incorporated the Pacific Mail Steamship Company to deliver mail between Panama and the United States. Aspinwall wasn't interested in the shipping profit as much as in the vision of connecting the oceans with a rail line across the Isthmus of Panama, merging the railroad he envisioned with steamship routes on both oceans to create a somewhat "seamless" connection between the coasts.

With the U. S. shipping contract in place, Aspinwall sought permission from New Granada to construct an "iron road" across the Isthmus of Panama. Aspinwall negotiated with New Granada exclusive rights to build a railroad connecting Panama City on the Pacific side with a yet to be determined point on the Atlantic side. New Granada granted the railroad over 250,000 acres of land for construction. The agreement granted six years for construction and rights to operate the railroad for forty nine years. After twenty years, New Granada had the option to purchase the railroad outright for the cost of the initial stock offering, or $5 million.

With the help of the U. S. Topographical Corps Colonel George W. Hughes, a route across the Isthmus was mapped. The survey team arrived in the middle of the rainy season, getting a graphic introduction to the challenges of the Isthmus of Panama. Meanwhile, Aspinwall returned to New York and incorporated the Panama Railroad Company in April 1849, issuing fifty thousand shares of stock at a fixed price of $100 a share.

The only logical point for the Pacific terminus was the city of Panama which, at the height of Spain's exploitation of the New World, had been the richest city in the world. The site for the Atlantic terminus was not as straightforward. The first site chosen was Portobelo, discovered and named by Christopher Columbus on his fourth voyage to the New World in 1502. Portobelo had been the storage point for the gold and silver that was loaded onto the Spanish treasure fleet for the journey to Europe. But George Law, who had the concession for the Atlantic steam ship route, heard of the plan, managed to buy up all the land around Portobelo, and then offered it for sale to the railroad at a highly inflated price.

After considering several other Pacific sites, the railroad settled on a swampy island known as Manzanillo, in Limon Bay. The decision was made to start on the Atlantic side, cross the lowlands, and climb the continental divide to cross the mountains at the lowest place, which was also the shortest route across the Isthmus.

Fessenden N. Otis describes the choice of Manzanillo: "The island, cut off from the main land by a narrow firth, contained an area of a little more than one square mile. It was a virgin swamp, covered with dense growth of the tortuous, water-loving mangrove, and interlaced with huge vines and thorny shrubs, defying entrance even to the wild beasts common to the country. In the black, slimy mud of its surface alligators and other reptiles abounded; while the air was laden with pestilential vapors, and swarming with sand-flies and musquitoes [sic]. These last proved so annoying to the laborers that, unless their faces were protected by gauze veils, no work could be done even at midday."[8]

In the winter of 1849 construction began unceremoniously with Colonel George Hughes and Captain John Williams driving a stake into the ground to mark the spot where construction would begin.

The original engineers contracted for the job, Colonel G. W. Totten and John C. Trautwine, were so intimidated by the daunting challenge of Panama that they asked that their contracts be withdrawn. The company decided to do the job itself, but hired the two engineers to supervise the project. They hired Indigenous people to begin hacking their way with machetes through jungle, marshes and swamps with snakes, crocodiles, bugs, and mosquitoes but of course at that time no one had made the connection between mosquitoes and disease.

Against All Odds

Otis writing in 1861, of course long before the Panama Canal, wrote,

"Thus unostentatiously was announced the commencement of a railway, which, from the interests and difficulties involved, might well be looked upon as one of the grandest and boldest enterprises ever attempted."[9]

Baldwin and his surveying crew were forced to wade through swamps and hack through virgin jungle to lay out the rail line. They managed to build some huts in order to get out of the constant rain and protect supplies, but at night the mosquitoes forced them to return to ships anchored in the bay. Eventually, Baldwin would have a wooden cabin designed and built for the bayous of Louisiana, constructed and shipped from New Orleans.

Indigenous workers, perhaps recognizing folly more quickly than the newly arrived North Americans, deserted the project in droves and it was necessary to recruit workers from elsewhere. Colonel Totten brought in 40 workers from Cartagena, "descendants of the old Spanish slaves, a peaceable and industrious race."

"With their increased corps the clearing progressed rapidly; but the rainy season soon settling in, the discomforts to which they were subjected were very great. The island was still uninhabitable, and the whole party were forced to live on board the brig [anchored in the bay], which was crowded to capacity. Here they were by no means exempt from the causes which deterred them from living on shore, for below decks the vessel was alive with musquitoes [sic] and sand-flies, which were a source of such annoyance and suffering that almost all preferred to sleep upon the deck, exposed to the drenching rains, rather than endure their attacks. In addition to this, most of their number were kept nauseated by the ceaseless motion of the vessel. Labor and malorious influences during the day, exposure and unrest at night, soon took a toll upon their health, and in a short time more than half the party were attacked with malarious fevers. Having neither a physician nor any comfortable place of rest, their sufferings were severe."[10]

Any realist looking at Panama and the minimal progress being made would certainly have predicted failure, except for an event that occurred at John Sutter's Mill in Coloma, California.

Gold!

On January 24, 1848 James W. Marshall, a foreman working in Sutter's lumber mill, found shiny metal in the tailrace of the mill. He took it to Sutter and the two tested the metal and confirmed that it was in fact gold. The person least excited about the discovery of gold at Sutter's Mill was John Sutter himself. Sutter was a Sacramento pioneer with plans to build an agricultural empire around Coloma. Gold did not fit into his plan, so Sutter attempted to keep the discovery quiet, fearing a mad rush of gold seekers.

At the time gold was discovered, California was still part of the Mexican territory of Alta California. Conveniently California was ceded to the United States after the end of the Mexican-American War by the Treaty of Guadalupe, signed on February 2, 1848. It may have been more than Sutter's reluctance and commitment to agriculture that kept the discovery quiet.

Rumors of the discovery began to spread. The first public announcement came on March 14, 1848 when the *Californian* announced, "In the newly made raceway of the Sam Mill recently erected by Captain Sutter, on the American Fork, gold has been found in considerable quantities ... California, no doubt, is rich in mineral wealth; great chances here for scientific capitalists. Gold has been found in almost every part of the country."

Without CNN or the Internet it took a while for the news to reach the East coast. It wasn't until August 19, 1848 that the *New York Herald* reported the discovery of gold. Finally, on December 5, 1848, President James Polk confirmed the discovery in an address to the U. S. Congress.

And the rush was on!

San Francisco, which at the time had a population of about a thousand, initially became a ghost town as everyone who possibly could, headed off to search for gold. Eventually things settled down and merchants realized that gold could also be mined by selling supplies and Levi's to the gold seekers, and providing needed services like saloons, gambling houses, and prostitutes. Waves of gold seekers, known as "Forty Niners," lived in tents and wood shanties and the population exploded to 25,000 in just two years. Just as John Sutter feared, his workers left to look for gold, squatters invaded, tore up his land, and stole his cattle.

Over 300,000 became infected with "gold fever" and dropped everything to rush off to California in search of their fortune.

There were three ways to get to California:

"The Plains Across" - the long, exhausting and at times dangerous journey across the American continent known as the "California Trail."

"The Horn Around" - the long, arduous journey by boat around the Southern tip of South America that could take 5 to 8 months sailing some 18,000 nautical miles [33,000 kilometers or 20,505 miles].

"The Isthmus Over" - though more expensive, was the fastest way, and this was, after all a Gold rush. People would sail from the East coast to Chagres in Panama, which almost overnight became a rowdy shanty boom town. From Chagres they would follow the same path the Spaniards and pirates had used across the continental divide to reach Panama City, where they would board another ship bound for San Francisco. It could take a week or more to slog through the jungle across the Isthmus.

About half of the gold seekers arrived in San Francisco by ship.

Nothing could have been better for William Aspinwall and his Pacific Mail Steamship Company. Aspinwall's first ship, the CALIFORNIA, was launched in 1848 and made its way down around the Horn to Panama City intending to carry mail and supplies from Panama to San Francisco.

When it arrived in Panama, the CALIFORNIA was mobbed by about 700 gold-seekers willing to pay any price to get to California. The ship finally sailed overloaded with four hundred lucky would-be gold millionaires. When she reached San Francisco her entire crew, except for the captain, elected to jump ship and go off to look for gold. The ship was stuck for almost four months in San Francisco while a new, and more expensive, crew was located.

Ships bearing goods and people from around the world arrived in San Francisco only to have their crew dessert for the gold fields. Soon the waterfront of the boom town of San Francisco was loaded with abandoned ships some of which were turned into stores, warehouses, and primitive lodging.

In Panama workers pressed on, constructing a single rail line through the jungle. Workers began arriving from Colombia, Jamaica, and the United States. A group of fifty Irish arrived from New Orleans along with a medical doctor, the brother of Colonel G. W. Totten. Housing was constructed and materials and supplies began arriving with regularity. There were about a thousand workers and the "railroad" was just two miles long, but eager gold seekers were willing to pay just for the privilege to walk along the railroad right-of-way.

But the railroad was quickly running out of money, requiring the principals to dig into their own pockets to keep the project moving. When news reached New York that California-bound passengers were using what little railroad was actually in existence, suddenly the value of the stock and subscriptions soared.

Aspinwall's first steamship.

San Francisco Harbor, 1850.

By 1852 the railroad stretched from Navy Bay eight miles beyond the settlement of Gatun[11]. The tiny settlement on Manzanillo island at Navy Bay was renamed Aspinwall and passenger trains met every incoming steamer to take the "Forty Niners" by rail twenty-three miles across the Isthmus.

Attempting to cross the Chagres River, the railroad met disaster when the bridge was swept away. The builders of the railroad, like the Canal builders who would follow in later years, couldn't conceive of a river that was "often rising forty feet in a single night."[12]

Undaunted, the railroad pushed on eventually managing to bridge the river. Efforts were doubled and the work force was increased.

"Their working force was increased as rapidly as possible, drawing laborers from almost every quarter of the globe. Irishmen were imported from Ireland, Coolies from Hindostan, Chinamen from China. English, French, Germans, and Australians, amounting in all to more than seven thousand men, were thus gathered in, appropriately as it were, to construct this highway for all nations."[13]

What is interesting is that this "highway for all nations" was constructed by men of all nations, just as the Panama Canal would be constructed in later years by workers from all over the world. And, just as with the construction of the Canal, disease and death were constant companions.

"It was soon found that many of these people, from their previous habits and modes of life, were little adapted to the work for which they were engaged. The Chinamen, one thousand in number, had been brought to the Isthmus by the Company, and every possible care taken which could conduce to their health and benefit. Their hill-rice, their tea, and opium, in sufficient quantity to last for several months, had been imported with them - they were carefully housed and attended to – and it was expected that they would prove efficient and valuable men. But they had been engaged upon the work scarcely a month before almost the entire body became affected with a melancholic, suicidal tendency, and scores of them ended their unhappy existence by their own hands. Disease broke out among them, and raged so fiercely that in a few weeks scarcely two hundred remained. The freshly-imported Irishmen and Frenchmen also suffered severely, and there was found no other resource but to reship them as soon as possible, and replenish from the neighboring provinces and Jamaica, the natives of which (with the exception of the North men of America) were found best able to resist the influences of the climate."[14]

With the flood of "Forty Niners" willing to pay a premium to ride the rails for just eight miles, and then pay more just to walk along the route of construction, investors in New York eagerly put up the money that enabled the railroad to shift construction into high gear.

From Sea to Shining Sea

The railroad continued pushing across the Isthmus encouraged with crews working simultaneously on the Atlantic and Pacific sides. Working round the clock the work was pushed to completion. On January 27, 1855 the last rail was laid in the rain and darkness and the very next day the first locomotive went from sea to sea.

The entire road was 47 miles [76 kilometers] and climbed over the continental divide with a maximum grade of 60 feet [18 meters] to the mile [1.6 kilometer]. The railroad had cost $6.5 million, over $138 thousand per mile, making it the most expensive railroad ever built based on cost per mile.

Rushed to completion in order to profit from the gold rush demand, the railroad was far from finished. A lot of the work was temporary. Temporary bridges needed to be replaced with permanent structures, ballasting needed to be completed, and warehouses and stations needed to be completed. Never-the-less, thanks in large part to the gold rush, the little railroad was making money hand over fist. The railroad paid off its indebtedness, established a sinking fund, and was paying dividends to stockholders.

During the peak Gold Rush years [1853-1860] California was exporting an average of $70 million of gold per year through the port of San Francisco according to custom-house manifests. Around half of this gold was shipped across Panama by the Panama Railroad with no loss. Reportedly over $700 million in gold was carried on the railroad between 1855 and 1867 without any loss … around $11.2 billion today!

Initially the gold was so plentiful in California that individuals could find it by simply panning for gold in the riverbed. Eventually the easy picking gold was gone and by 1853 most of the mining was being done by more advanced methods which required initial capital investments and machinery. The stereotyped individual miner image with his Levi jeans, suspenders, hat, and pan was for the most part just a memory. Some gold-seekers made money during the Gold Rush, but most were lucky to just cover their expenses. The big winners were the people who supplied the Forty Niners with equipment and services, people like Levi Strauss, owners of boarding houses and brothels and, of course, the Panama Railroad that made it possible for folks to get to the Gold Rush and for those who had either made money or not lost it all, to get back home.

Though the Gold Rush was over, the Panama Railroad had established itself as the first railroad to link the oceans. The little railroad that could was the first "transcontinental," or at least trans-Isthmian, railroad. The first transcontinental railroad in the United States would not open until 1869.

Most of the supplies and material for the Gold Rush had been shipped across Panama using the railroad. The gold had been shipped back East on the railroad. The railroad had proved itself to be the fastest and most dependable way to move freight across the Isthmus. The railroad had freight cars handling large quantities of gold and silver as well as "timber, anchors, and chains of the largest size, cannon shot and shells, iron-work in pieces of twenty-five tons, heavy machinery, guano, whale-oil, etc., more or less of which are daily passing over the road."[15]

Keeping the rain forest at bay on the Panama Railroad.

"A glance at the geographical situation of the Isthmus of Panama, in its relation with Australia, China, Japan, and the Sandwich Islands [Hawaiian Islands], will discover the capacity of the transit to shorten the distances from those countries to the markets of the United States by so many thousands of miles as must make it an eventual necessity for the trade, at least a large portion of it, to seek this, the only direct route between the Atlantic and Pacific oceans."[16]

- The distance from New York to Sydney Australia via Cape Horn is 12,870 miles [20,712 kilometers], via Panama 9,950 miles [16,013 kilometers]; in favor of Panama 2,720 miles [4,377 kilometers].
- The distance from New York to Honolulu, Sandwich Islands via Cape Horn is 13,560 miles [21,822 kilometers], via Panama 6,800 miles [10,944 kilometers]; in favor of Panama 6,760 miles [10,879 kilometers].
- The distance from New York to Hong Kong, via Cape Horn is 17,420 miles [28.035 kilometers], via Panama 11,850 miles [19,071]; in favor of Panama 5,570 miles [8,964 kilometers].
- The distance fro New York to Japan, via Cape Horn is 16,710 miles [26,892 kilometers], via Panama 10,220 miles [16,448 kilometers]; in favor of Panama 6,490 miles [10,445 kilometers].

The Gold Rush may have been over, but travelers still came to transit Panama en route to other destinations, and, then as now, just to experience Panama. Today's tourists experience a far different railroad and a different route across the Isthmus, since much of the original route of the railroad lies underneath today's Panama Canal.

Riding The Rails

The big thrust for growth of the railroad as the Gold Rush wound down was not so much passenger traffic, but cargo.

The Isthmus was the logical, most convenient, fastest, and cheapest way to move goods around the world. Two freight trains ran daily leaving Aspinwall at 2:00 p.m. and Panama at 9:00 a.m. Mail was carried at twenty-two cents a pound, coal at $5 a ton, first class freight in boxes or bales was fifty cents a cubic foot. All freight charges were paid in gold.

F. N. Otis' *Illustrated History of The Panama Railroad* was intended as the "Businessman's Handbook For The Panama Railroad And Its Connections" with not only rates, connecting schedules, customs duty and rules and regulations, but also detailed information on the emerging markets of the day: California, Oregon, Vancouver, Washington Territory as well as the Latin American markets of Costa Rica, Nicaragua, San Salvador, Guatemala, Honduras, New Granada [what is now Panama and Colombia], Ecuador, Peru, Bolivia, Chile, and Mexico.

A morning passenger train left Aspinwall on the Atlantic side every day but Sunday at 8:15 a.m. and arrived in Panama at 12:15 p.m., and the train from Panama left at 9:00 a.m. and arrived at 1:00 p.m. Special trains were added when passenger steam-ships arrived at Aspinwall. "This arrangement has been made solely with a view of affording the passenger the greatest degree of comfort and convenience ... "[17] First class fare was $25 for adults, children ages 6 to 12 half price, and children under 6 paid a quarter of the adult price. Second class was $10. Personal baggage was 10 cents a pound.

Otis gives a unique and very special account of what the traveler experienced crossing the Isthmus in 1861 on the Panama Railroad.

When a traveler in 1861 arrived in Navy Bay, first visited by Christopher Columbus, he found ships from many countries at anchor and tied up. Since the Midlack-Mallarino Treaty not only gave the United States a concession for a railroad, but also gave the right to intervene militarily, Navy Bay became a rendezvous point and refueling station for the U. S. Navy in the Atlantic, and often U. S. Navy frigates would be at anchor in the harbor.

Walking into the railroad terminus at Aspinwall, a traveler passed stores and shops displaying items imported from Europe and the States. The Panama Railroad company was housed in a two-story brick building that also served as the Aspinwall office of the Isthmus Telegraph Company, connecting both sides of Panama. There were a few hotels offering rooms costing from $1 to $4 a day. "Probably the best accommodation will be found at the Howard City, and Aspinwall hotels. Usual charge for first class passengers $3 per day. Second class passengers are accommodated at the other houses at considerably lower rates. It is well to have the terms well understood beforehand."[18]

As the train pulls out of Aspinwall you would have seen the railroad wharf with both sail and steam ships, and stacks of cargo waiting to be shipped by the railroad across the Isthmus.

"Bales of quina bark from the interior were piled many tiers deep and reached to the iron triangular-braced roof of the edifice. Ceroons of indigo and cochineal from San Salvador and Guatemala; coffee from Costa Rica, and cacao from Ecuador; sarsaparilla from Nicaragua, and ivory-nuts from Porto Bello; copper ore from Bolivia; silver bars from Chili; boxes of hard dollars from Mexico, and gold ore from California; hides from the whole range of the North and South Pacific coast; hundreds of bushels of glistening pearl-oyster shells from the fisheries of Panama lay heaped along the floor, flanked by no end of North American beef, flour, bread, and cheese, for the provisioning of the Pacific coast, and English and French goods for the same markets; while in a train of cattle-cars that stood on one of the tracks were huddled about a hundred meek-looking lamas from Peru, on their way to the island and of Cuba, among whose mountains they are used for beasts of burdens as well as for their wool."[19]

The first community you would have passed was named Mingillo. This contemporary account is interesting not only because of the detailed description, but also the imperialistic view of a different culture.

"A few lusty half-naked negroes, descended from the African slaves of the old Spanish dominion (who form a large proportion of the littoral population of the Isthmus) are generally seen supplying their customers with fish, cassava, bananas, plantains, and many other fruits and vegetables of the country, from out the *bongoes* [dug out wooden canoes] which lay alongside the wharf, or, grouped on the shore over smoking kettles of *sancoche* [Panamanian chicken soup - still a favorite], ladling out this favorite compound to their native patrons. Large quantities of the vegetable ivory-nut [*tagua*] are also brought here by the natives for barter and sale. Sometimes a few aboriginal Indians [Kuna] from the region of San Blas (some 60 miles down the coast) may be seen here. Rather under the medium stature, they are broad-shouldered and muscular, with straight black hair and high cheek-bones of the North American tribes. They have a peculiar interest from the fact that they belong to a tribe never subjugated by the Conquistadores, but who have maintained unwavering hostility to the Spanish since the first discovery of the country, and have cherished such a jealousy of their independence that, to the present day, no white man has been permitted to land upon their shores. Their usual dress consists of a simple fold of cloth tied about the loins, although they are not infrequently seen clad after the manner of the Spanish natives, in a loose shirt and loose cotton or hempen trousers. Though apparently apathetic and uncommunicative, there is a considerable degree of intelligence in their expression, and a conscious independence in their bearing, that gives one a fair idea of the races which Columbus and his followers found here in the days of old."[20]

As the train moved on you passed Johnson's Ice House, a thriving business on the Isthmus, Aspinwall House, the company hotel, the railroad hospital, and a company recreation building with library, club room, and lecture hall. The recreation building was intended to provide workers with alternative recreation to the bars and brothels.

The lush jungles and tropical foliage through which the track passed proved fascinating to visitors from Northern climates. Leaving Manzanillo island the road ran through vast mangrove swamps. Though the swamps and standing water had created health problems for the workers building the railroad, by 1861 F. N. Otis was all but enthusiastic about lack of disease on the Isthmus.

"It may interest the general reader to know that more than 196 thousand passengers have been transported over the [rail] road during the five years ending in December, 1859, and it is not known that a single case of sickness has occurred during or in consequence of the transit since the entire opening of the road in 1855. The diseases contracted by persons in transit previous to that time were of a purely malarious character, and identical with the intermittent (fever and ague) and bilious fevers of the Western States, always unavoidable while the transit was performed upon mules and in open boats, occupying from two to five days, the traveler frequently obliged to live upon the vilest food, and sleep upon the wet ground or in the but little less comfortless huts of the natives; the comfortable railway carriage, and the passage from ocean to ocean reduced to *three hours*, having fully demonstrated a *perfect* immunity to the traveler from all those varieties of sickness long popularly recognized under the head of *Panama Fever* ... the congestive forms of fever among the laborers and residents which, during the earlier days of the road, were the chief causes of mortality, are now rarely met with, and the whole line of the transit will, in point of healthiness, compare favorably with many of the equally recent settlements in the Western States." [Emphases by Otis][21]

Regrettably, this was not the experience of the French and Americans when they worked on the construction of a canal across the Isthmus.

After passing across the mangrove swamp and through lush rain forest seven miles from the start, the train would arrive at Gatun Station, located on the Eastern Bank of the Chagres River. The railroad station was a two-story framed building which also served as the residence of the local superintendent and railroad workers. On the other side of the river was the village of Gatun which consisted of around fifty huts made of cane and palm. Prior to the railroad people travelling across the Isthmus would arrive by dug out canoes and stop in Gatun where "eggs were sold four for a dollar, and the rent for a hammock was two dollars a night."

The road would cross the Chagres River on an iron truss and girder bridge that was 97 feet [29.6 meter] long, and then start climbing uphill, passing the Lion Hill Station, then dropping down to a stop know as "*Ahorea Lagarto*" or "hang the lizard," so called because a Spanish regiment had once stopped there with its banner featuring a lizard, the insignia of the Order of Santiago.

As the train moved deep into the rain forest, travelers were in awe of the tropical vegetation.

"A mile or so farther on the forest becomes less lofty, and the traveler soon passes what may easily be mistaken for the overgrown ruins of some ancient city: walls, watch-towers, tall columns, and Gothic arches are on either hand, and it will be difficult to realize that Nature alone, with a lavish and fantastic hand, has shaped this curious scene out of myriads of *convolvuli*; whole clumps of trees covered by them, so that they appear like the remains of huge fortifications; tall stumps of palm look like broken columns overgrown with verdure and when they lean together, as in several instances is the case, great Gothic arches are formed."[22]

Travelling along the river the train arrived at another station called "*Buyo Soldado*" or "the Soldier's Home."

"From this point beautiful views up and down the river are visible, while across, the high opposing bank stretches back in a broad plateau, covered with low foliage, from among which occasional tall trees shoot up, until it meets a range of distant hills. Continuing your course, with an occasional view of the river, which winds like a great serpent along this tortuous valley, you come upon the native town of "*Bueno Vistita*" (beautiful little view)."[23]

Travelling along the Chagres River through the rain forest, the train arrived at Frijoli Station. To this day frijoles, a pea-like fruit that grows on a bush-like tree, slow cooked over an open fire so as to absorb some of the smoky flavor and then and ladled over rice, are a Panamanian delicacy.

Since this area is now forever lost, under the Panama Canal and Gatun Lake, it is worth remembering ... "Here, during the dry season, may be seen the gorgeous scarlet passion-flower, as well as the purple variety, in great abundance. Occasionally small gangs of natives are seen engaged in clearing away the recent growths along the track with their *machetas*. The machete is a sort of hiltless broadsword, from two to three feet in length, heavy, straight, and pointed, with a handle of wood or bone, and is the universal companion of the native of this country; with it he cuts his path through the tangled forest, clears his little plantation, builds his hut; with it, too, he plants his crops and reaps them; it is usually his only weapon of offense and defense; and from the half-grown boy to the gray-headed patriarch, you seldom find one, walking or sleeping, without his cherished machete."[24]

Later we will talk about the Panama Railway, the direct descendent of the Panama Railroad, and the train which carries hundreds of shipping containers, as well as tourists, across the Isthmus of Panama today. One cruise line, hyping the shore excursion on the Panama Railway, says that you can watch for wildlife as the train rumbles through the rain forest. Well, "watch" is the operative word! You can "watch" all you want, but no self-respecting wildlife is going to hang out beside the train tracks in the middle of the day, and even if it did, you'd never see it rolling along at forty miles an hour.

However, back in the day it was different ... "This section is rich in its variety of the birds, beasts, reptiles, and insects peculiar to intertropical America. Here are found frequent colonies of the oriole, or hanging-bird, whose beautifully-woven nests, often two or three feet long, may be seen [hanging] by scores from the trees. Several richly-colored varieties of parrots and toucans, trogons, tanagers, humming-birds, etc., abound. Grouse and the crested wild turkey are found on the higher grounds of the interior. The tapir is occasionally found in the river and marshy grounds adjoining. Monkeys in variety, the opossum, the ant-eater, the peccary, or wild hog, the sloth, the deer, bear, cougar, and two or three varieties of tiger-cat are native here. Among the many varieties of the lizard tribe which abound is the iguana, which grows to a large size, viz., from 3 to 6 feet in length, and is eagerly sought for by the natives for its flesh, which is tender and delicate as a chicken, and also for its eggs ...

"Land-crabs abound in great numbers, and are esteemed as a delicate article of food. The most common variety is of a pale blue color, and as large as half a cocoanut. Stories are told of their rapacity and carnivorous tastes that almost surpass belief. It is said that the largest animals, dead or wounded past resistance, are frequently reduced by them to whitened skeletons in a single night. There are several other smaller varieties, some of which are beautifully colored. Among the venomous insects, the tarantula, the centipede, and the scorpion are frequently met. Among the troublesome insects are white, red, and black ants, musquitoes [sic], sand-flies, fleas, *garapatos*, or wood-ticks, and the *chigoe,* or jigger, which not only bites, but burrows under the skin, and there deposits its eggs, which, if not speedily removed, will hatch out a troublesome nest of minute worms, producing great inflammatory disturbance in the part. As, however, they are at first very superficial, and enclosed in a little membranous sac, this is easily removed entire with a needle, and no farther trouble ensues; they are fortunately not common here, and seldom annoy any but the barefooted native. Venomous snakes, though occasionally seen, are not common. The boa constrictor is native here, and sometimes is found from 12 to 18 feet in length; it is, however, exceedingly rare to hear of any serious injury having been done by any of them. The alligator[25], which is found more or less plentifully in all parts of the Chagres and its tributaries, and the adjacent streams and swamps, frequently attacks and destroys dogs and cattle, and occasional instances have occurred where the natives, imprudently venturing into the waters infested with them, have fallen a prey to their rapacity."[26]

The railroad left the Chagres and moves through deep clay and rocky cliffs to the meadow-lands of Matachin, which was the spot where the railroad was completed, when the rail lines from both the Pacific and Atlantic met. There were several side branches at Matachin where trains from either side meet. Locals would meet the trains to sell candy, fruit and snacks to passengers.

The journey would continue through the Rio Obispo valley crossing the river several times before reaching Rio Obispo station. Here the trains would start climbing with a maximum grade of sixty feet per mile, past the Empire Station to the Summit Station, the highest point on the railroad.

A little further on you would come to a tiny settlement known as *Culebra* or "the Snake" which is where the railroad had ended in 1854. Back then, at the height of the rush for gold, passengers arriving on the train from Aspinwall "were compelled to mount upon mules, and flounder on through heavy sloughs and rapid streams, along the borders of deep ravines and over precipitous mountains, exposed to drenching rains in the wet season, and broiling sun in the dry, not infrequently attacked and plundered by banditti, with which the road was then infested, until, after a whole day's labor and peril, they arrived in Panama, only twelve miles distant."

"Culebra at that time was a thrifty place, boasting two or three hotels, imported ready-made from the United States, into which often more than a thousand men, women, and children were promiscuously stowed for a night. There were also twenty or thirty native huts, about twelve feet square, each of which was considered of ample dimensions to house a dozen wayworn travelers, only too thankful to find a spot of dry ground upon which to spread their blankets ..."[27]

Once the line was completed Culebra quickly became a "vestige ... of its former estate." When completed the rail line went through a third of a mile cut through the clay summit, about forty feet deep, and then began descending to the Pacific again at the same rate as it had climbed to the summit,

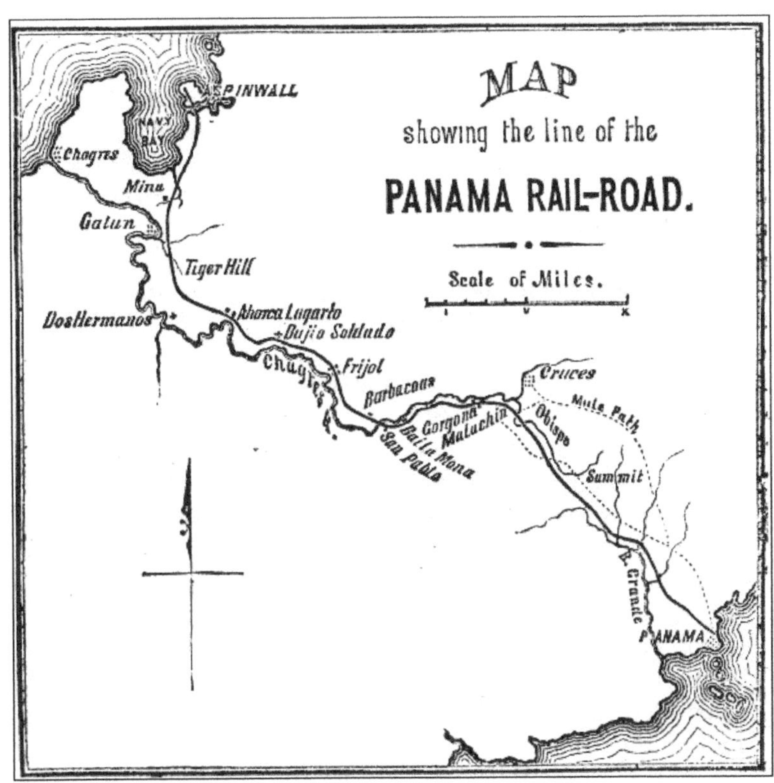

Train leaving for Panama City 1857.

sixty feet to the mile. The final stretch was more scenic including a basaltic cliff partially destroyed with yet with enough remaining "to strike the beholder with admiring wonder, on contemplating this curious formation, at the still visible regularity and beauty of its crystallization, and with awe when he reflects upon the gigantic internal forces that have resulted in its upheaval."[28]

The train continued along the Rio Grande through a beautiful valley called *Paraiso* ("Paradise").

"From Paraiso the road continues on over ravines, and curves around the base of the frequent conical mountains, gradually descending until the low lands and swamps of the valley of the Rio Grande are passed, when looming up in the distance is seen the high bald head of Mount Ancon, whose southern foot is washed by the waters of the Pacific Ocean. On the left rises 'Cerro de los Buccaneros' ('the hill of the Bucaneers'), from whose summit the pirate Morgan, on his marauding march across the Isthmus in 1670, had his first view of ancient Panama, and where he encamped on the night previous to his attack and pillage of that renowned city. Crossing by bridges of iron the San Pedro Miguel and Caimitillo (narrow tide-water tributaries of the Rio Grande), the Rio Grande Station is passed. From thence, through alternate swamp and cultivated savanna, the muddy bed of the Rio Cardenas is crossed; when, leaving the Rio Grande to the eastward, a fine stretch of undulating country around the base of Mount Ancon is brought into view, enlivened by native huts and cultivated fields. About a mile farther on may be seen the long metallic roofs of the railroad buildings of the Pacific terminus peeping out from a grove of cocoa-trees, and a little beyond them, to the right, the Cathedral towers, the high-tiled roofs and dilapidated fortifications of the city of Panama, while through the intervening foliage occasional glimpses of the 'ever peaceful ocean' assure the traveler that the transit of the Isthmus is nearly accomplished, and a few minutes more brings him safely into the spacious passenger depot of the Railroad Company at Panama."[29]

Seven steam ship lines and four sailing vessels provided

connections between Panama and New York, San Francisco, Oregon, California, Liverpool, Bremen, Bordeaux, Mexico, Nicaragua, Costa Rica, Salvador, Guatemala, Ecuador, Peru, Bolivia and Chile

The very existence of the Panama Railroad and the convenience of moving goods across the Isthmus made it possible for people to speculate about the feasibility of a canal across the Isthmus as a path between the seas.

Moving Onward

When the United States bought the French rights to build a canal, they got the railroad rights as well. Since the canal followed the route of the railroad along the Chagres, it cost the United States $9 million to relocate the railroad.

When the Carter-Torrijos Treaty turned what remained of the Panama Railroad over to Panama, the railroad was antiquated and losing money.. Nine passenger trains ran daily beginning at 5:00 a.m. The main engines were already twenty-five years old. Getting equipment was not easy because the railroad was not a standard gage. The number of employees increased dramatically after Panama took over the railroad, but many of these were political administrative jobs without the requirement to even show up at work. Maintenance was neglected and conditions became so bad that the U. S. military prohibited their personnel from using the railroad. Shipping rates rose and service became so erratic that the Canal ceased to use it. The railroad reverted to what John Stevens once described as "two streaks of rust and a right of way" and was losing an estimated $4 million a year.

Panama's aggressive process of privatizing many of the assets it acquired with the Canal turnover eventually included the railroad. In 1998 the Panama Canal Railway Company was formed as a joint venture between Kansas City Southern Railroad and Mi-Jack Products, an independent intermodal terminal operator with a fifty-year concession to rebuild and operate the line. The company invested $80 million to renovate and renew the railroad.

Today the Panama Canal Railway, the direct descendant of the Panama Railroad, has one passenger train which makes a journey each morning from Panama City [Balboa] to Colon, and during the cruise season carries cruise passengers on excursions between the two cities. Thousands of cruise passengers each season, roughly September to May, make this journey from one side of the Isthmus to the other.

The Panama Canal Railway's main business is transporting shipping containers across the Isthmus. Panama is the only place in the world where it is possible to transship containers in-bond from the Atlantic to the Pacific in under four hours. Often container ships have containers stacked too high to meet Canal restrictions, and so they can offload extra containers at one end of the Canal and by the time they reach the other end the containers are waiting to be reloaded. Because containers can be transshipped in bond, they can be sent from the Pacific port to the gigantic Colon Free Zone on the other side of the Isthmus

PANAMA RAILROAD.

7. The French Effort

Ferdinand de Lesseps, dubbed "the greatest Frenchman who ever lived," saw a great opportunity and seized it. De Lesseps, sometimes also called "the great engineer" even though he was a promoter and not an engineer, was riding high after his triumph in creating the Suez Canal.

Although canals had been built in ancient Egypt, those efforts had long since been covered over by shifting sands. De Lesseps, who for most of his life had been a diplomat, was able to parlay his connection with Sa'id Pasha of Egypt for permission to construct a sea level canal.

Until you've sailed across the Suez, and spent a long day gazing out at mile upon mile of sand, you really can't appreciate what a phenomenal achievement it was to link the Mediterranean with the Red Sea. When the Suez Canal opened in 1869 it was like when the first man landed on the moon. It was a fantastic achievement of the French, who were called "the great engineers" because all across Europe they were building fantastic bridges and structures.

Riding high after Suez, a canal across Central America seemed the next logical step. There were two possible routes, one across Nicaragua and the other across Panama. Nicaragua was the longer route, but it was able to use the vast expanse of

Lake Nicaragua in the middle of the country.

France wasn't the only player. The United States, by now the primary user of the Panama Railroad, needed a cheaper and more efficient supply line to the West. Several U. S. surveying expeditions studied routes across both Nicaragua and Panama, and even Mexico. The United States had been quietly negotiating with both Colombia, for Panama, and Nicaragua. Great Britain was also talking about a possible canal.

As mentioned, the idea of a canal across Panama had been around since the earliest Spanish explorers. Riding on the success of Suez, and sensing the time was right for a canal across the Isthmus, the French sent over a preliminary exploration team in 1876. Their report recommended a canal design that would include locks and a series tunnels through the mountains. De Lesseps, already committed to the idea of a sea level canal like Suez, didn't like their recommendation and sent over a second team in 1877. This team basically mapped out the route along the original Panama Railroad, which is somewhat the route the Canal follows today. They called for just one tunnel through the continental divide at Culebra.

It was a ready made environment for a promoter like de Lesseps.

Matthew Parker, in *Panama Fever*, writes, "Paris in the spring of 1879 was awash with financial speculation. Money was more plentiful and mobile than ever before … Penalties for debt and bankruptcy had been eased, and restrictions on lifting shares had been lifted. In the Paris bourse, young stockbrokers noisily wheeled and dealed betting on pretty much anything and often making huge sums for themselves."[30]

Meanwhile, a concession to build a canal was negotiated by the French with Colombia, since Panama was then part of Colombia. The concession gave the French a lease for ninety-nine years without paying any compensation to Colombia, and at the end of the lease the canal would revert to Colombia.

Sometimes people say, "I thought the United States had a ninety-nine-year lease," confusing the French agreement with Colombia with the agreement the United States would wrest from the newly minted Republic of Panama.

The Greatest Frenchman

In 1897 De Lesseps called the "Congres International d'Etudes du Canal Interocéanique" in Paris to consider a Canal across Central America, knowing in advance what he planned to do, and looking for an official endorsement. Instead of getting a quick rubber stamp to his plan, he got a heated debate.

There were fourteen plans offered for consideration. Proposals included several requiring tunnels through mountains and lock systems. Only one of the engineers had any construction experience in the tropics, and he argued for a canal that using locks. De Lesseps had organized the conference with only one purpose, and that was to have his plan rubber-stamped. Before the final vote half of the conference walked out in disgust.

The resolution for a sea level canal passed with only eight of the remaining delegates opposed. The "no" votes included the engineer with the tropical experience who always said a sea level Canal wouldn't work and Alexandre Gustave Eiffel, of Eiffel tower fame. Of those voting in favor, only one, Pedro Sosa of Panama, had ever actually been in Central America.

"Greatness" was the operative word for the French. The Franco Prussian War in 1870 had crushed France, both militarily and emotionally. The Second French Empire was replaced by the Third French Republic. France was determined to be great once again, this time not by war, but through the greatness of engineering achievement that had been evidenced by the opening of Suez, just a year before the crushing Franco Prussian War.

De Lesseps pitching his plan for a Suez Canal

Cartoon of the day showing de Lesseps dividing the continents.

De Lesseps could have retired after his triumph in Suez, but the time and the conditions were right for de Lesseps to lead another French engineering triumph. De Lesseps was not an engineer, nor had he ever been to Panama or the tropics, but the idea of building yet another grand canal captivated him. Several survey teams were dispatched and if they returned with less than favorable reports, de Lesseps simply sent out another group of surveyors.

Back in the United States it looked like the States would finally get a canal, only one built and controlled by the French.

De Lesseps kicked his promotion efforts into high gear. In February, 1880, he went to New York to raise money, meeting with the American Society of Civil Engineers and the Geographic Society. The "greatest Frenchman who ever lived" went to Washington, where he met with President Rutherford Hayes, and testified to the House Interoceanic Canal Committee. He went to Boston, Chicago, and several other large American cities raising interest and capital. On the way home he stopped in Liverpool where he received a warm reception.

Back home in France he found his countrymen eager to invest, often investing their life savings in this great project of France.

One of the Canal landmarks you will pass on your voyage is known as "Gold Hill." Why "Gold Hill"? Turns out the overeager and over optimistic writer of a prospectus for the French Canal Company, lured investors by saying, "this mountain is full of gold and it is believed that the ore from this place alone will be worth more than will be the total cost of the canal construction." Who could resist an investment pitch like that? The French enthusiastically bought into the project snapping up shares of the company, demanding to buy more shares than were available.

The French arrived in Panama in 1881 with one local paper enthusiastically comparing de Lesseps plan to link the oceans with Columbus' discovery of America. Confidence and optimism prevailed; after all, all they had to do was move a few mountains and dig a canal. De Lesseps declared that Panama would be easier than Suez. The work was begun with great pomp, ceremony and celebration. Lavish state dinners and balls were held with de Lesseps, already seventy-five years old, dancing through the night.

The French were so confident of success they ordered 150 thousand kerosene torches sent to Panama, to be used in the grand midnight parade that would celebrate the completion of the canal.

Since de Lesseps was a trained diplomat and not an engineer, he assigned his son Charles the task of supervising the daily work. De Lesseps himself handled the important work of promoting and raising money for the project from private subscription. His boundless confidence, enthusiasm for the project, his consummate faith in the miracles of technology, and promises of huge return were irresistible to investors.

With the Monroe Doctrine[31] in hand, the United States looked askance at the French moving ahead with a canal that the United States had intended to build on what U. S. President Rutherford Hayes considered to be "virtually part of the coast line of the United States." Reluctantly viewing the French Panama project as a private and not a state project, the United States chose to sit back, watch, and criticize. De Lesseps dismissed American opposition as "a phantom and a bugbear."

The French effort failed for several reasons.

The first was mismanagement.

> At stockholder expense, de Lesseps built himself a grand house on the continental divide for $100,000, equal to about $2 million in today's money. He also built a summer house at La Boca for $150,000, about $3 million today, and ordered a private rail car for him to travel around Panama for $42,000 or about

Celebrating the start of the French Canal

Ferdinand de Lesseps 1805 – 1894.

$840,000 in today's money.

Willis Fletcher Johnson, writing of *Four Centuries of The Panama Canal* describes the mismanagement: "When a $50,000 building was needed, a $100,000 building was erected, at a corrupt cost of $200,000."[32]

One of de Lesseps early acts was to order snow shovels from France. Johnson recalls seeing, after the French had left, warehouses full of "thousands of snow shovels."

"Apparently, agents were sent all over France, asking manufacturers if they had any surplus stocks of goods of which they wished to rid. If the answer was affirmative, as of course it usually was, they were told to ship the goods to Panama. But they were nothing that was wanted or could be used there … no matter; ship them along. So they sent cargo after cargo, of the most useless things, from hairpins to grand pianos. Almost every week the men at Colon were surprised by the arrival of a ship load of things they had not ordered, did not want, and could not use."[33]

Contracts were let in the same random way in which supplies were ordered. Over two hundred different firms were contracted without any coordination.

Machinery was shipped from France, the United States and Belgium. Equipment was constantly being modified and used in experimental combinations. There were no spare parts, and parts were not interchangeable, so work sites were littered with discarded and inoperative equipment all testifying to poor planning.

De Lesseps second grand visit to Panama.

Compagnie Universelle du
Canal Interocéanique de Panama
Société Anonyme
2E SÉRIE Capital Social 300,000,000 de Francs 2E SÉRIE
Émission de 500,000 Obligations
Obligation Nouvelle
au Porteur
Remboursable à Mille francs
No 048,399
Par délégation
Un Administrateur
Le Président Directeur
Ferd de Lesseps

Canal Interocéanique de Panama 24
Oblig. No 048,399

Canal Interocéanique de Panama 23
Oblig. No 048,399

Canal Interocéanique de Panama 22
Oblig. No 048,399

Canal Interocéanique de Panama 21
Oblig. No 048,399

Canal Interocéanique de Panama 20
Oblig. No 048,399

Stock certificate from the French Panama Canal Company.

De Lesseps plan for a sea level canal was flawed from the start.

The engineers whom de Lesseps ignored were right: a sea level canal across Panama would never work, largely because of the continental divide. It is said that if de Lesseps had continued, that the French would *still* be digging.

The French had absolutely no concept of what life in the tropics was like. They had no idea of the amount of rain that could fall, and how quickly it could fall. It wasn't just the mud and mudslides, it was the water itself. They had no idea of the tremendous amount of water that could come down the Chagres River, rushing into the sea.

The Chagres could rise and flood in an hour, sweeping away men and materials. Isthmus is one of the wettest places on earth where rain can fall at what would be an hourly rate of 4 inches [10.2 centimeters] per hour. The French had no idea what to do with all the water flowing from the Chagres River. The United States would come along and wisely utilize all of this water … and even to this day, it is the water generated by the Chagres River that allows the Canal to function.

It was becoming clear to nearly everyone, except Ferdinand de Lesseps, that a sea level canal would not work. Eventually, and reluctantly, he agreed to change, but ... suddenly, there was no more money. The company was broke ... 20,000 men had died ... and there was no canal.

The French not only didn't understand the disease problem they would encounter in Panama, but at the time no one understood the cause of the disease, let alone had any idea how to treat or control the illnesses.

Whole towns were thrown up without adequate sanitation. The rain pooled everywhere. Shanty towns sprang up without any form of public order. There was little for workers to do in their off hours but drink and fornicate. Colon had over 150 bars, and one street, "Bottle Alley," was nothing but forty bars. Workers who got sick were simply terminated so the subcontractors didn't have to pay for hospitalization. Men who died on the job were sometimes just rolled down the hill and buried under tons of spoil.

It rains in the rain forest. All of that rain, plus all of the excavation equals mud and standing water, the perfect breeding ground for disease-carrying mosquitoes. Only the French simply did not understand the tropical diseases they would face. Medicine had only vague theories of how diseases like malaria and yellow fever were spread. They thought that perhaps the diseases were spread through some kind of swamp vapors. No one had made the connection with mosquitoes.

Stylish Victorian interiors featured rooms overloaded with furniture and palm trees giving the space a colonial touch. Now the French came to Panama with beautiful foliage everywhere, so they decorated their houses and porches with beautiful palms in pots standing in saucers of water. Ooops! To control the plague of ants that is common in Panama, and keep the ants out of patient beds, in hospitals they put bowls of standing water under the four posts of the beds ... standing water ideal for breeding mosquitoes. Those who were admitted to hospital for any reason had a seventy-five percent chance of dying

Workers wrote their wills before leaving for Panama: a few had the foresight to bring their coffins with them from France.

French machinery at work.

Abandoned French machinery.

Old French engine found while dredging the Canal.

> A West Indian worker named Alfred Dottin recalled, "Death was our constant companion. I shall never forget the trainloads of dead men being carted away, daily, as if they were just so much lumber. Malaria Malaria with all its horrible meaning those days was just a household word. I saw mosquitoes, I say this, without fear of exaggerating, by the thousands attack one man. There were days when we could only work a few hours because of the high fever racking our bodies – it was a living hell."[34]
>
> The medical understanding and technology needed to conquer the Isthmus did not exist.

Most importantly, the French failed because they were ahead of their time: the technology to perform the Herculean task simply didn't exist.

> Each of five excavators working on the Atlantic side could remove 392 cubic yards [300 cubic meters] each day, but lack of spoil trains defeated their work. The equipment wasn't the right type, and was too small and too light. French bucket-chain excavators got caught and halted by stones and rock.

If you drive along the side road from Panama City to Colon, just before the bridge across the Gamboa River and the Gamboa Resort Hotel, you will pass a tiny hillside cemetery beside the road known as Mount Hope Cemetery or the French Cemetery. This is the resting place of some of the workers of the Panama Canal from the French period, many of whom came from Martinique, Jamaica, and St. Lucia. It is estimated that 20,000 workers died during the French era, but nobody knows for sure. The French recorded only people who died in hospitals, but people were dying so fast that many never made it to hospital.

"The Panama Affair"

Not surprisingly the French effort ended in dismal failure. The money had run out. The stock was worthless. Millions of French investors had lost everything. For years to come in France the French canal effort would simply be referred to as "The Panama Affair."

Except for the recriminations and trials that would consume France over the next several years, the grand French Panama adventure had ended. De Lesseps and his son and Eiffel, of Eiffel tower fame, were tried and sentenced to prison. In the end it was decided that although the canal was plagued by mismanagement that there was no malfeasance or intent to defraud and the so principals never actually went to jail.

De Lesseps would retire from public eye and eventually become a senile old man, maybe still dreaming of his years of glory, maybe not.

A "new" Panama Canal Company was organized, but with insufficient working capital, and a public that had soured on the idea of a canal, the idea was abandoned and the rights to build a canal were eventually sold to the Americans.

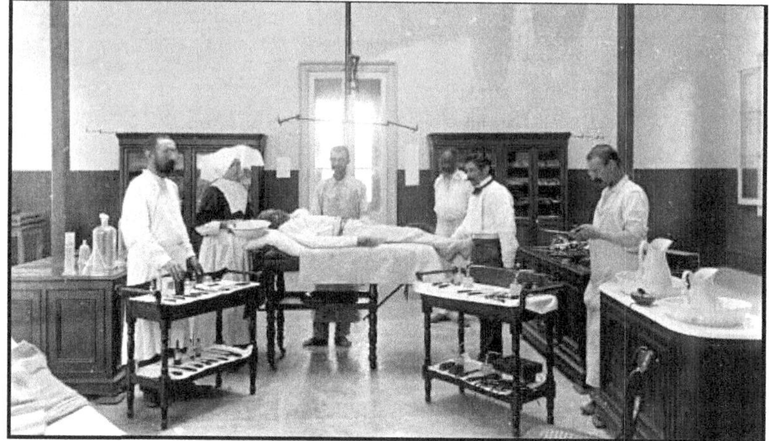

French Hospital Ancon around 1900.

The trial of de Lesseps and the French canal promoters.

8. Banana Republic

The TV show "Survivor" was one of the productions that led to a revolution in television and introduced a whole string of "reality" shows, if you can call being marooned on a deserted island with a dozen or so supposedly "normal" self-obsessed characters selected for their "eye candy" appeal, along with a full Hollywood production crew, any sort of reality. But the show was a hit and the first shows were filmed on the Pearl Islands of Panama. Contestants sought to outdo one another to "outwit, outplay, outlast" and be the ultimate "Survivor" who walks away with the money.

If there was any "survivor" of the French Canal effort it was de Lesseps' chief engineer, Philippe Bunau-Varilla, who not only managed to avoid being convicted and sentenced in France, but also eventually managed to acquire stock in a new French Canal company, and exercise some control of the French rights to build a canal across Panama.

The Frenchman, Bunau-Varilla, would be a key player not only in selling the French rights to the United States, but in writing the treaty that gave away the swath across Panama known as the U. S. Panama Canal Zone.

Essential to U. S. Growth and Defense

Since the United States from the beginning had been angling to build and control a canal across Central America, they weren't saddened by the French failure.

California [1850] and Oregon [1859] had both become states, so there was a need in the States to move material and people across the country. Although the transcontinental railroad was completed in 1869, it was still developing and although cheaper and faster than a wagon train, it was a slow and expensive way to transport everything needed to supply a growing Western United States. The Spanish American War in 1898 demonstrated the military need for a Canal. When the battleship USS MAINE was blown up in Havana Harbor, the nearest battleship was the USS OREGON in San Francisco. It took sixty-seven days to bring the USS OREGON around the Horn to Havana from San Francisco. As the war came to a close the United States acquired the Philippines, Guam, Puerto Rico, and a permanent U. S. Naval base at Guantánamo Bay. The United States had also thrown out the Hawaiian monarch and annexed the Hawaiian Islands.

As the U. S. empire grew, there was clearly the need for a strong U. S. Navy, and the need for a canal to conveniently and quickly move ships between the Atlantic and Pacific to protect U. S. interests.

The United States always had a sense of entitlement to any future canal, based on a broad interpretation of the Monroe Doctrine. So when U. S. President Rutherford Hayes said that he considered Panama to be "virtually part of the coast line of the United States," he was simply expressing the U. S. party line.

U. S. President William McKinley was assassinated by an anarchist in 1901 and his popular Vice President, Theodore Roosevelt, became president.

Roosevelt was born with a silver spoon in his mouth and was sickly as a child. But, as a federal bureaucrat, later no-nonsense Commissioner of Police in New York City, then Assistant Secretary of the Navy, and finally Vice President, Roosevelt carefully cultivated his image. When the Spanish American War broke out, Roosevelt had resigned his Navy position to go off to battle leading a voluntary U. S. Cavalry regiment the newspapers nicknamed the "Rough Riders."

Rudyard Kipling wrote of Theodore Roosevelt, "The universe seemed to be spinning around and Theodore was the spinner."

Roosevelt expanded the Monroe Doctrine in what is called "The Roosevelt Corollary to the Monroe Doctrine" which stated, "All that this country desires is to see the neighboring countries stable, orderly, and prosperous. Any country whose people conduct themselves well can count upon our hearty friendship. If a nation shows that it knows how to act with reasonable efficiency and decency in social and political matters, if it keeps order and pays its obligations, it need fear no interference from the United States. Chronic wrong doing or an impotence which results in a general loosening of the ties of civilized society ... may force the United States, however reluctantly, in flagrant cases of such wrongdoing or impotence, to the exercise of an international police power."

Nicaragua or Panama?

The big question in the United States wasn't whether or not to build a canal, but where the canal should be built … Nicaragua or Panama? The issue was hotly debated in Washington, throughout the country, and in scientific circles.

There were those in government, and who influenced government, who had vested interests and lobbied accordingly. Both routes had their advocates, and the same arguments present before the French failure, were still in play. Panama was shorter, but would require considerable effort to get over the continental divide, and would require a lock

Philippe Bunau-Varilla 1859 – 1940

Teddy Roosevelt leading his "Rough Riders"

system. Nicaragua, although a longer route, could take advantage of Lake Nicaragua, and could be a sea level canal.

Unfortunately, Nicaragua decided to celebrate its live volcanoes by putting them on their postage stamps, one of which showed Nicaragua's famous Momotombo volcano in full eruption.

As the debate in Congress raged on, just days before the Senate was scheduled to vote on the route the canal should take, Bunau-Varilla remembered the Nicaraguan stamps. "Rushing about to every stamp dealer in Washington he managed to purchase ninety all together, one for each senator. He pasted the precious stamps on sheets of paper and below each typed out: 'An official witness of the volcanic activity on the isthmus of Nicaragua.'

"The stamp arrived at the office of every member of the Senate with the morning mail on Monday, June 16, three days before the deciding vote."[35]

Of course Panama had volcanoes then, and now. I live on the slope of one! But the "stamp lobby" successfully created fear and doubt and proved to be an inexpensive and effective lobbying effort. On June 19, 1902, the Senate voted forty-two to thirty-four in favor of a canal through Panama.

Now that Panama had been decided on as a location, all the remained was for the United States to get Colombia to give up a swath of land across the middle of its Panamanian territory.

Roosevelt assigned his Secretary of State, John Hay, to negotiate a treaty with Colombia that would give the United States rights to build a canal across Colombia's Panamanian territory. The Hay-Haran Treaty was approved by the U. S. Senate on January 22, 1903. But when the Colombian charge d'affaires, Dr. Tomás Herran, took the treaty home to be ratified, the Colombian legislature took one look at it and unanimously said, "No way Jose!"

Political cartoons reflecting the debate of the day … Panama or Nicaragua?

Meanwhile, the Frenchman Bunau-Varilla was hustling around Washington, peddling shares in the New French Canal Company, which he controlled, first asking $109 million, and then cutting his price to a fire-sale, bargain basement price of $40 million.

When Panama had joined Bolivar's Gran Colombia, it never intended just to be part of Colombia, but that's what happened when Gran Colombia dissolved. Panama's relations with Colombia deteriorated. The Thousand Days War between factions in Colombia raged on from 1899 to 1903, sucking Panama into a conflict in which they really had little interest. As the war continued it became more oppressive and cruel, with the population forced to take part in fanatical ways, including having young boys conscripted as boy soldiers. Panamanians began asking, "Why?" This was not the stuff of Bolivar's dream Gran Colombia.

In September 1902 the United States sent U. S. troops to Panama to protect the U. S. owned Panama Railroad. In November, with strong United States encouragement, a peace treaty was signed between the warring factions on the battleship USS WISCONSIN.

The move toward independence from Colombia was quietly gaining support across Panama.

Things moved quickly in Washington. Buneau-Varilla and company had actually prepared a "new country kit" to share with their connections in Panama which included, amongst other things, a suggested constitution and a silk flag for the new country! Thankfully the Panamanians threw it all in the dump.

Meanwhile, in the fast-moving world of international politics and intrigue, on October 10, 1903 Philippe Bunau-Varilla met with Roosevelt to warn him of imminent rebellion in Panama.

Child soldiers in Panama 1895.

Impatient to build the canal, Roosevelt supported Panama's independence movement. He dispatched warships to both sides of the Isthmus blocking sea approaches, conveniently just in time for Panama to declare separation from Colombia on November 3, 1903. The only casualties were a shopkeeper and a donkey.

On November 6 there was an official declaration of separation from Colombia and on November 7, conveniently the United States immediately recognized the status of the Republic of Panama. When Colombia sent troops to quell the rebellion, the United States just happened to have warships sitting off Panama to repel the Colombians. On November 13, 1903 the United States formally recognized the Republic of Panama, as did France and fifteen other countries.

The "Survivor" is the one who walks away with the money.

Twelve days later, claiming to represent the newly created Republic of Panama, the Frenchman Bunau-Varilla granted the United States a strip of land across Panama and the rights to build the canal and in return the United States agreed to protect the new country. Bunau-Varilla had not lived in Panama for the previous sixteen years, nor would he ever return to Panama, but had purchased influence through financial assistance he had provided to the rebels, including among other things, the unused "new country kit."

"The high contracting parties have resolved for that purpose to conclude a convention and have accordingly appointed as their plenipotentiaries - The President of the United States of America, John Hay, Secretary of State, and The Government of the Republic of Panama, Philippe Bunau-Varilla, Envoy Extraordinary and Minister Plenipotentiary of the Republic of Panama, thereunto specially empowered by said government ..."

On November 18th the Hay-Bunau-Varilla Treaty was signed and called for the United States:

- To maintain the independence of Panama;
- To have use, occupation and control of zone 10 miles [16 kilometers] wide splitting Panama in half;
- To pay Panama $10 million initially and after nine years pay $25 thousand per year with Panama having no future share in profits.

It is important to note that *no Panamanian signed the Treaty.* The treaty was never-the-less ratified by both sides, despite Panamanian complaints. The new country of Panama was dubbed the "Banana Republic" and had the choice to accept the treaty or have all U. S. support for their new country withdrawn.

Lest those of us accustomed to U. S. manipulation of international affairs just assume Panama was solely created at the convenience of Washington, R. M. Koster and Guillermo Sanchez point out, "Panama was always a separate national entity [and] was never organically integrated into Colombia. The chief reason was Panama had achieved independence from Spain on her own. The authors of this independence, perhaps frightened by their own audacity, then began to fear a Spanish reconquest of the Isthmus ... Panama was both small and thinly populated, with no troops and few weapons. That is when the idea came up for Panama to join with a larger nation ... [Colombia] then governed by Simón Bolívar in a confederation called Gran Colombia. Bolivar was almost a mythological figure, almost a divinity. His prestige drew Panama into a union with Colombia. In no one's mind in Panama, however, was this union intended to be permanent. When the danger of Spanish reconquest was over, Panama would return to independence."[36]

"By the time Bunau-Varilla ... and Teddy Roosevelt came on the scene, a revolutionary conspiracy was already in progress. But those directing it were realists. They knew Panama's weakness and the strength of Colombia's veteran army. They seized the moment when a coincidence of interests presented the best chance for independence. Here it is that Panama's national aspirations became bound up with the irresistible expansionism of the United States, the political ambitions of Theodore Roosevelt, and the turbulent intriguing of Bunau-Varilla. But the principal separatist impulse came from within Panama ... [Other countries had achieved their independence with help from other nations] And Panama's founding fathers were no less brave, generous, far-seeing, or fallible than those of any other country."[37]

On February 3, 1904 U. S. Marines clashed with Colombian troops attempting to re-establish Colombian sovereignty in Panama and twenty days later the United States paid Panama $10 million for the Canal Zone. U. S. "Gunboat Diplomacy" insured that Panama remained independent.

Colombia did not recognize the Republic of Panama until 1921 when the United States paid Colombia $21 million in "compensation" to buy a kind of Colombian recognition of legitimacy. The United States would continue to intervene in Panama's political affairs until 1936 when the United States agreed to limit the use of its troops to the Canal Zone and the annual rent on the Canal was increased.

In later years when Roosevelt was criticized over U. S. actions in Panama he famously replied, "I took Panama while Congress talked about it."

Political cartoon of the day calling into question the convenient birthing of this new country nicknamed the "Banana Republic."

The Roosevelt Corollary to the Monroe Doctrine.

9. Let The Dirt Fly

The first order of business in constructing the canal was for the United States to evaluate what the French had done, and see what French equipment could be used. It turned out that most of the French equipment was rusted and useless and about the only thing that could be used were some of the French buildings. This was actually to the benefit of the United States since it forced them to invent new machinery that was adequate to do the job.

War on the "family cat" or "all the beasts of the jungle?"

If the Americans were to be successful, they had to control disease and death. In 1904 Dr. William Gorgas took over as the chief sanitary officer. Gorgas was able to build on the work of his commanding officer, Dr. Walter Reed, who had developed insights of a Cuban doctor, Dr. Carlos Finlay, to prove that yellow fever was transmitted by mosquitoes. First in Florida, then in Cuba, Gorgas had attacked yellow fever. Gorgas had survived yellow fever and was now immune. He knew that he needed to eradicate mosquitoes on the Isthmus before new workers arrived, became infected, and died.

Previously unscreened offices and houses got window screens and screen doors. Mosquito nets were distributed.

Fumigation brigades went house to house spraying against mosquitoes in homes, cisterns and cesspools. Gorgas instituted sanitation programs across Panama, drained swamps, and much of the Canal Zone was sprayed with a mixture of carbolic acid, resin, and caustic soda. Clean running water was introduced to do away with the need for standing water containers that could breed mosquitoes. Workers were required to take daily doses of quinine.

Without Gorgas the Canal would never have been possible. Thanks to Gorgas, yellow fever was completely wiped out in Panama with the last reported case in 1905.

Often when people are planning a cruise through the Canal they visit their local public health office or seek out a tropical medicine specialist. Then they come on the ship laden down with malaria pills and having received yellow fever shots ... and gotten stuck with a $500 medical bill.

Pay your money and take your choice, but yellow fever is not a problem in Panama and hasn't been since 1905. Malaria? Unless you are planning to visit a remote part of the Darien jungle … and I have no idea why you would want to do this unless you are going to break bread with Colombian rebels or visit the illegal jungle lab of a Colombian drug lord … you don't have to worry about malaria. If you get malaria, in most cases it is readily cured by the same pills you take to prevent it. Hear out your doctor and make your own decision, but $500 is $500, and might be better spent on Panama tours or Embera Indian basketry.

The greater problem today, in Panama, South and Central America, the islands of the Caribbean, and Southern United States is dengue fever for which there is no preventative pill or cure. So Panama is very concerned about controlling mosquitoes. But on the ship … in the Canal … you're not going to need any bug spray. The breeze alone will keep you bug-free.

Do as you wish, and of course listen to your physician, but as for me, I wouldn't even think about taking malaria pills ... and I live in Panama.

Malaria, unlike yellow fever, does not confer immunity and you can get it again, so malaria was the cause of more deaths during the French and U. S. construction periods than yellow fever. During the first year of the American effort, 1905, nearly everyone, including Gorgas, had contracted malaria.

Gorgas said, "If we cannot control malaria, I feel very little anxiety about other diseases. If we do not control malaria our mortality is going to be heavy." Gorgas said that getting rid of the mosquito that carried yellow fever carrier was like "making war on the family cat," but the campaign against the malaria-carrying mosquito was "like fighting all the beasts of the jungle."

The task to eradicate disease-carrying mosquitoes from the Isthmus was almost as big as the task of building the Canal itself. Vegetation around houses and buildings was removed. More than a hundred square miles of swamp was drained. Ditches were installed so water would not pool. Thousands of minnows were hatched and released and spiders, ants, and lizards were bred and released to feed on adult insects. A mixture of carbolic acid, resin, and oil was sprayed monthly in areas where standing water might collect. Tourists who came to Panama to observe the Canal construction said the entire Isthmus smelled like an oil refinery.

John Wallace was the first man in charge of the U. S. construction effort. Wallace tried picking up where the French had left off, but without support from Washington ended up frustrated and resigned.

Teddy Roosevelt's famous remark regarding the Canal effort, after the convenient creation of the Republic of Panama, was, "Let the dirt fly!" The man who finally made the "dirt fly" was John F. Stevens, the second man in charge of the American effort.

Dr. William Gorgas surveying sanitary conditions.

Sanitation brigade in what is today Casco Viejo.

The Railroader

Steven's background was as a railroad engineer and his ability to design a railroad was critical. Virtually none of the equipment the French had left was useable. Everything that was needed for Canal construction had to be brought to the Isthmus and distributed efficiently along the construction line. Stevens rebuilt the Panama Railroad from the ground up and developed special cars that could be loaded and unloaded quickly.

By comparison to the Americans, the French had used a very primitive rail system. Stevens developed a complex system of railroad tracks at different levels within the Culebra Cut that would enable the spoil to be removed. The tracks could be moved as necessary so that the spoil trains kept pace with the excavation, thus enabling the giant steam shovels to keep working continuously.

Later Stevens would comment, "This is no reflection on the French, but I cannot conceive how they did the work they did with the plant they had."

The size of the work force tripled in six months. To support this rapidly growing workforce Stevens built entire communities including housing, mess halls, YMCAs, hospitals, hotels, schools, churches, laundries, and cafeterias. Communities were designed from scratch. Complex schedules were devised so that the work never stopped and trains carrying the spoil of rock and dirt were at the right place at the right time.

It was Stevens who pushed for a lock canal, rather than a sea level canal. Congress voted approval of the lock plan by a narrow margin, the margin being the difference between U. S. success and a repeat of the French failure.

With all systems "go" and work proceeding efficiently and on schedule, in 1907 Stevens suddenly retired, without giving any explanation other than it was "personal."

Presidential photo op on a Bucyrus steam shovel in Panama.

President Roosevelt and party viewing Canal construction first hand.

Frustrated by the loss of Stevens, Roosevelt decided to go to Panama himself to survey the situation on the ground.

In 1907 Roosevelt went to Panama, the first president in history to leave the United States while in office. He chose to visit in November at the height of the rainy season, because he wanted to see Panama at its worst and understand the challenges faced. He visited construction sites, talked to workers, and even had an early presidential "photo op" while sitting at the controls of a steam shovel in Culebra Cut.

Roosevelt viewed the building of the Canal as a mighty battle, pitting the United States against the unbelievable challenge of building a route between the oceans.

Someone Who Could Not Resign

Determined not to lose another capable leader, Roosevelt appointed someone who could not resign, then Lieutenant Colonel George Washington Goethals of the U. S. Army Corps of Engineers. Goethals was an Army man used to taking orders. Determined that Goethals get it done, Roosevelt gave Goethals absolute authority over the project, answerable only to the Secretary of War and the President himself.

Accepting the challenge, Goethals said, "I am no longer a commander in the U. S. Army. I now consider that I am commanding the Army of Panama, and that the enemy we are going to combat is the Culebra Cut and the locks and dams at both ends of the Canal, and any man here on the work who does his duty will never have any cause to complain of militarism."

Although Goethals never wore his military uniform in Panama, eventually he became *General* George Washington Goethals. A West Point Graduate, Goethals not only had experience in military organization and command, but understood engineering and construction of locks and dams.

Long before OSHA, this charcoal sketch by William Van Engen illustrates how workers were lifted in and out of the lock chambers

The popular image was that the United States was digging the Canal, but the truth was that almost the entire world became involved. Panama and the United States alone couldn't provide all the "grunt" labor to dig the canal, so the United States began recruiting and importing laborers from all over. They came by the thousands from Greece and Europe, from China and Asia, and from the islands of the Caribbean.

Generally there were no more than 5,000 Americans employed. Almost all of the down and dirty workers came from the rest of the world. Like the French, the Americans looked to the nearest source of cheap labor, the Caribbean. Almost 20,000 laborers came from Barbados alone, representing about thirty to forty percent of the adult men of Barbados.

Keeping such a diverse, transient, mostly male population relatively healthy and controlled, required the Canal Zone from the start to be a highly ordered and regulated society.

Gold or Silver?

Canal workers were paid in either gold or silver. U. S. workers, mostly white, were paid in gold, and everyone else was paid in silver. Of course today any U. S. citizen would be delighted to be paid in either gold or silver! The pay car had separate windows for people being paid in gold and in silver. Thus began the distinction that ruled life in the Canal Zone and became a euphemism for racism, a highly stratified system of "gold" and "silver."

Many of the Americans who worked on the Canal came from the Southern States where segregation was the norm and that way of life was followed in the Canal Zone. Signs on toilets, drinking fountains, shops, and railway cars noted "gold" or "silver," the Canal's way of saying "white" or "colored." Those paid in gold were all white Americans, and those paid in silver were all persons of color, including local Panamanians.

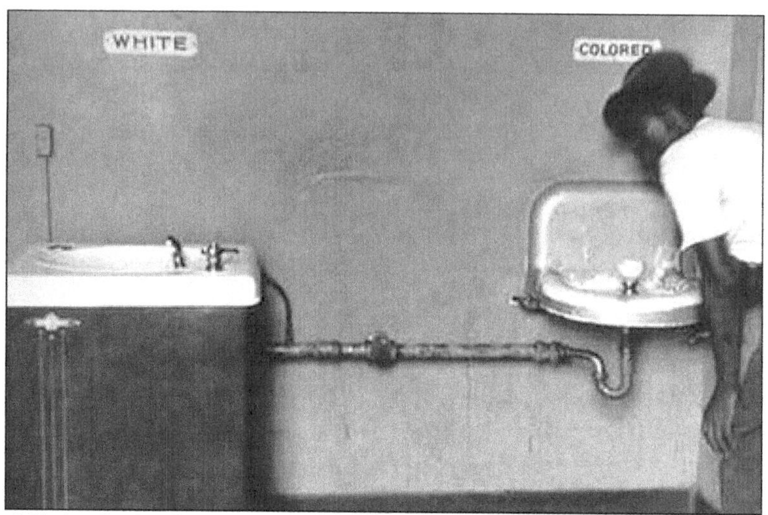

Life in the U. S. Canal Zone was strictly segregated, generally euphemistically labeled "silver" and "gold."

The pay car: originally non-white laborers were paid in silver, and white American workers were paid in gold.

A stated goal of life within the Canal Zone was to prevent "intermingling of the races." Most Panamanians working within the Zone were people of color who had menial jobs and quite naturally came to resent not only the system, but the United States and its occupation of the Canal Zone.

Built Tough in the U. S. A.

The French effort had been compromised by scores of independent contractors who were poorly coordinated and by inadequate machinery that wasn't standardized. The United States had one contractor: the U. S. Army Corps of Engineers. The fact that the equipment left behind by the French was unusable proved to be a blessing for the United States. The United States simply built its own equipment.

The first patent for a steam shovel was acquired by William Otis, a Philadelphia engineer, in 1839. The steam shovel proved to be a boon to railroad construction. Two companies in the United States, Marion Steam Shovel Company and Bucyrus-Erie Shovel Company, built the machines that were instrumental in the construction of the Canal. One hundred and two shovels were used in the Canal construction, two-thirds of these built by Bucyrus and the others by Marion.

The Bucyrus shovels each weighed 95 U. S. tons [86 metric tons] and could lift up to 30,000 pounds [13,607 kilograms] of rock.

Another essential component of success that the French had lacked was a railroad capable of moving 232 million U. S. tons [210 million metric tons] of spoil. Just as William Gorgas had been the key to success in controlling tropical diseases, John Frank Stevens, the second man in charge of the Canal construction, was the key to creating the infrastructure that made the Canal possible.

Moving Mountains

To complete the Canal it was necessary to somehow get over,

under, or through the mountain. The Canal builders decided to cut an 8.75 mile [14.1 kilometer] stretch through the continental divide from Gamboa to the little town of Pedro Miguel on the South. Ships would be lifted up to the level of a newly created lake and then sail across the Isthmus 85 feet [25.9 meters] above sea level. To get the ships through the continental divide the cut through the mountain would have to take it from 210 feet [64 meters] to 40 feet [12.2 meters] above sea level.

Holes were drilled and filled with explosives to loosen the dirt and rock. Gigantic steam shovels would pile the spoil on railroad cars that would haul it away to fill or dump sites. This is where the railroad system designed by John L. Stevens would prove essential. Wooden flatcars, each carrying 19 cubic yards [14.5 cubic meters] of spoil, would be pulled by long trains to the designated dump sites. Stevens had designed a unique rail car where both sides could be dropped and a huge scoop dragged along the line of cars that efficiently pushed the spoil off the sides as it was winched along.

More than 100 million cubic yards [about 76.5 million cubic meters] of spoil had to be hauled away from the excavation site and dumped. Part of the spoil was used to link four small islands on the Pacific side to create a breakwater which is today known as the Causeway or Amador Peninsula running over three miles [4.8 kilometers] out into the Pacific. Spoil was also used as fill to create the town of Balboa and what became the Fort Amador military reservation.

The unstable nature of the geology of Culebra and the frequency of heavy rains in Panama made earth slides a constant threat to Canal builders. During the French era land slides would sweep away both machinery and people burying both under tons of earth. On October 4, 1907 after several days of heavy rain, 500,000 cubic yards [382,277 cubic meters] of material slid into the cut and the slide continued for ten days moving an average of 14 feet [4.3 meters] every twenty-four hours.

The genius behind the massive Culebra excavation was a young engineer, David Gaillard, a graduate of the United States Military Academy at West Point. Goethals brought Gaillard with him and put the young engineer in charge of the Culebra Cut excavation.

The cut was the most difficult part of the construction taking nine years to excavate, during which 100 million tons of rock were removed and the mountain was cut down from 210 feet [64 meters] to 40 feet [12.2 meters].

Gaillard was evacuated from Panama in 1913 with what was thought to be nervous exhaustion. It turned out that Gaillard had a brain tumor and he died at the age of fifty-four, only nine months before the opening of the Panama Canal. In recognition of his achievement, Culebra Cut was renamed Gaillard Cut. Outside the Miraflores Visitor Center is a memorial plaque to David Gaillard and the men who did the "impossible."

Culebra Cut or Gaillard Cut is one of the special wonders of the Canal. Here is where you should stand with your mouth open, gaping in awe at what men and machines were able to achieve over a hundred years ago.

A Colonial Outpost

While the Americans dug away, there was an underlying resentment building amongst Panamanians. Whereas the French, being French, and convinced that they were the all-knowing engineers of the world, kept to themselves, many Panamanians expected something different from the United States. After all, the creation and security of Panamanian independence from Colombia had been somewhat of a joint effort, so Panama expected to have more of a role in the U. S. Canal project. They expected a piece of the pie. What they got instead was a country divided in two by a self-governed

David Gaillard 1859-1913.

Memorial plaque to David Gaillard outside Miraflores Visitor Center.

ten-mile swath across their country that was totally controlled and administered by the United States without Panamanian participation.

In addition to the Canal the United States was building a colonial outpost that mirrored as much as possible life back in the States to the exclusion of Panamanians. That gives you some idea of the feelings of resentment that Panamanians felt about the Canal Zone. And it helps you understand what was behind U. S. President Jimmy Carter's statement, at the turnover of the Canal at the turn of the century,

"We didn't understand clearly enough the feeling of many Panamanians that the arrangement implied an element of colonialism and subjugation and not an equal representation ..."

The Wonder of the World

The Panama Canal incredibly was completed ahead of schedule, under budget and without any corruption or scandal.

David McCullough writes of the completion of the Panama Canal, "Its cost had been enormous. No single construction effort in American history had exacted such a price in dollars or in human life. Dollar expenditures since 1904 totaled $352 million … By present standards this does not seem a great deal, but it was more than four times what Suez had cost ... and so much more than anything before ever built by the Unites States government as to be beyond compare. Taken together, the French and American expenditures came to about $639 million."[38]

People always read that cost and think, "Wow! That's a lot of money, but look at what they were able to do for that amount," not always realizing that, in today's dollars, with inflation, that $639 million is well over $16 billion!

The greater cost was in the cost of human lives. Hospital records during the U. S. construction era record 5,609 lives were lost from disease and accident. The estimate for the French era is 20,000, although because people were dying so rapidly during the French era, accurate hospital records were not kept. It is likely that the number of people who died during the 10 years of the French effort far exceeds the estimate of 20,000. Adding the deaths during the French era would likely bring the total deaths to some 25,000 based on an estimate by Gorgas. However, the true number will never be known, since the French only recorded the deaths that occurred in hospital.

Again, McCullough, "The total volume of excavation accomplished since 1904 was 232,440,945 cubic yards and this added to the approximately 30, million cubic yards of useful excavation by the French gave a grand total, in round numbers, of 262 million cubic yards, more than four times the volume originally estimated by Ferdinand de Lesseps for a canal at sea level and nearly three times the excavation at Suez."[39]

No Fanfare

Two of the most memorable events in the life of the Panama Canal happened without fanfare.

On August 15, 1914, with the world preoccupied by a World War, the SS ANCON carrying cement made the first official crossing westbound from the Atlantic to the Pacific

Almost a century later, on September 4, 2010, a Chinese freighter carrying a cargo of steel, the MV FORTUNE PLUM, became the one millionth ship to transit the Canal going from the Pacific to the Atlantic, four years ahead of the 100th Anniversary. For whatever reason the Panama Canal Authority wasn't paying attention and missed the historic event! It was weeks before someone noticed that the millionth ship had passed through the Canal without pictures or fanfare. The Canal de Panamá had to chase down the FORTUNE PLUM to arrange to present a plaque commemorating the historic event.

"A Work of Civilization"

Engraved in the rotunda of the Panama Canal Administration building are these words of Theodore Roosevelt:

"It is not the critic who counts, not the man who points out how the strong man stumbled, or where the doer of deeds could have done them better. The credit belongs to the man who is actually in the arena; whose face is marred by dust and sweat and blood; who strives valiantly, who errs and comes short again and again; who knows the great enthusiasms, the great devotions, and spends himself in a worthy cause; who, at the best, knows in the end the triumph of high achievement; and who, at the worst, if he fails, at least fails while daring greatly, so that his place shall never be with those cold and timid souls who know neither victory nor defeat."

David McCullough, in his book *The Path Between The Seas: The Creation of the Panama Canal, 1870-1914,* writes:

"The creation of a water passage across Panama was one of the supreme human achievements of all time, the culmination of a heroic dream of over four hundred years and of more than twenty years of phenomenal effort and sacrifice ...

Primarily the canal is an expression of that old and noble desire to bridge the divide, to bring people together. It is a work of civilization."[40]

SS ANCON making the first official transit of the Canal 1914.

Goethals watched the first transit from his private train along the shoreline.

10. How It Works

On a world map the Isthmus of Panama appears as a tiny sliver of land joining the continents together. At its narrowest point, about where the Canal is located, the Isthmus is about 30–120 miles [48–193 kilometers] wide. So it would seem that if you dug a channel across this narrow point you could link the oceans, which is exactly what de Lesseps thought. The problem was that the Isthmus isn't flat. The American Cordillera, a chain of mountain ranges forming the backbone of the Americas and part of the Pacific Ring of Fire, runs through Panama. A sea level Canal would have to dig through and create a channel dug *below* sea level.

A Water Elevator

The solution was to build what is, in effect, a water elevator, raising the ship from sea level on one ocean, enabling the ship to sail across the Isthmus, and returning it to sea level at the other ocean. For the record, sea level is sea level. Although tidal levels may vary, sometimes greatly, between oceans, sea level is sea level.

As we have noted, cutting through the continental divide was an enormous challenge requiring the mountain to be cut down from 210 feet [64 meters] to 40 feet [12.2 meters] above sea level.

The locks on both sides act as a "water elevator" to lift the ship 85 feet [25.9 meters] above sea level to the level of Gatun Lake, and then lower it again on the other side.

On the Atlantic side this is accomplished using three locks that are grouped together known as Gatun Locks.

On the Pacific side there are two locks at Miraflores and one at Pedro Miguel separated by a small man-made lake. There are several reasons why the locks were split on the Pacific side. First, there wasn't sufficient bedrock at Pedro Miguel to support a three-step lock complex. Second, there were two rivers in the area, Rio Cocoli and Rio Grande, which had to be taken into account so as not to interfere with the shipping channel. Early plans called for one step at Pedro Miguel and an artificial lake, much like the present-day Miraflores Lake, to receive the outflow of the two rivers. The final set of locks was placed at Miraflores. The Rio Grande River still flows into Miraflores Lake. As part of the Canal expansion program, the Cocoli River has been rerouted for the construction of the Boriquen Dam that will create the Pacific Access Channel to the new Pacific lock system.

Water

In order to create the body of water that would enable the ship to sail across the Isthmus, it was necessary to create a huge dam and in the process flood several towns. Since the Canal route roughly follows the route of the original Panama Railroad, several of these towns were important stopover points when crossing the Isthmus by rail. The names of the lock complexes were taken from the names of several of the towns that were flooded in order to create the lake.

The Canal uses only fresh water. Not only would salt water have a corrosive effect on the cement and the metal, but the challenge of the Canal historically has been what to do with all the water that flows into Gatun Lake during the rainy season from the Chagres River. It is not unheard of in Panama to have rain falling at times at 3 to 4 inches [76 to 102 millimeters] an hour.

Each time a ship transits the Canal, through the original locks, 53.4 million U. S. gallons [202,000 cubic meters] of fresh water is passed into the sea. With some 14,600 vessel transits per year, this represents a huge demand for fresh water.

Gatun Dam

Originally there was a gap in the hills around the Chagres Valley of about 1.2 miles [1.9 kilometers]. This gap was filled with material excavated from Culebra Cut and the Gatun lock site to create a dam 2,100 feet [640 meters] thick at the bottom, 7,500 feet [2,286 meters] long along the top and 98 feet [30 meters] thick at the top. At the normal level of Gatun Lake the top of the dam is 30 feet [9 meters] above the lake level.

Gatun Dam is an earthen dam built across the Chagres River, constructed between 1907 and 1913. The dam creates the large, artificial Gatun Lake that allows ships, once they are lifted by the Gatun Locks up 85 feet [25.9 meters] above sea level, to sail across the Isthmus of Panama. The dam, lake, and locks are all named to honor the town of Gatun which was flooded in order to create the Canal.

To create the dam two parallel walls of stone were built and then clay, dredged out of the river base of the Chagres River, was pumped into the center of the walls to create, in effect, a solid core of natural material within the dam.

The dam contains some 22 million cubic yards [16.8 million cubic meters] of material, and weighs some 30 million short tons [27 million metric tons]. It covers 290 acres [1.17 square kilometers] of ground. There is enough earth and rock in Gatun Dam to build a wall almost 5 feet [1.5 meters] high and a foot [.3 meters] thick around the Earth at the Equator!

Construction of the dam was itself a stunning engineering achievement, eclipsed only by the simultaneous excavation of the Culebra or Gaillard Cut. When it was completed Gatun

Dam was the largest earth dam in the world and Lake Gatun was the largest man-made lake in the world.

From Gatun Locks you can see part of the dam and the spillway which regulates the flow of excess water from Gatun Lake. The crest of the spillway dam is 16 feet [4.9 meters] below the normal lake level. The spillway dam has fourteen electrically operated gates, each 46 feet [14 meters] wide by 20 feet [6 meters] high. These gates are used to control the flow of water and the height of water in Gatun Lake. The capacity of the spillway is 140,000 cubic feet [4,100 cubic meters] of water per second, which is more than the maximum flow of the Chagres River.

Panama has a tropical climate with temperatures constant throughout the year, in the Canal area averaging 86 degrees Fahrenheit [30 degrees Celsius]. The rainy season, or "green season" as the tourist people prefer, is May through December and the dry season is January through April. Even during the rainy season it does not rain all the time. When it rains, it rains! Tropical downpours, not drizzle, are typical in Panama. The area of the Panama Canal gets an average of 75 inches [1,905 millimeters] of rain a year, most of it during the rainy season.

Sometimes, during the rainy season so much water is pouring into Gatun Lake that the lake needs to be lowered and the spillway gates are opened, which is a spectacular sight that always draws locals to watch. Should this not be sufficient to lower the lake, the culverts in the locks theoretically could release an additional 49,000 cubic feet [1,400 cubic meters] of excess water per second, probably flooding part of Colon in the process.

A hydroelectric power plant at the Gatun Dam produces power that in the U. S. Canal days was just used for the operation of the Canal. Today the plant provides enough electricity for the Canal as well as additional power which is sold onto the Panama grid. Under Panamanian operation, the

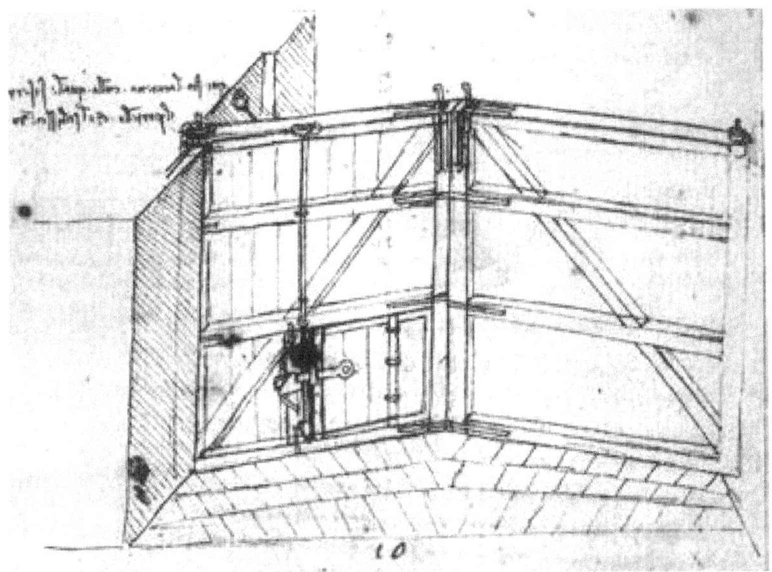

Leonardo da Vinci's design for mitered lock gate.

Panama Canal gates using de Vinci's design.

Canal generates significant revenue from the sale of surplus electricity.

Since rainfall is seasonal in Panama, Gatun Lake also acts as a water reservoir, allowing the Canal to continue operation through the dry season. Gatun Lake is fed primarily by the Chagres River which is in turn fed by dozens of tributaries upstream. Gatun Lake not only enables ships to sail across the Isthmus, but it also solved one of the great problems in constructing a canal: what to do with all that water! Above Gatun Lake, on the Chagres River, is another smaller dam called Madden Dam which helps control the rush of water and creates another artificial water storage area called Alajuela Lake.

Locks

The Chinese were using locks already in the 9th century. In medieval Europe locks were in use in the Lowlands by the 13th century. An Italian civil engineer, Bertola da Novate, constructed a network of eighteen locks in and around Milan in the 14th century. The perpetual problem of holding water in the lock was solved by Leonardo da Vinci who came up with a design for double-leaf doors hinged on chamber walls and sealed by water pressure. That same basic design of the Milan canals is used by the Canal's current lock gates.

Each steel lock leaf is 65 feet [19.8 meters] wide, 7 feet [2.1 meters] thick, and from 47 to 82 feet [14.3 to 25 meters] high and weighs from 390 to 730 tons. The largest gates are at Miraflores Locks and were so designed because of the vast tidal variances on the Pacific side. Tides on the Atlantic are only 1 or 2 feet [.3 or .6 meters] whereas on the Pacific they can run as high as 23 feet [7 meters].

The lock leaves are hollow, so for repairs and maintenance they can be lifted out by one of the Canal's giant cranes and floated off to be repaired. Of course that requires shutting down a traffic lane and causing delays, so the new lock complexes now under construction for the expansion of the

When the gates are closed raised walkways allow workers to cross.

The Gatun Lock control house.

Canal will use the rolling-type gates which are more efficient and easier to maintain.

There are walkways across the lock gates that allow Canal workers to pass from one side of the lock chamber to the other. When the gates are closed and about to open, a bell warns workers and the rails collapse into the gate. Sometimes you will see the red lights flashing on the center wall and hear a siren. This is a warning that hazardous cargo is on the ships and no open flames, smoking or electrical tools are permitted.

One safety concern always has been the failure of the lock gates, perhaps caused by a runaway ship hitting a gate. This could not only unleash a flood, but drain the entire lock system and even Gatun Lake.

Originally the locks had chain barriers stretched across the lock to prevent a ship from ramming a gate. These were lowered into the lock floor when it was time for the ship to pass. These "fender chains" were designed to stop ships up to 10,000 tons, but with ships getting much larger and the expense of maintaining the chains they were removed in 1980.

Extra safety against flooding the system and draining Gatun Lake is provided by an extra set of gates at both ends of the upper chambers on both sides. All four gates would all have to fail to create a disaster. The additional gates are 70 feet [21 meters] from the operating gates.

Each lock chamber is 110 feet [33.5 meters] wide and 1,000 feet [304.8 meters] long. The lock chambers are seven stories high. The maximum draft is 39.5 feet [12.04 meters] in tropical fresh water, which is a slightly different than in salt water or cold fresh water.

Panamax vessels navigate under-draft-depth restrictions that do not allow them their full cargo capacity. Part of the expansion program is to increase the depth of the locks to make it possible for vessels to carry a full load of cargo.

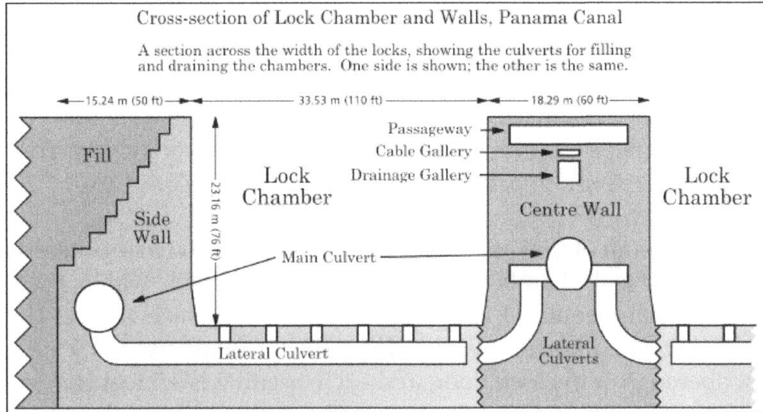

[41]Remember, the Main Culverts are the size of the tunnels dug underneath the Hudson River to take trains into New York City!

Double lock gates protect Gatun Lake water supply in the event of an accident in the locks.

One of the most fascinating things about the Canal is the way in which water from Gatun Lake flows through the locks. Deep within the walls are huge culverts 18 feet [5.5 meters] in diameter. When the Canal was built the tunnels were the same size as the tunnels under the Hudson River in New York that were built to bring the railroad into New York City.

The design of that allows water to flow from the main culverts into the lock chambers is amazing. From the side wall in the lock chamber are 11 lateral culverts, each of which is 6 feet [1.8 meters] in diameter. Each side wall lateral culverts has 5 openings in the lock floor, and each opening is 4.5 feet [1.4 meters] in diameter, or a total of 55 openings. From the center wall culvert are another, similar, 10 lateral culverts each with 5 openings, or a total of 50 openings. So you have 105 openings and the bottom of the lock floor allowing the chamber to fill quickly and without motion or turbulence. The same openings used to fill the chamber are used to spill or empty the lock. It all happens so smoothly you hardly know the ship is being lifted or lowered until you happen to look at a ship in the next chamber or a point on shore.

The upper chambers have an additional culvert on the side wall which because of its shape is called the "T culvert" and it has an additional five openings in the chamber floor. So the upper chambers have 110 openings.

The lockmaster at each lock has the responsibility for handling ships in the locks. The control house is the center of operations. The pilot, lockmaster, and control house operator are in constant radio communication.

Since all the equipment of the locks is operated electrically, the whole process of locking a ship up or down is controlled from a central control room located on the center wall of the upper flight of locks. The controls were designed to minimize the chances of operator error so an actual model of the locks with moving components to mirror the actual state of the locks was designed by General Electric. An operator could see at a glance exactly the position of all locks and valves. Interlocks were built into the controls so that no component can be moved if another is not in the right position. Today the system is controlled by a Microsoft system … point and click!

Once the ship is inside the chamber and the lock gates are closed, the entire process takes about thirty minutes. Depending on the combination of culverts selected by the lockmaster the actual raising or lowering of the ship takes from eight to fifteen minutes. Assuming everything flows smoothly the ship will be in the lock complex about an hour. This depends not only on the lockage of your ship, but also the ship ahead of you.

Sometimes the process gets delayed and everything does not move on schedule. The width and draft of the ship ahead of you may cause it to take longer to move from chamber to chamber or in and out of the locks.

The Canal has thirty-nine tug boats and usually two will be standing by to assist as necessary and, if necessary, nudge the ship into the correct position to enter the locks. At some times of the year the wind blows from the north, sometimes quite strongly, so a Panamax ship can act like a huge sail, and the tugs are sometimes essential.

There are two "lanes" through the lock complexes and in the case of Gatun each lane has three lock chambers. They are bi-directional and you can go in either direction. All this is done to maximize the number of ships passing through the Canal.

There is no way of knowing in advance whether you will be assigned left or right side. Today the pilot , lockmaster, and marine traffic control are all linked by computer, but the traditional way to indicate which side of the lock would be used was a giant arrow at the entrance to the lock. The arrows may also be positioned to give vessels various orders while they wait for the lock to clear.

The pilot maneuvers the ship to the approach wall where the line handlers attach the cables of the locomotives to the vessel.

The arrow is an additional communication tool.

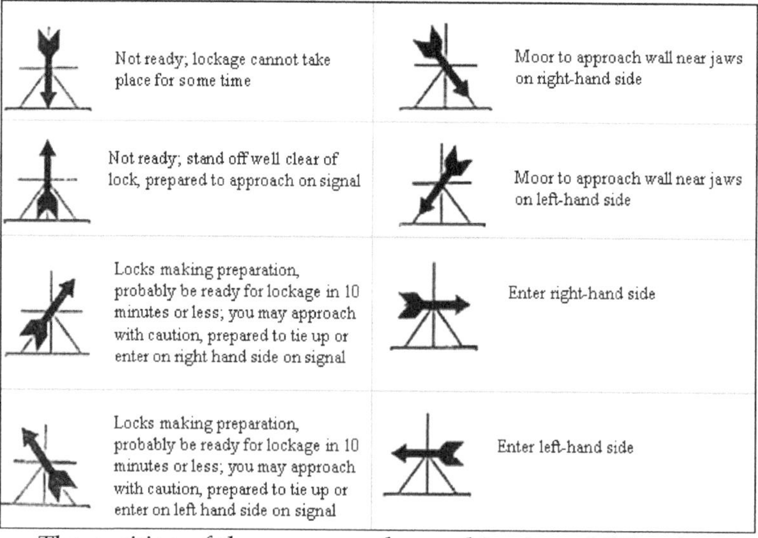

Not ready; lockage cannot take place for some time	Moor to approach wall near jaws on right-hand side
Not ready; stand off well clear of lock, prepared to approach on signal	Moor to approach wall near jaws on left-hand side
Locks making preparation, probably be ready for lockage in 10 minutes or less; you may approach with caution, prepared to tie up or enter on right hand side on signal	Enter right-hand side
Locks making preparation, probably be ready for lockage in 10 minutes or less; you may approach with caution, prepared to tie up or enter on left hand side on signal	Enter left-hand side

The position of the arrow can be used to give additional orders to the vessel.

As the pilot calls out maneuvers to the captain, the vessel continues forward with assistance from the tug at the stern. When the ship reaches the first chamber of the lock, line handlers will attach the cables of the remaining locomotives to the vessel and draw them tight to stabilize the ship for entry into the chamber.

Together with the locomotives and tugs and under its own power, the ship moves into the first chamber, where gates close behind the vessel's stern to lock it into the chamber.

In order to tie the ship up to the "mules" or locomotives, lines have to be passed from the shore to the ship. This job is handled by the Panama Canal line handlers. Over the years they have tried many ways to get the lines from the vessel to the shore. They've tried everything including shooting the lines on board, which ended up putting out a few people's eyes. So it turns out that the very best way is to send a little rowboat to bring the lines from the ship to the engines

Here's this high-tech cruise ship with our sophisticated, computerized bridge ... and the little row boat is still the best way!

As we enter the locks you will notice some round things that look like giant tires on the Canal walls. These are the "bumpers" ... just like in a pinball machine ... designed to roll and keep the Canal walls from putting a hole in the ship hull should the ship accidentally drift or make too sharp a turn. Nobody wants to bring the "family" ship back with a giant gash in the hull ... or paint off the fender ... but the fact is the cosmetic paint on the hull of many ships passing through the Canal takes a beating.

"Mules"

The locomotives used to assist ships during their lockage are often referred to as "mules" through animals were never used in Panama. In the early history of canals in the Europe and the United States actual mules were used to pull barges along.

So it is because of that history, that the engines used in Panama came to be called "mules."

There have been three generations of locomotives, the first built by General Electric, the second built by Mitsubishi, and the current generation built by Mitsubishi. The newest were assembled in Panama, and each cost $1.9 million. The Canal has a hundred of these electric engines, powered by a third rail, geared to run on tracks. Each locomotive weighs 50 tons and operates with two 290 HP traction units with a towing capacity of 178 to 311.8 kilo new tons depending on their speed. Their maximum return speed is 16 kilometers per hour which is important when a lockage is completed and the engines have relay down the center track back to the beginning.

Each locomotive has two powerful winches controlled by the driver to take cable in or pay it out as ordered by the pilot. Ships travel through the Canal using their own power. The locomotives have several important functions:

- Keeping the vessel centered;
- Assisting in towing if needed;
- Stopping the forward motion if needed as a safety feature.

As a ship makes its way through the locks the pilot is continually giving commands to the locomotive operators by radio. The bells and lights on the locomotives are additional ways of communicating and confirming commands.

The green light means the locomotive is at the selected speed. While travelling connected to a ship the locomotive speeds can be 1, 2 or 3 miles per hour. When returning to handle another ship the locomotives go 6 to 9 miles per hour.

The yellow light designates the number one center wall locomotive for the lockage. It is important for the pilot to know where his number one center wall machine is located, particularly when they are returning to connect to the ship.

The red light is a visual signal for the bell. Sometimes the pilot is too far away to hear the bell.

The white lights over the cables are known as the cable fairlead lights. The original purpose for these lights was to illuminate the area when the cables were being retrieved. They have evolved into becoming a signal for the pilot. Cable lights on means the cables are not attached to the ship. Cable lights off means the cables are attached to the ship.

The locomotive bells are an additional means of communication between the pilot and the locomotive operator. Two "distinct taps" on the locomotive bell means the cable is attached to the ship. Two strikes of the bell indicate the operator has received the order and can comply. Three strikes means the operator cannot comply with the order. Continual ringing of the bell means there is a problem or emergency.

The locomotive horn indicates an immediate problem or emergency.

For generations electric locomotives have been used to assist ships through the locks, but the size of the new locks would have required twelve to sixteen mules. So ... the mules will disappear in the new lock chambers. The size of the new locks makes it possible to use two of the existing tug boats, one at each end of the ship, allowing for a more efficient transit.

The number of locomotives or "mules" that are used depends on the size of the ship. The Canal is kind of like an a la carte restaurant. There is a basic toll that's based on the size and amount of cargo plus all the extra fees. Although on a cruise people come on as guests, after eating all that spectacular food, they end up being classed as "cargo," the reality is that cruise ships are charged according to the number of berths regardless of the weight of the "cargo."

Line handlers preparing to bring lines out to the ship.

Even with all the modern technology, that tiny little rowboat brings the lines out to the ship.

When it was built, the concrete construction of the Panama Canal was the largest ever undertaken and the record remained until the construction of the Hoover Dam in the 1930s. Pedro Miguel was the first lock complex, completed in 1911, and Miraflores was finished in 1913.

Since much of the concrete in the Canal is over a hundred years old, the Canal Authority spends a great deal of money to repair and replace deteriorating concrete. It is believed that within the Canal walls there still are pockets of concrete which have not completely dried.

Passing through the locks it is hard to imagine the immense size of the culverts deep within the walls that carry the water necessary for the lock chambers to work.

Operation

The Canal de Panamá, which operates the Canal, is an autonomous government legal entity with exclusive charge of the operation, administration, management, preservation, maintenance, and modernization of the Canal so that the Canal may operate in a safe, continuous, efficient, and profitable manner. Because of its importance and uniqueness, the Canal de Panamá is financially autonomous and has its own, non-political hiring and operational authority. An Administrator is appointed for a seven-year term, and may be re-elected for an additional term. There is an eleven-member board of directors, nine appointed by the president and one by the legislature. An advisory board is composed representatives from the world's largest shipping firms and representatives from the biggest customers.

The New Locks

We will talk more about the Panama Canal expansion project later, but for the moment you should know that the new locks will be different not only in size but also in operation.

- Instead of the existing swing or mitre gates, the locks will have rolling gates which are easier to maintain.

A center cog track enables the locomotives to climb the walls.

Up close and personal with a Panama Canal "mule."

- While all of the fresh water used in the original locks gets flushed into the sea, the new locks will feature water saving basins that will recycle sixty percent of the fresh water.
- For generations electric locomotives have been used to assist ships through the locks, but the size of the new locks would have required twelve to sixteen mules. So ... the mules will disappear in the new lock chambers. The size of the new locks makes it possible to use two of the existing tug boats, one at each end of the ship, allowing for a more efficient transit.

The existing chambers will continue to be used for smaller vessels increasing not only the size of ships that can use the Canal but the number of ships that can transit on a given day.

.

11. A Complicated Marriage

The relationship between Panama and the United States is almost like a complicated marriage of convenience with moments of cooperation and mutual support, an eruption into a brutal separation, and then, finally, bound by historic ties, evolving into a relationship of mutual respect and friendship.

Would the Republic of Panama exist without the United States?

Undoubtedly, Panama eventually would have achieved independence from Colombia. Panama signed up to be part of Bolivar's Gran Colombia, not just part of Colombia. Panama was separated from Colombia not only geographically but also emotionally. Panama was the "spout" on the "teapot" that was Colombia, separated geographically by the enormous and impenetrable Darien jungle. Colombia was leaning on Panama conscripting troops to fight essentially Colombian, not Panamanian, wars, without giving anything back in return. So a split was probably inevitable, but had it occurred without U. S. encouragement and backing, it would have taken longer and come at great cost in terms of human life.

The United States had one interest in the newly minted Republic of Panama: a canal. Panama's interest in the United States was the security of its independence and the economic benefit the canal construction would bring. Whereas the French had come in as the glorious French engineers who "knew it all," ignored the local wisdom, and failed miserably, Panamanians expected that the United States would build a canal with more of a sense of partnership with the locals, providing opportunities for jobs, contracts, and purchasing food and materials.

The Hay-Bunau-Varilla Treaty provided that the United States would have a zone ten miles wide in which to build a canal, and that within that zone the United States would act "*as if* it were sovereign." In fact the United States took over the ten-mile zone and established it *as* sovereign U. S. territory, with no "if." The Canal Zone split Panama in half. Even without fences, it was a sore point for many Panamanians just knowing that they could not pass from one part of their country to another without passing through a strip controlled by the United States.

The partners in this marriage of convenience had entered into the relationship with vastly different expectations. As the century wore on American dominance in the relationship became a major issue.

U. S. Colony in Panama

The United States created a Canal Zone, which, although physically in Central America, could have been a township anywhere in the Southern United States, just picked up, and dropped down in Panama. The Canal Zone had its own shopping areas, with all food and goods shipped in from the States without any tax going to Panama, its own hospitals, post office, police department, laws, courts, railroads, schools, fire departments, sewage, churches, theaters, recreation, values, life-style ... you name it. It was totally separate and totally unequal. The intent of the Canal Zone, from the beginning, was to keep everything separate. The Canal Zone was built on the premise that it was necessary not only to keep the races separate, but to keep the U. S. colonists separate from the Panamanian locals.

Bill Benny, who lived and worked in the U. S. Canal Zone, notes, "I would not deny that early on in the beginning of the Canal Zone there wasn't some Jim Crowe thinking going on, but this only mirrored what was going on in the United States. I believe the evolution of the Canal Zone as a quasi modern day colonial holding came about innocently. In the early days of construction there just was not the infrastructure available to support the Canal effort. Whether it was supplying a workforce, housing of workers, feeding, clothing or providing for well being of the workers, Panama just did not have what was required. What was here was a typical boomtown mentality. When the workers got $1 then prices went up by $1.10. From everything I have read, a stable workforce was pretty elusive in the early days with attrition about even with hiring. It was not until some semblance of hometown USA came along that they were able to end the constant turnover."

The piece of the pie for many Panamanians was low wage, menial jobs and to be treated as inferiors. Benny says, "Up until the 50s the Panamanians did occupy the jobs at the lower end of the spectrum for the most part. I think before that the security of the Canal played an important part in keeping U. S. citizens in key jobs. In too many people's minds the Canal was just too important to 'farm' out. You could argue that it was all way overdone, and with 20/20 hindsight, I'd agree.

"Panamanians could have been made a much more important part of the Canal operation much earlier. That started to change with the Eisenhower-Remon Treaty in 1955."

The Eisenhower-Remon Treaty of 1955 updated and amended the original Hay-Buna Varilla Treaty of 1903. Some of the more interesting provisions included increasing the annual payment from for the Panama Canal from $430,000 to $1.93 million, Panama lowering the 75 percent tax on national liquors sold in the Canal Zone, allowing Panama to charge taxes to Panamanians working in the canal and for U. S. railroads, and to allow Panamanian companies the right to service and provision ships transiting the Canal. Two other provisions of interest were the United States had "beautify" the U.S. Embassy in Panama, and was to construct a bridge over the canal, which today is the Bridge of The Americas.

One of the most significant provisions of the Eisenhower-Ramon Treaty was to eliminate the Gold/Silver Roll and to treat Panamanian and U. S. workers equally.

Bill Benny recalls, "By the time I started working for the Canal in the mid 50s, virtually all State-side recruitment had stopped except for pilots, teachers and doctors. Panamanians could be found in most key positions. If they weren't there it was only because a vacancy had not come along in the department. In most cases I think the Canal officials were more progressive and open minded than many of the elected leaders in the States and they put it to positive change whenever they could."

You could live your entire life in the Zone without ever leaving ... or going into Panama! And many people did, but not everyone. There is the image of a so-called "fence of shame" separating Panamanians from the U. S. Canal Zone residents. One Canal Zone resident recalls, "You could find a few Canal Zone residents who were aloof and disliked the locals, but just a few, just as you could find Panamanians who hated gringos for no other reason than they were gringos." Judging from the number of Panamanians today who have dual citizenship, because one parent was a U. S. citizen who lived in the Canal Zone, the fence was pretty porous. And, "There are many folks, 'Canal refugees', who live in Florida, share a Panamanian heritage and still have a fondness for Panama and the Canal." [42]

Once the Canal was completed, life was good in the Zone. Goods, even although everything had to be imported from the States, cost about the same as they did at home. Military personnel stationed in the Canal Zone could shop at the PX commissary where imported U. S. goods were sold cheaper than in stores. Panama Canal employees enjoyed this privilege until 1984. Canal workers rented housing from the Canal which provided maintenance. From the mid 50s onward all U. S. citizen employees were entitled every two years to a vacation to their home of record, wherever that was, and the Canal would pay transportation. In 1984 it was changed to a *yearly* return home.

You had life as in the States, only without snow. Multiple generational families lived in the Zone. Some of these U. S. children of the Zone and ex U. S. military or Canal people who choose to remain and retire in Panama are known as "Zonians." Talk to any of these people who grew up in the Canal Zone and they will tell you their privileged life was a "paradise."

The United States had twenty military installations in the Canal. [See list of "U. S. Military Installations in Panama 1904-1999" at the end of this book.] These provided jobs and despite the containment of the Zone, contributed to the local economy. All those jobs gave ordinary Panamanians a way to see the way others lived and the benefits these "*extranjeros*" enjoyed.

On the whole relations between U. S. citizens living in the Canal Zone and Panamanians were amicable. Benny recalls, "Too often the relationship between those in the Zone and Panamanians has been characterized by clichés, painting a picture of a band of neo-colonialists ensconced comfortably within their compound oblivious to what went on outside. Most of the time it was just normal people doing normal things without any regard to which side of the 'border' they were located."

He continues, "Whether you were an U. S. citizen who spent almost all your time within the confines of the Zone, or a garden variety gringo like me, or even what is affectionately termed a Panazonian, many Panamanians were exposed to

Omar Torrijos, Maximum Leader of the Panamanian Revolution 1929-1981.

Panamanian students protest during the "flag wars."[43]

U. S. culture and Zone residents to Panamanian culture. When he spoke English, former Panamanian President Demitrio Lakas sounded just like Lyndon Baines Johnson, probably because he went to school in Texas. Former Panamanian President Martin Torrijos managed a McDonald's in the States. Many of the high placed officials as well as ordinary Panamanians were heavily influenced by U. S. culture. On a person to person level there usually was nothing out of the ordinary. We all gained a lot from each other. The lower levels of government and the Canal administration cooperated on a regular basis. Only when it was convenient or had some political purpose was the Canal Zone a dedicated whipping boy for the crisis du jour. At one time General Omar Torrijos blamed a drought in western Panama on the United Sates because he Canal was using all the water!"

Change

The Zone had intentionally been built on blatant discrimination between "gold," usually American and usually white, and "silver," usually other nationalities and people of color.

Back in the States, as Bob Dylan would note, the times were "a'changin'." Segregation was coming to an end in the bastions of the Confederacy. Two hundred thousand people, led by Dr. Martin Luther King, Jr., had marched on Washington. The Civil Rights Movement in the United States was in full swing.

Life had changed internationally as well. Colonialism was out: new countries were emerging with the freedom to control their own destinies. Yet in Panama the Canal Zone was still part of a U. S. colonial empire.

In 1960 President Dwight D. Eisenhower, in response to Panamanian protests outside the U. S. Canal Zone, ordered a Panamanian flag be flown next to the American flag in front of the Canal Headquarters building. In January 1963, President John F. Kennedy, recognizing a deteriorating situation in

Panama and aware of the sensitivities of many Panamanians, who resented all the U. S. flags being flown in the Canal Zone, extended Eisenhower's order and issued an Executive Order that on non-military bases in the Zone, wherever a U. S. flag was flown, a Panamanian flag should also be flown.

The Zonians resented Kennedy's policy and his meddling in their paradise and sued in the Canal Zone's Federal District Court, which reluctantly and unhappily upheld the presidential order. Before the policy could be carried out, Kennedy was assassinated in Dallas, and the federally appointed Canal Zone governor immediately took it upon himself to rescind a presidential order.

The result is sometimes referred to as the "flag wars," but the name infers a hostility that wasn't initially involved. Ric Winstead, whose father worked in the Canal Zone, recalls that the initial reaction in the Canal Zone to Kennedy's order wasn't so much against the idea of Panamanian flags, as much as it was a budgetary issue. Remember, the Canal Zone was a company town where the company paid for everything, so who was going to pay to design and build all of these flag poles and furnish the flags? Whose budget would be tapped for the improvements?

U. S. high school students, listening to dinner table conversations and their parents frustrations with the new order, picked up the tension and reacted in an adolescent way. The Canal Zone was, for the most part, a giant military post and ROTC was a big deal on the U. S. high school campuses in the Zone. Within the Canal Zone residents began to view the order to fly Panamanian flags in the Zone as a weakening of U. S. control and "ownership" of the Canal Zone. Gradually the flag issue moved from a budgetary issue to a challenge to national pride and sovereignty, and, a threat to their "entitled" existence.

The flags of both sides became not only national symbols, but symbols of the tension created by the United States presence in Panama. Panama at the time was ruled by military strongman Omar Torrijos and political pressure in Panama was building for Panamanian ownership of the Canal.

History as a living fact consists not so much in what actually happened as in what people believe to have happened. Therefore it should not be surprising that Panamanians and U. S. citizens living in the Canal Zone at the time interpret the events of January 1964 differently.

Bill Benny recalls that, "On or about January 7th the U. S. flag was no longer flying at Balboa High School. A student raised a small U.S. flag which was later taken down by school officials. Students from a nearby junior college came and put up another U. S. flag which became jammed halfway up the flag pole. Students began to gather around to prevent the school from lowering the flag. Parents joined the group and for the next several days keep watch that school officials did not lower the flag.

"The afternoon of January 9th a large group of Panamanian students came into the area. The Canal Zone kept them away from the flagpole but allowed them to congregate across the street. Police allowed a smaller group of Panamanian students to come across to the flag pole with a silk Panamanian flag they wanted to raise in place of the American flag. The students were not allowed to raise the Panamanian flag but they were allowed to sing various patriotic songs, presumably the Panamanian national anthem."

This proved less than popular with some of the U. S. students and there was some scuffling during which it is believed that the Panamanian flag was torn in the hedge surrounding the flagpole area.

Benny recalls, "During that brief incident I did not see any physical exchanges between the groups. It all happened so fast and appeared to be over after the Panamanian students went back over the hill. The U. S. crowd also began to thin. I left for work. It was only after work that I heard things had really boiled over."

Ric Winstead, who lived as a teenager on the hill above the entrance to the Canal Zone overlooking what is today Avenida de los Mártires, recalls that when the confrontation erupted at the flagpole he ran back to his house on Ancon Hill to make sure it was secure. He watched as a growing angry mob of kids marched down his street. He remembers a neighbor, a full U. S. Army Colonel, went out into his front yard with a shotgun and fired it into the air, presumably in an independent, misguided, and reactionary attempt to disperse the demonstrators, but the sound of a shotgun blast only inflamed the situation. From in front of his house above the entrance to the Canal Zone, he watched as rioting broke out and students attempted to pull down a section of fence. As the evening progressed and the demonstration became a full-scale riot, he remembers hearing the bullets from both sides flying through the palm trees.

Rioting broke out across the country and Panama broke off relations with the United States When it was over, twenty-one Panamanians including six teenagers, and four U. S. soldiers were dead, and as many as five hundred civilians were injured. Today in Panama, January 9 is a national holiday and celebrated as the "Day of The Martyrs."

Panama celebrates two "independence" days as national holidays ... smart people these Panamanians ... the first celebrating independence from Spain and the other separation from Colombia. If there were a day to celebrate independence from the United States it would be January 9th. It was a day when Panama stood up and demanded to control its destiny.

A photographer from *Life Magazine* happened to catch the moment as students climbed a street light pole at the entrance to the U. S. Canal Zone as the boy reached the top of the light pole and planted the Panamanian flag. That picture was chosen as the cover of the very popular *Life Magazine* and inside was a story about the deteriorating situation in Panama.

Thousands of commuters pass this monument each day, many without a clue that this monument is to teenagers who dared to challenge U. S. occupation of the Canal Zone and began the movement that eventually returned the Canal Zone and Panama Canal to the people of Panama.

Most Americans were totally unaware of life in the Zone, let alone the feelings of Panamanians, and the Zonians preferred it that way, lest someone rattle their cage. Suddenly ordinary U. S. citizens realized that all was not well in Panama. This incident, and the outrage it provoked in the United States as well as Panama, was a precursor to the decision to transfer the Canal Zone back to Panama.

Life Magazine editorialized, "As owner and operator of the Canal Company, the U.S. government has blindly allowed the Canal Zone to turn into a pretty fair imitation of a colony, complete with a colonial mentality. In the Zone, discrimination against Panamanians has existed since the beginning, backed up by wage differentials, special privileges for Americans and all the paraphernalia of extra-territoriality. Isolated and pampered, permitted to stay on as settlers instead of being rotated back to the states, the few thousand Zonians developed a misplaced sense of patriotism which made them roundly disliked and which -- as expressed by the high school kids and their flag -- touched off the latest anti-American demonstrations."[44]

As late as 1987 the United States was still calling the road between the former Canal Zone and Panama City "4th of July Avenue" while the Panamanians called it "Avenue of The Martyrs." Today, if you drive into Panama City coming across the Bridge of the Americas, as you drive along the Avenue of The Martyrs you will pass by an ordinary looking street light post, with three teenagers immortalized in bronze climbing the pole and at the top flies a Panamanian flag.[45]

Benny reflects the opinions of many who lived in the Canal Zone at that time, when he says, "The leaders of the Panamanian government and the Guardia Nacional (then also the police) were derelict in not trying to quell the disturbances. They chose to let things get out of hand fearing the risk of criticism that they were on the side of the gringos. They made a decision based on what was best for them politically and not what was in the public good."

Vultures

Panama has a very ugly black bird with a huge wingspan that you often see flying in groups high in the sky. We call them "The Panamanian Air Force," but they are actually turkey vultures that perform the valuable task of cleaning up road kill and disposing of dead animals. In Panama they have a saying that "Politicians are like vultures: during the day they fight over the same road kill, but at night they all go home to the same tree to roost." So many of the politicians during the day fight over this and that, but they intermarry, and all belong to the same clubs, go to the same parties and hang out together.

One notable Panamanian politician was Arnulfo Arias, notable because he was elected president three times, yet he never finished a term in office because he was always thrown out by a military coup.

[At the age of 63, Arias married an 18-year-old interior decorator, Mireya Moscoso, who would later serve as president from 1999–2004. In 1984 at the age of 83, Arias ran again for president and although polls showed a substantial lead, election results were manipulated by Noriega so that Noriega's hand-picked man was elected.]

In 1968 Arias was overthrown by the National Guard in a military coup led by General Omar Torrijos. Although Torrijos never assumed the role of president, preferring the title "Maximum Leader of the Panamanian Revolution," Torrijos ran the country from 1968-1981 as a military strongman. To this day, Omar Torrijos is the most popular figure ever to live in Panama. Torrijos was a social reformist, a populist who empowered the Indigenous, redistributed wealth, opened universities formerly reserved for the privileged few families to all Panamanians, and in spite of being a military strongman opened up government.

Omar Torrijos liked to parade around with ordinary people and Indians in his battle fatigues, smoking a big cigar, just like another Latin American military strongman, Fidel Castro. All of this made the United States nervous and the CIA needed an insider to keep an eye on Torrijos. They already had just the man surreptitiously on the CIA payroll, a young officer named Manuel Noriega.

Noriega was born in Panama City, raised by his grandparents and ended up in Chiriqui province. He was a career soldier having been educated at military school in Peru, trained at the U. S. School of the Americas in the Canal Zone, as well as at Fort Bragg in the United States.

Noriega was commissioned in the Panama National guard and in 1968 was made a Lieutenant. Nobody is quite sure how or why Noriega came to the attention of Torrijos, but Torrijos took the young Lieutenant under his wing. Sometime in the late '50s Noriega started working for the CIA. He provided the ideal CIA "insider" to keep an eye on General Torrijos.

It was Omar Torrijos who negotiated the United States withdrawal from Panama and the turnover of the Canal Zone and the Panama Canal with U. S. President Jimmy Carter. Torrijos had the reputation as a "man's man" who liked hard liquor, cigars, and women. He established a friendship with a stereotypical "man's man," movie actor John Wayne. It is said that during the negotiation for the treaties, Jimmy Carter used John Wayne to help smooth over some rough spots with Torrijos as well as getting Wayne to encourage his politically conservative Orange County friends to support the treaty. Supposedly out of gratitude, Omar Torrijos gave John Wayne the island of Taborcillo, off the coast of Panama. The island is now being developed as a resort called "John Wayne Island."

The Torrijos-Carter Treaties were signed on September 7, 1977. Supposedly, Torrijos had started celebrating early, and showed up for the signing noticeably drunk, slurring his speech, and needing assistance for the photo op that followed

Signing of the Carter-Torrijos Panama Canal Treaties.

Then CIA Director Bush [41] and Manuel Noriega.

Omar Torrijos died in a small plane crash in 1981. Nobody knows for sure why the crash occurred. Panama, just like the United States, has its share of conspiracy theorists. Some claim the crash was caused by the CIA and others say it was engineered by Noriega. Weather conditions for small planes can turn deadly flying over Panama's mountainous interior very rapidly. Most likely Omar Torrijos death was just what it appears on the surface, an unfortunate accident.

"The Dictatorship"

Torrijos death left a gaping void in leadership. Noriega, a member of Torrijos party and head of the secret police, managed to leverage his secret police power to close down all opposition, and emerge as Torrijos' successor.

Panamanians don't like to talk about "the dictatorship" just like most Americans don't like to talk about Spiro Agnew, the Nixon presidency, and Watergate. It was a dark period when anyone who criticized was likely to be beaten or disappear. You will find that a number of Panamanians will have a four or five-year period of their history where they worked abroad.

There is no doubt that Noriega was a military dictator and a thug who brought a great deal of grief to Panama and in the process robbed the country blind. There also is no doubt that Noriega worked for the CIA, probably as early as the late '50s and that during some periods of his employ he was being paid more than the president of the United States.

It's not that Noriega wasn't worth his keep. Noriega maintained friendly relations with Cuba and Fidel Castro and was useful to the United States in back-channel communications and negotiation with Cuba. He helped the Reagan administration by serving as a channel to send illegal aid to the Contras in Nicaragua.

Noriega's image in the States was increasingly being portrayed as a drug kingpin. In an effort to "clean up" his image, Noriega sought the support of Oliver North. At one point, according to Congressional testimony, North supposedly said to a meeting of the Reagan administration's Restricted Interagency Group: "I can arrange to have General Noriega execute some insurgent -- some operations there -- sabotage operations in that area. [Nicaragua] It will cost us about $1 million. Do we want to do it?"

North flew to London to meet with Noriega and the two supposedly discussed developing a commando training program for the Contras in Panama, with Israeli support, and of plans to sabotage targets in Nicaragua.

The very idea of such conversations is reprehensible to most Americans. The plans were supposedly aborted when the Iran-Contra scandal came to light in 1986.

Relations with Noriega deteriorated rapidly. Former CIA chief George H. W. Bush was Vice President with an eye on the Oval Office for himself. Noriega would turn out to be a Frankenstein-like monster.

Noriega sought to manipulate the situation to his continued advantage defying and taunting the United States in an effort to shore up his deteriorating leadership. The United States increasingly portrayed Noriega as a drug mastermind, while at the same time the U. S. Department of Justice was investigating the CIA for importing crack cocaine into Los Angeles and selling it to raise illegal money for the Contras.

Former CIA spymaster George H. W. Bush, when running for president, attempted to pass off his relationships with Noriega noting that the last seven American administrations had paid off Noriega.

Retired Navy Admiral Stanford Turner, who took over the CIA from George Bush in 1977, paints a different picture. "Bush is in the government during the Ford administration and Noriega is on the payroll. Bush is out of the government during the Carter years and Noriega is off the payroll. Bush comes back and so does Noriega. Those are the facts, and you have to figure out for yourself what they mean."[46]

There were increasing tensions between Panama and the Canal Zone. Although many U. S. assets in Panama had already been turned over, many in Panama believed the now Republican U. S. administration would renege on the deal agreed to by a Democrat administration before the "Grand Prize" of the Panama Canal was scheduled to be awarded in December 1999.

And there was good reason for concern. In 2002 the Texas Republican Party, the party of U. S. President George H. W. Bush, still had the following plank in its platform:

"The Party urges Congress to support HJR 77, the Panama and America Security Act, which declare the Carter-Torrijos Treaty null and void. We support re-establishing United States control over the Canal in order to retain our military bases in Panama, to preserve our right to transit through the Canal, and to prevent the establishment of Chinese missile bases in Panama."

In February 1988 Panamanian President Eric Arturo Devalle removed Noriega as commander of the National Guard only to be overthrown himself by Noriega. In March Noriega declared a "state of emergency" and took total control. In April 1988 U. S. President Ronald Regan addressed the deteriorating situation in Panama declaring a "national emergency" and freezing all assets.

"A State of War"

In May 1889 Noriega called for elections but when voters rejected his hand-picked candidate he nullified the election. In response President George H. W. Bush, in the light of "massive irregularities," called for Noriega to step down, recalled the U. S. ambassador and beefed up U. S. troops in the Canal Zone.

Bush: "On May 7, the people of Panama, by an overwhelming

margin of votes, braved repression, intimidation, and fraud to choose democracy over dictatorship. They sent a clear and unmistakable message. They wanted an end to dictatorship and restoration of elected democratic government. But this act of self-determination was brutally repressed before the eyes of the entire world. Noriega answered the cry of his people with beatings and killings. The candidates chosen by the Panamanian people will not be allowed to take office today, as required by the Panamanian Constitution. Panama is therefore, as of this date, without any legitimate government."

The situation in Panama continued to deteriorate as Noriega foiled an attempted coup and had the leaders executed.

On December 15 the Noriega-dominated legislature used the phrase that a "state of war" existed between the United States and Panama, a statement Noriega would later say represented the attitude and actions of the United States toward Panama and not vice versa. Even had Panama "declared war" on the United States, it would be a little like a flea on the back of an elephant saying, "I'm going to get you Mr. Elephant!" At any rate, for whatever reason and some believe that it was in reaction to the press image of George H. W. Bush as a "wimp," the United States took this declaration of "war" seriously, perhaps with good reason. Although tiny, and although the Canal was at the time under U. S. control, the Canal was actually in Panama. Subsequently it came to light that Noriega did indeed have an actual plan to destroy the Canal; all Noriega had to do was pull the trigger.

Panama was in political and economic shambles. The United States had agreed to turnover the Canal just before the Millennium. Panamanians were ready for change and fully expected that eventually the United States would negotiate Noriega's retirement. To add to the U. S. embarrassment an unarmed U. S. Marine in civilian clothes was killed by Panamanian soldiers after running a Panamanian military check point.

The Invasion

On December 20 at 12:01 a.m., as Panamanians were preparing for Christmas, the Panama Canal was closed. At 1:00 a.m. at U. S. Fort Clayton in Panama, U. S. officials installed Guillermo Endara as Panama's new President in a secret ceremony. Endara would have been president had not Noriega invalidated the electoral results. Almost immediately the United States began a massive invasion of the Republic of Panama. For the first time in modern history the United States invaded another country without being at war.

Instead of the negotiation Panamanians expected, operation "Just Cause" was launched with 26,000 troops invading tiny Panama, attacking with tanks and aircraft. At least six times as many civilians as Panamanian military died in "Operation Just Cause," according to Physicians for Human Rights. The exact numbers are still being argued, but Physicians for Human Rights estimated 300 civilians and 50 military were killed, another 3,000 injured and 15,000 left homeless. It is said that in this nation of 3.7 million people, where everyone is related, almost everyone has a family member or knows someone who was killed or injured by the U. S. invasion. Most Americans like to think that Panama, like the rest of the countries the United States invades, is grateful for U. S. intervention. Although most Panamanians ape any U. S. fashion or brand and genuinely like the United States and Americans, and although they were happy to be rid of Noriega, the violence with which it was accomplished remains a sore spot.

Bush: "General Noriega's reckless threats and attacks upon Americans in Panama created an imminent danger to the 35,000 American citizens in Panama. As President, I have no higher obligation than to safeguard the lives of American citizens. And that is why I directed our Armed Forces to protect the lives of American citizens in Panama and to bring General Noriega to justice in the United States ...

Operation "Just Cause."

Tragically, after the Invasion the United States had no plan.

"At this moment, U. S. forces, including forces deployed from the United States last night, are engaged in action in Panama. The United States intends to withdraw the forces newly deployed to Panama as quickly as possible ... Tragically, some Americans have lost their lives in defense of their fellow citizens, in defense of democracy. And my heart goes out to their families. We also regret and mourn the loss of innocent Panamanians.

"The brave Panamanians elected by the people of Panama in the elections last May, President Guillermo Endara and Vice Presidents Calderon and Ford, have assumed the rightful leadership of their country. You remember those horrible pictures of newly elected [Panamanian] Vice President [Guillermo 'Billy'] Ford, covered head to toe with blood, beaten mercilessly by so-called 'dignity battalions.' Well, the United States today recognizes the democratically elected government of President Endara. I will send our Ambassador back to Panama immediately.

"Key military objectives have been achieved. Most organized resistance has been eliminated, but the operation is not over yet: General Noriega is in hiding. And nevertheless, yesterday a dictator ruled Panama, and today constitutionally elected leaders govern."

Many Panamanians lost everything as a result of the invasion. After the invasion Panama was in chaos; the United States had no plan. The old police force was in hiding and there was no law. The United States had "liberated" Panama only to bring incredible hardship, chaos, and anarchy in the streets. There was wide-spread looting. Many small businesses were destroyed. Larger business, unable to collect, went bankrupt.

As his government fell, Noriega moved around hiding out from U. S. forces, eventually taking refuge in the Vatican Embassy, home of the Papal nuncio. Noriega had taken the U. S. Army's Psych Ops training but was now himself the target. The United States blasted the residence with rock music day and night until Noriega surrendered.

If they had rap music Noriega would have given up in several hours!

Noriega was arrested and hustled off to prison in Miami as a POW. Originally sentenced to forty years, the sentence was reduced to thirty years, and with good behavior Noriega ended up serving seventeen years. As a POW he was entitled to be addressed as "General" (albeit of an army of one, since Panama had abolished the military). Noriega had a suite of rooms in prison, exercise machines, telephone, and was provided with "general" uniforms at U. S. taxpayer expense. Noriega, after serving his prison sentence in the United States was extradited to France to serve a prison sentence for money laundering serving, not as a make-believe "general," but as just another prisoner.

In December 2012 Noriega was extradited from France to Panama and currently resides in a simple, nondescript Panamanian prison where Noriega has an ordinary cell with some accommodation made due to his poor health and for his security. Some of his friends, family, and old PRD party friends would like to see him under house arrest due to his age and infirmity. But with the PRD out of power, it is highly unlikely that Noriega will get house arrest since he faces additional very serious charges and sentences already handed down for multiple murders, kidnapping, and corruption.

News photographers have captured occasional pictures of a frail, old man in a wheelchair being escorted to hospital with high security to receive treatment. Most Panamanians are much more concerned about inflation, pay raises, and the latest fashions in stores at the gigantic Panama City malls. At best, Noriega is an interesting bit of history. It is doubtful that Noriega even recognizes the booming country to which he returned.

The Aftermath

The role of the United States in Panama will always be the

topic of discussion and controversy. There are differing opinions amongst Panamanians and Americans even to this day. Some U. S. citizens question why we turned the Canal over to Panama. And there are many criticisms of the U. S. Invasion of Panama.

When I talk on cruises I'm always aware that there will be mixed opinions amongst my usually heavy U. S. audience. On one particular Canal cruise on one side of the theater I had a man who was a career Army officer who taught at the U. S. War College. He had a definite opinion! On the other side of the room was a "bird colonel," a career Army man, and a graduate of West Point, whose life-long friend and West Point roommate was a General in the U. S. Southern Command who resigned in opposition to the Bush Administration's policy in Panama. He had a very different opinion![47]

So not everyone agrees, even within the U. S. Army, but the important thing is to look at history and try and learn from it.

Everett Ellis Briggs, U. S. Ambassador to Panama from 1982 to 1986 says, in regard to the U. S. Invasion, "Almost everyone in government, however, shares some of the blame."

While in prison in Miami, Noriega, with the help of Peter Eisner, an American journalist who had covered Panama, wrote his memoirs. About two thirds of the book is Noriega's as-told-to story. It is a measured book, not at all the ramblings of a mad-man dictator, and like the memoirs of every head of state, self-justifying. The other third of the book is Peter Eisner's analysis. Eisner writes, *"The shambles of U. S. actions and responsibility in Panama were the result of the actions of rigid and ruthless ideologues; Noriega was the target, but the responsibility lies with a country whose citizens should not be so complacent as to fall for the rhetoric."*[48]

Rather than launch a full-scale military invasion, Eisner suggests it would have been cheaper and more effective just to have loaded a bomber with $100 bills and flown low over Panama dumping the money out the door.

There are amazing parallels between the CIA's involvement with Noriega and the U. S. invasion of Panama and the U. S. invasion of Iraq and the aftermath. Perhaps the United States and its citizenry should review history more often, and maybe as citizens we should, in Eisner's words, "not be so complacent as to fall for the rhetoric."

When the Carter-Torrijos treaty was signed the United States almost immediately began withdrawing and gradually turning over Canal operations to Panama, but it was not until December 31, 1999 exactly as the new millennium began that Panama once again achieved full sovereignty over its territory and the Panama Canal.

Following the Invasion, Panama had to deal with the aftermath and destruction of the Invasion as well as the United States closure of military bases. Although Panama gained back property, buildings, and infrastructure, many jobs were lost hurting the country economically. Combining the war damage and the sudden loss of jobs and revenue, Panama went through some tough economic times. It was not until several years after the turnover of the Canal that the money started to flow.

Many people look at the turnover only in terms of what the United States "gave away" or "lost." What they fail to realize is that the United States was unloading a lot of liability. The United States had operated the Canal as a service, just breaking even. Panama came in and started operating the Canal as a very profitable business. Had the United States hung onto the Canal it would have had to have changed the way it was operated, but there were generations of special interests to deal with. The United States turned over to Panama enormous military bases, but the bases in Panama were no longer needed by the United States and were an enormous budget drain. The concept of war had changed and the United States was now dependent the ability to rapidly deploy a slimmed down military.

On December 14, a few days before the new millennium and the actual turnover of the Canal, former U. S. President Jimmy Carter joined Panamanian President Mireya Moscoso, King Juan Carlos of Spain, and various Latin American leaders at a ceremony celebrating the turnover of the Canal.

Conspicuously absent were U. S. President Bill Clinton, Vice President Al Gore, and the U. S. Secretary of State, Madeleine Albright.

Carter said, *"We didn't understand clearly enough the feeling of many Panamanians that the arrangement implied an element of colonialism and subjugation and not an equal representation . . ."*

Panama and the United States moved into the new millennium with a new relationship based on mutual respect, trust, and cooperation. Panama and the United States are not only linked by historic ties, and the fact that many Panamanians have joint Panamanian-U.S. citizenship, but by the commitments of the Carter-Torrijos Treaty. There were actually two treaties. The first treaty turned over the Canal and the Canal Zone to Panama. In the second treaty the United States agreed to defend the neutrality of the Canal in perpetuity

So, far from being over, the relationship has just moved on to a different level. Today the United States and Panama relate as neighboring sovereign states each vitally important to the other. Panama has yielded to U. S. bullying to change its long tradition of private banking and allow the U. S. access to Panamanian banking records in order to secure U. S. ratification of a Free Trade Agreement.

12. Moving Forward

As the clock ticked onward on December 31, 1999, much of the world was worried about Y2K issues, fearing prison doors flinging open, planes crashing and apocalyptic chaos, as our computerized society was confounded with new double-zero digits. Panama, however, was in a mood of national celebration. A huge digital clock at the base of Ancon Hill, just below the Panama Canal Headquarters, ticked off the minutes until the turnover of the Panama Canal, that magic moment ... when the countdown clock reached zero! As the time grew nearer anticipation grew and thousands flocked onto Ancon Hill. It was not only a new millennium, but more importantly for Panama, a symbolic new beginning and actual ownership of its Canal.

A lot of people think that at 11:59 p.m. on December 31, the last U. S. employee to leave the Canal threw the keys to the Panamanians and said, "Here. Good luck!" The reality was that the signing of the Canal Treaties in 1977 began a long process of U. S. disengagement and Panama taking an increasing role in management of the Canal. Almost immediately the United States began unloading expensive-to-operate and obsolete military facilities, gradually turning them back to Panama. By the time Panama formally acquired the Canal, Panama had increasingly been involved in its operation for twenty years.

The new millennium signified a new beginning for Panama. The dark days of the dictatorship were over and Panama had survived both the dictatorship and the U. S. Invasion. Panama had lived without an army and in a democracy for ten years, and, at last, the Panama Canal belonged to the people of Panama.

"On December 31, 1999, the Panama Canal ceased operations under U. S. administration and became a corporate entity of the Panamanian government ... From that time, the business model that adequately served the Canal for 86 years under U. S. administration became obsolete. The Panama Canal, under the new legal framework, began its turnover from break even operation company, whose main objective was recovering costs, to a public efficient entity with clear profitable goals."[49]

Immediately the new Canal de Panamá began to formulate business objectives and plans to achieve these goals.

- Objective 1 - To increase profitability in a sustainable manner for the benefit of the country.
- Objective 2 - To expand the range of services and products in order to exploit market opportunities.
- Objective 3 - To implement business practices that enhance good corporate governance.
- Objective 4 - To efficiently manage the volume and quality of the water resources of the Panama Canal Watershed.
- Objective 5 - To increase productivity through excellence in performance and the wellbeing of human resources.[50]

Since the Panama Canal was turned over to Panama,

operations have improved significantly. Panama has been successful in running the Canal as a very profitable business venture. The Canal de Panamá is an independent agency of the government and operates outside of the government and its tradition of patronage and favoritism to members of the political party in power at the moment.

Major improvements have been made on the Canal infrastructure, widening, deepening and expanding channels, improving visibility, refurbishing locks, and updating equipment. New equipment has been installed including the latest generation of electric mules and more efficient and powerful tug boats.

- Operating efficiency has improved;

- Waiting time has decreased by thirty-five percent;

- Transit times have decreased by twenty-five percent;

- There has been a thirty percent reduction of accidents;

- There has been continuing upgrading and maintenance with the Canal has spending $1.5 billion in improvements to the original Canal since the turnover apart from the expansion project;

- The United States ran the Canal as a federally operated service with tolls just covering operating costs. Panama runs it as a very profitable business. The Canal now generates $2.4 billion[51] per year.

It is hard for people outside of Panama to realize the significance the Canal has for Panamanians and how much it is the focus of national pride. In Panama there is a saying, "Panama is the heart of the universe, the bridge of the world." It is location, location, location, along with the Canal that make Panama strategic.

But the Canal faces significant challenges.

At the time of the turnover the Canal had already been in operation for eighty-five years. The Canal was running for the most part exactly as it had always run, still operating, and still a wonder of the world. But the world had changed. At the time of construction no one could have imagined a ship that could carry eighteen thousand twenty-foot containers!

Traditionally the largest ships were Panamax ships, meaning they were the largest ships that could fit through the Canal. As ship-building technology improved, it became more economical to operate larger ships and shipping lines began building Post-Panamax ships, ships that by design were too large to fit through the Canal. The economies of scale of the Post-Panamax ships were significant enough that it was worth having to make the longer trip around Cape Horn.

As ships have gotten bigger the Canal de Panamá realized the necessity of enlarging the Canal. This was nothing new. The United States began a program to enlarge the Canal and in effect build a "third lane" back in 1939. They started and actually began digging access channels, but World War II came along and the project had to be abandoned. After the war there was never money to finish the project. The current expansion or amplification project is once again a "third lane" project and, interestingly, has been able to use some of the channels that were dug by the United States back in the '30s.

The Canal realized that in order to remain competitive and for Panama to continue to be the crossroads of the world, it was necessary to expand the Canal to accommodate the larger ships that are more efficient to operate, hold more containers, and hence reduce shipping costs.

At the time of the turnover Mireya Moscoso, whose administration was dogged by accusations of fraud and misuse of funds, was President of Panama.

Moscoso was followed by Martin Torrijos, the illegitimate son of former military strongman Omar Torrijos. Being Torrijos illegitimate son carried no censorial weight in Panama: it was a mark of pride for Martin and many believe helped him to secure the Presidency. Martin Torrijos was partially raised in the United States, worked at Mc Donald's, and graduated from Texas A&M. Torrijos tried to crack down on corruption, which in Panama, as in many Latin countries, has been the accepted way of doing business.

It was Martin Torrijos who proposed a plan to expand, or "amplify," the Panama Canal, which his father Omar Torrijos had secured for Panama. On September 1, 2004, Panamanian President Martin Torrijos proposed what was initially projected to be an $8 billion expansion of the Panama Canal. The figure was later revised downward, perhaps to gain voter approval, an estimate of $5.25 billion.

In order to proceed, Panama needed a national referendum to approve the Canal Expansion. Tabloid-size proposals were distributed all over the country. Arguments were made for and against the Canal Expansion program. The country was covered with posters and flags urging a "Si!" or "No!" vote. The Indian workers on my coffee farm had vigorous discussions about the merits of the proposal. On October 22, 2006 the expansion program was approved by 78 percent of the people of Panama.

The original plan was that of the $5.25 billion expansion program, $3 billion would come from retained earnings, and the rest from bilateral and multilateral lenders, led by the Japan Bank for International Cooperation, European Investment Bank and the Inter-American Development Bank. The money would be repaid by gradually increasing tolls and revenue.

On September 3, 2007, with former U. S. President Jimmy Carter in attendance, work began on the Canal Expansion project. The project was originally scheduled for completion in 2014 during the 100th Anniversary of the Canal.

Sometimes called the "Third Lane" project, the expansion involves creating two new sets of locks, one on the Pacific and one on the Atlantic to accommodate the Post Panamax ships.

The project includes:

- Deeping and widening of the Atlantic entrance channel.

- New approach channel for the Atlantic Post-Panamax locks.

- Atlantic Post-Panamax locks with three water saving basins per lock chamber.

- Raising the maximum Gatun Lake operating water level.

- Widening and deepening of the navigational channel of the Gatun Lake and the Culebra Cut.

- New approach channel for the Pacific Post-Panamax locks.

- Pacific Post-Panamax locks with three water saving basins per lock chamber.

- Deepening and widening of the Pacific entrance channel.

The new locks will not only be larger than the current locks, but they will operate somewhat differently.

- Instead of using the current "swing" or miter gates, they will use rolling gates which are easier to maintain.

- Instead of using the traditional "mules" or electric engines to keep the ship centered, the locks will be large enough to accommodate a tug at both ends of the vessel.

- The locks will have water saving basins which will allow sixty percent of the water to be recycled.

- The "third lane" refers to the construction of the two new lock chambers and approach channels, but does not mean that another entire Canal channel is being dug across Panama.

- Most importantly the size of the lock chambers will be increased.

- Width: currently 110 feet [33.53 meters] - new 180 feet [55 meters]

- Length: currently 1,000 feet [304.8 meters] - new 1,400 ft [427 meters]

- Draft: currently 39 feet [12 meters] – new 60 feet [18.3 meters]

Sensitive to the popular and negative image of the lack of transparency and corruption that has plagued Panama for much of its history, the Canal de Panamá focused on maintaining the independence of the Canal administration and bent over backwards to at least give the appearance of transparency in the bidding process.

Competing bids were submitted from major companies from all over the world and were kept sealed in transparent boxes in a bank vault until they were publicly opened and the due diligence begun. One of the major competitors was Bechtel, the largest U. S. construction company, which has an outstanding record of completing similar gigantic projects around the world. It came as a surprise to many, and a disappointment to U. S. interests, when the contract was awarded to a consortium led by Sacyr Vallehermoso S.A. (Spain) who bid $1 billion less than Bechtel. The other

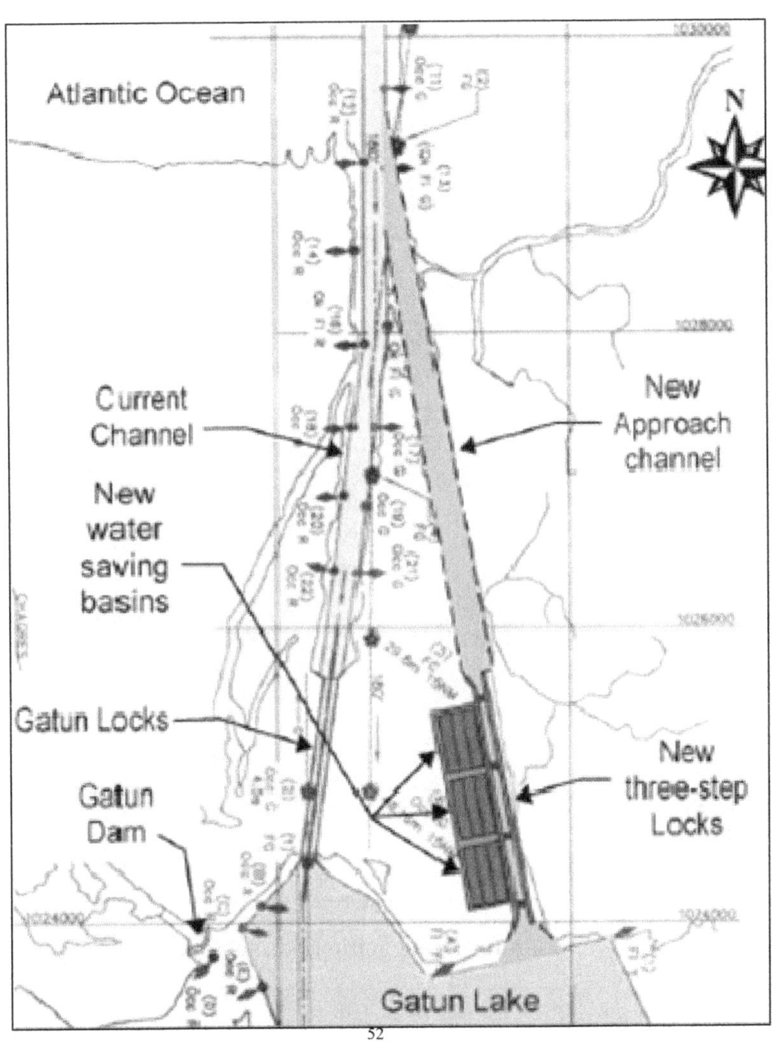

52

Plan for new Atlantic lock system.

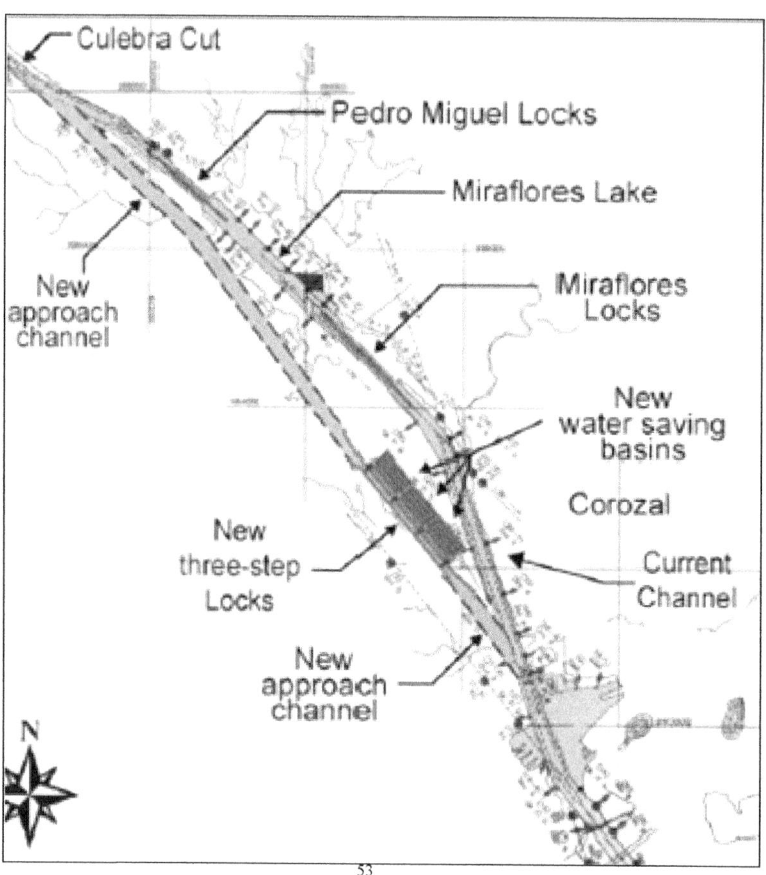

53

Plan for new Pacific Lock system

consortia members are Impregilo S.P.A. (Italian), Jan de Nul N.V. (Belgian), Constructora Urbana, S.A. (Panamanian and run by the first cousin of the Panama Canal Administrator), Montgomery Watson Harza (American), IV-Groep (Dutch), Tetra Tech (American), and Heerema Fabrication Group (Dutch). The ACP, now officially Canal de Panamá, declared Sacyr to have the "best value" proposal.

At the time U. S. Ambassador Barbara J. Stephenson sent a confidential cable home, since released by Wikileaks, calling into question the acceptance of Sacyr's low bid offer and predicting, "… that during construction, Sacyr will attempt to renegotiate the price with the ACP." Later Stephenson cabled Washington describing Sacyr as "a bankrupt company sustained only by the Spanish government."

That is exactly what has happened. Additional studies of the geology surrounding the existing Canal and a developing theory that the weight of the water in the locks and basins might create new, hitherto unknown faults, caused engineers to strengthen the locks design, exacerbating the cost problem.

In the opening months of 2014, the originally proposed date for opening the new "third lane," and with work only 70 percent complete, Sacyr began demanding additional compensation to the tune of $1.6 billion. First threatening, and then stopping all work. Ten thousand people were thrown out of work when a halt was called to construction, while the contractors haggled with the Canal de Panamá for more money.

Panamanian friends, now living in Spain, tell me this is "business as usual in Spain" and in part the reason for Spain's financial problems. Pouring massive amounts of concrete is difficult in Panama during the rainy season. Sacyr conveniently waited until the dry season, the time when the massive amounts of concrete must be poured, to make their demands which many view as terrorist extortion tactics.

One way or another the Canal Expansion will be completed, sooner or later. This being Panama, later is more likely. The projected date for completion has now been pushed to the beginning of 2016.

This has implications for the government of Panama which receives a cash contribution from the Canal, a direct check written to the government, now approaching $1 billion a year. The government was expecting the Canal to generate a contribution of $1.25 billion a year for 2014 and 2015.

The Canal now is projected to cost $7 billion, $1.5 million more than initially budgeted. Should Sacyr prove unable to complete the work, the Canal de Panamá has threatened to take over the work and complete it independently, which could be a boom to Panamanian companies with government connections. Even if Sacyr completes the work, the incident of stopping work on the Canal is a big blow to the prestige of the Canal which is the focus of Panamanian pride and the flagship for Panamanian business excellence.

Storm Clouds

- *Northwest Passage* - If global warming continues, it is conceivable that the Northwest Passage will provide an alternative route to the Panama Canal, but most experts do not see the Northwest Passage as a viable route for at least the next two decades.

- *Nicaragua* – The idea for a Nicaraguan canal has been around as long as the idea for a Panama Canal. In 2006 the Nicaraguan President Enrique Bolanos declared there was sufficient demand for two canals and proposed a $25 billion canal across Nicaragua. The proposal has met strong opposition by environmentalists, but most importantly collided head on with the world financial crisis and reduced demand. When it looked as if this idea was dead, China entered the fray, and plans are moving ahead

In June 2013 Nicaragua gave Hong Kong-based HKND Group was given a fifty year concession to build the canal. The Nicaraguan government will get a minority share of the profits generated by the canal but feels the project will lift the overall standard of living in Nicaragua, one of the poorest countries in Central America. HKND's owner, Wang Jing, claims to have lined up global investors and claims he can build the canal in less than six years, now with an estimated cost of $40 billion. Critics challenge the company's credentials, experience, and fear the environmental impact of a sea level canal.

Panama considered this potential competition and decided that even if this scheme or other schemes materialize, there would be sufficient demand for the Panama Canal. And the Expansion Program might just dissuade potential competitors, such as Nicaragua. Panama's big advantage is not just that it already has the Canal, but also has experience operating the Canal, the infrastructure of ports, logistics, and the Colon Free Zone, the second largest in the world.

- *Triple-E Ships* – Just as when the Canal was first designed and no one could anticipate the eventual size of vessels, even before the new, larger locks are completed, the Canal de Panamá is going back to the drawing boards to plan for yet another expansion in order to accommodate the newest generation of ships.

  Maersk, the world's largest shipping company, has built the world's largest ship, 1,312 feet [400 meters] in length and 193.6 feet [59 meters] wide is too large to fit into the new locks. The Triple-E ship, one of which is already in service, with twenty more are on order, uses less fuel, has a smaller CO_2 footprint, and requires less than two dozen crew members, delivering an economy of scale by carrying eighteen thousand twenty-foot containers. The ship will sail on the Asia to Europe route which represents the largest container trade route in the world.

> Even the Maersk E-class ships, which only carry around fifteen thousand twenty-foot containers, and are 1,299 feet [396 meters] in length and 183.7 [56 meters] wide, are too large to use the new locks.

	Existing Locks	New Locks
Length	1,050 feet [320.04 meters]	1,400 feet [427 meters]
Width	110 feet [33.53 meters]	180 feet [55 meters]
Draft	41.2 feet [12.56 meters]	60 feet [18.3 meters]

Economic Impact

Since the turnover of the Canal, Panama has been on an economic roll and despite a world economic down turn, Panama's economy continues to grow.

Panama faced tough times when the United States started closing down bases and pulling out of Panama after the 1977 Treaty. All those U. S. jobs and contribution to the economy suddenly disappeared. But eventually money began to flow from the Canal operation. In the eighty-six years the United States operated the Canal in Panama it had paid the original $10 million, plus $250,000 per year after the first nine years, or a total of $29.25 million, which would equate roughly to $688.25 million in today's dollars. That would average about $77 million a year in today's dollars. In the first year of Panama's ownership and stewardship of the Canal, the Canal made a direct transfer to the national treasury of $252 million.

During the *first four years* of Panamanian operation the Canal made direct contributions to the national treasury of $1.1 billion plus all the additional indirect contributions to the national economy such as salaries, taxes, procurement, and local business.

Today the Canal writes an annual direct check to the government of Panama for about $980 million. It's estimated that by the time the Canal expansion is finished the annual contribution of the Canal will be $1.25 billion a year and remember, this is in a country of 3.7 million people.

Panama's current government is headed by Juan Carlos Varela, a businessman whose family business is the largest liquor distillery in Panama. Varela graduated with an engineering degree from Georgia Institute of Technology. In the last election he partnered with Ricardo Martinelli as Vice Presidential candidate in a coalition that managed to defeat the major political party and get Martinelli elected. Varela and Martinelli had a falling out, and although he continued as Vice President, Varela campaigned for the Presidency against Martinelli's hand-picked candidate. Although Martinelli enjoyed a 60 percent approval rating and was responsible for pushing major infrastructure and investment projects, in 2014 Varela went from running third in the polls to winning election.

As a result of living through the Noriega years, Panamanians have a deep set fear of concentration of power, and seem to prefer changing governments every five years. In Panama a sitting President or his relatives are not allowed to immediately run for reelection.

As a result of the lessons learned in "the dictatorship," Panama, like Costa Rica, has abolished the military. Of course Panama can afford not to have an army since the United States has committed to protect the neutrality of the Panama Canal in perpetuity.

Different

The Canal de Panamá is not building a new Canal that will parallel the existing Canal, as some folks mistakenly imagine, but another lane with the necessary approach channels. The present locks will continue to be used, but the new lock complexes will allow for larger vessels. All traffic will feed into the existing Canal route which is being enlarged and deepened as part of the expansion project.

The new locks will be different not only in size but also in operation. Instead of the existing swing or miter gates, the new locks will have rolling gates which are easier to maintain. And the new locks will feature water saving basins that will recycle sixty percent of the fresh water.

For generations electric locomotives have been used to assist ships through the locks, but the size of the new locks would have required twelve to sixteen mules. So ... the mules will disappear in the new lock chambers. The size of the new locks makes it possible to use two of the existing tug boats, one at each end of the ship, allowing for a more efficient transit. New and far more powerful tug boats are being added to the Canal fleet.

The new locks will use more efficient rolling gates which are also easier to maintain.

The existing locks will continue to be used for smaller vessels.

When the new locks open, how will you know which locks your ship will use? If it is a post Panamax ship, obviously it will have to use the new locks. Vessels small enough to use the existing locks will likely continue to do so. I suspect that the Canal will work with cruise lines to give them preferential treatment for a price. For me, an ideal transit would use the original locks on one side and the new locks on the other side.
.
There were a lot of doomsayers who predicted Panama couldn't manage the Canal, and that it would fall apart once the turnover took place. The reality is that the Canal is doing better than ever!

Panama Canal SWOT

'SWOT" is a standard business term for "strengths, weaknesses, opportunities, and threats" used in analyzing a business plan or examining an existing operation.

Panama Canal Strengths

- Location, location, location – at the center of the world
- Ideal logistic hub for the Americas
- One hundred year history
- Well-developed infrastructure of ports, facilities and logistics
- Neutral country and neutral Canal
- Under terms of Torrijos-Carter Treaties the United States guarantees to protect the neutrality of the Canal in perpetuity, so Panama does not have the cost of maintaining a military
- Panama's overall economic strength, although that strength is heavily tied to success of Canal
- Second largest free zone in the world, second only to Hong Kong
- Tocumen International is quickly becoming the airline "Hub of The Americas"
- Tradition of political independence of Canal Administrator
- Neutral country and neutral Canal
- Under terms of Torrijos-Carter Treaties the United States guarantees to protect the neutrality of the Canal in perpetuity, so Panama does not have the cost of maintaining a military
- Panama's overall economic strength, although that strength is heavily tied to success of Canal
- Second largest free zone in the world, second only to Hong Kong
- Tocumen International is quickly becoming the airline "Hub of The Americas"
- Panama is outside the hurricane belt although a tropical depression in the Caribbean or a monsoon trough stuck over Central America can bring heavy rains and flooding
- Tradition of political independence of Canal Administrator

Panama Canal Weaknesses

- Panama's reputation for corruption and lack of transparency

- "Insider trading" perceptions in awarding contracts and choosing suppliers
- Potential for political interference although theoretically Canal is independent, but nothing really independent in Panama
- Contractual problems in completing Expansion Program, delays and cost overruns
- Vulnerable to world economic problems such as declining value of U. S. dollar, Venezuela devaluation of currency, European Union financial problems
- Declining demand due to world financial crises and alternative routes such as Suez Canal which can be profitable with larger, more fuel efficient ships
- In 2013 maritime cargo in Panama ports decreased by around four percent compared to 2012, which had already registered less cargo than in 2011
- Wide-open and visible asset making accessibility easier for potential terrorists and extortionists
- Depending on paying for Canal Expansion by continually increasing tolls as demand slows
- Being forced to halt construction of the new locks, even for a short time, because of financial problems and cost overruns was been a blow to confidence in the Canal administration
- Within Panama the Canal is the poster child for business success and stoppage of work on the Canal expansion, even for a short time, was a major blow to the prestige of the Canal de Panamá

Opportunities

- Widening of the Panama Canal will allow most LNG tankers to transit the isthmus and make natural gas from Gulf of Mexico ports "instantly economic" to transport to high-price Asian markets
- Continued expansion of Panamanian economy and role of Panama as distribution center for the Americas
- Ability to handle larger vessels makes shipping through the Canal more cost effective than other alternatives, i.e. cheaper and faster to ship a container from Asia to New York via the Canal, than ship it to

The new locks will use tug boats instead of mules to assist ships.

Conceptual view showing existing Miraflores Locks to the right and new entrance channel to new Pacific Locks on the left.

Los Angeles and truck or train it across the States
- According to Willys Delvalle, president of the Panama Maritime Chamber, "There is a need for leadership composed of government and private enterprise in order to improve efficiency, reduce costs, improve systems, eliminate old patterns that are obsolete and change the laws that are required to truly modernize the way to carry out the maritime business"

Threats

- Challenge of the future construction of a rival canal, two ports and a cross continent railway in Nicaragua
- Probably over next two decades competition from opening up of Northwest Passage
- Geological instability of region and earthquake potential
- Climate change affecting rainfall and the water supply necessary to operate the Canal
- Development threats in Canal area threatening watershed
- Panama's reputation for corruption and lack of transparency
- Wide-spread consumer dissatisfaction with "Made in China" goods causing decrease in shipping
- Movement toward bigger and bigger ships - even new locks will be unable to service the existing larger container vessels
- Potential terrorist target if not for its own sake, as a secondary target against major users such as United States
- Contractual problems with expansion affect expected Canal revenues to government and negatively impact Panama's economy

Security

In our post 9/11 world Canal Security is a major concern. Whereas in the past the Canal's neutrality and usefulness avoided conventional threats, since 9/11 the rules of engagement are different. Now you have fanatical groups

Conceptual view of new Pacific Locks, showing water saving basins. Existing Miraflores Locks are in the upper center of the image.

Sailors from Panama, United States, Chile, Colombia, Dominican Republic, Ecuador, and Peru participate in a U. S. sponsored PANAMAX training operation.

who aren't afraid to hurt themselves or to die in the process and are looking for spectacular targets of particular interest and concern to the United States.

There are several avenues of protection for the Panama Canal.

First, Panama is neutral country and the Panama Canal is open to everyone.

Part of Panama's defense has been the famous "Swiss strategy," a take-off of the phrase, "If you have them by the balls, their hearts and minds will follow." In this case, "If you have them by their money, their hearts and minds will follow." It worked for Switzerland and has worked with Panama, that is, until Panama, like the Swiss, caved in and gave the United States access to financial records destroying the traditional privacy of banking in Panama.

Panama's second line of defense is the United States. Panama abolished the army after the dictatorship. It doesn't need an army since it has the United States. Many people do not realize that there were actually two treaties signed in 1977. The first treaty turned the Canal over to Panama. In the second treaty the United States agreed to protect the neutrality of the Canal in perpetuity.

The Canal uses an Electronic Data Collection System that requires all pre-arrival information to be submitted to the Canal in advance so that a risk assessment can be made and to insure that all international security regulations are followed. Cargo manifests, crew and passenger lists are carefully monitored and checked against U. S. security databases.

Each year the United States sponsors and finances "Operation Panamax," a security exercise that simulates an attack on the Canal. The exercise involves as many as fifteen countries in addition to Panama. Additionally it provides the United States an opportunity to showcase military hardware for sale to friendly countries. Where in past years the United States military has spent lavishly on such exercises, to the tune of $20 million plus, budget constraints have caused the U. S. military to tone down the exercise to cut expenses.

13. Panama 101

When I lecture on ships I always ask the audience, "When I say 'Panama' what comes to mind?"

Generally I get the same set of answers:

Malaria
Yellow fever
Mosquitoes
Snakes
Money laundering
Drugs
Panama Canal
Noriega
Panama hats

It really sounds like a place you'd like to visit!

People labor under a lot of misconceptions.

For example, take *Panama hats*. Only one problem: Panama hats are made in Ecuador, not Panama. How did they become associated with Panama? At the time of the Canal construction, an enterprising hat salesman from Ecuador had an oversupply of hats and, because of the canal construction, brought the hats to Panama hoping to sell them ... and he did!

He discovered a great market for Ecuadorian hats which folks who visited Panama or worked on the Canal thought of as "Panama hats."

Panama hats were popularized when Teddy Roosevelt, the first U. S. President to leave the country while in office, came to Panama to see for himself the Canal construction. He wore a Panama hat in numerous photo ops which instantly made the hat a popular fashion accessory.

Noriega is a sick old man and ancient history. Noriega was arrested by the United States over twenty years ago. Noriega, after serving his prison sentence in the United States was extradited to France to serve a prison sentence for money laundering. In December 2012 he was extradited from France to Panama and currently resides in El Renacer Prison (interestingly meaning "rebirth") which is located right beside the Panama Canal just South of where the Chagres River flows into the Canal. It is a simple, nondescript Panamanian prison and Noriega has a simple cell with some accommodation made due to his poor health and to protect his security. Some of his friends and family would like to see him under house arrest due to his age and infirmity, but that is unlikely since he faces additional very serious charges and sentences already handed down for multiple murders, kidnapping, and corruption.

Panama Canal – I always thought it was good when folks mentioned the Canal, especially since they had plunked down thousands of dollars to cruise through the Panama Canal!

Drugs - Yes, a problem. Panama borders Colombia, has 1,547 miles [2,490 kilometers] of coastline, and is situated on the main route between Colombia and the United States, which is the world's largest consumer of illicit drugs. Although Panama law enforcement seizes tons of cocaine almost weekly, this will continue to be a problem in Panama, Mexico and elsewhere in the world as long as the United States continues its failed drug prohibition, providing the drug cartels enough money to buy off almost anyone.

Money laundering is no more a problem in Panama than Miami or Los Angeles. It is far more difficult to open a bank account in Panama than it is in North America. It's more convenient and politically acceptable for the United States to focus on money laundering outside the United States than in Miami and New York.

Snakes: we have a few, 127 to be exact, but only 20 of these are poisonous. You have a better chance of getting struck by lightening in Panama than getting bitten by a poisonous snake. If you live in Panama the "snakes in the grass" you need to look out for are dishonest contractors, promoters of various Ponzi schemes, and Americans on the lam from the law. Count yourself fortunate if you even see a snake in the wild. Of course it's the ones you don't see that can be problematic.

You always want to be the first person in the line walking through the jungle. First person, fer de lance snake thinks, "Damn it, here they come again!" Second person, "I'm really getting tired of this!" Third person ... bam!

Mosquitoes: we have some, but not what you might think. This is not Alaska or Wisconsin in the summertime! If you are coming from a country where yellow fever is present, Panama requires you to have a yellow fever vaccination. Unless you are leaving the typical tourist areas and heading off deep into the jungles of the Darien or Bocas del Toro, neither yellow fever nor malaria are of concern. What is of concern is dengue fever which is a problem throughout the Caribbean, Central and South America, and the southern United States. Dengue is transmitted by mosquitoes and for this reason Panama is vigilant in controlling mosquitoes.

Panama has been described as the "crossroads of the Americas" and even due to the Panama Canal, the "crossroads of the world."

Simón Bolivar was the great liberator of Latin America who is sometimes referred to as the "George Washington of South

America." In 1826, at the height of his power, he convened a congress of Latin American republics in Panama City. The building where the congress was convened is enshrined in the Ministry of The Exterior in Panama City. Long before the construction of the Canal, Bolivar said, "If ever the world were to have a capital it would be Panama."

So what is in Panama?

- 940 bird species
- 10,000 species of plants
- 200 species of mammals
- Mountain from which you can see two oceans
- Rivers where you ride 20 sets of rapids in an afternoon
- Greatest number of deep-sea fishing records in the world
- Seven Indigenous Indian cultures
- 125 animal species found nowhere else in the world
- Almost 1,500 miles of coastline

The Republic of Panama is a constitutional democracy with an elected president and national assembly, both serving five-year terms. As a result of its experience with dictatorship, both the president and vice president must sit out two additional terms [ten years] before becoming eligible for reelection.

Panama has no need for a military since, in the second 1977 treaty turning over control of the Canal to Panama, the United States agreed to protect the neutrality of the Canal and ipso facto Panama in perpetuity. The military was abolished after Noriega.

The National Police do have field uniforms that look like military fatigues, but they are police, not military. We do have two divisions of the national police, heavily supported overtly and covertly by the United States, which dress and look like military. The naval police look a lot like the U. S. Coast Guard and in fact drive U. S. Coast Guard boats. The

Panama City from Ancon Hill.

Cruise ships passing in Gatun Locks.

police assigned to protect the borders with Costa Rica and especially Colombia, look a lot like the U. S. Army commandos who help to train them.

Although called the Balboa, the Panamanian currency is in fact the U. S. dollar. In 1941 Panama briefly, seven days briefly, printed its own currency. Subsequently these notes were burned and now are only collector items. Panama does mint its own coins which are identical in size and weight to U. S. coins, and so U. S. and Panamanian coins are used interchangeably. If you end up with Panamanian coins, not to worry, they work fine in U. S. vending machines! Because of the short life span of paper dollar bills in the tropics and the high cost of shipping old currency back to the United States, the Panamanian government has issued a one Balboa coin that is equal to the U. S. dollar. The one Balboa coin is derisively called by locals "the Martinelli," after the President who introduced the coin. Prices will usually be marked "B" for Balboa, but it is in fact the U. S. dollar.[54]

Because Panama's currency is the U. S. dollar it has been very attractive to investors who like the security of the U. S. dollar. There are many international banks in Panama. Seventy percent of the economy is service based, which includes the Panama Canal. Panama is second only to Hong Kong in the number of offshore registered companies. The Colon Free Zone is the second largest free zone in the world.

Tocumen International Airport is the busiest airport in Central America and one of the most modern and technologically advanced airports in Central and South America. The airport is the home of Panama's Copa Airlines, and is a hub for flights to the Caribbean, North and South America, and, increasingly, Europe. International travelers discouraged by security delays in the United States, are increasingly choosing to connect through Panama.

Panama has enjoyed a booming economy with GDP growth of 8-12 percent a year before the world economic collapse. Even post-collapse, Panama has had 5-12 percent GDP growth when some countries were having negative GDP growth. While the ratings of other countries' bonds have been lowered, the rating of Panama's bonds has been increasing.

Panama is on an economic roll, awash in numerous projects in addition to the Canal expansion including, a score of new Dubai-like towers under construction, a new subway system already being expanded, a total traffic redesign for Panama City in progress, new airports and expansion of the existing Tocumen International Airport, new container ports, new highways, alternative energy projects, and development of what will be the second largest copper mine in the world. All of this has happened since the overthrow of Noriega … all of this in a country of 3.7 million people.

Panama has become a top international retirement destination. Baby boomer retirees are lured by a lush, tropical environment, lower cost of living, easy access to the rest of the world, easy permanent residence for pensioners, the U. S. dollar, and a neutral country with warm relations with the United States and the rest of the world.[55]

Indigenous Peoples

One of the great things about Panama is that there are seven living Indigenous cultures who have been here since before Columbus arrived. It's estimated that there may have been one to two million Indigenous inhabitants at the time the Spanish arrived.

East of the Panama Canal, the Kuna live on the San Blas islands and along the Caribbean coast. The Chocoes, more correctly known as the Embera and Wounaan, live in the jungles stretching into what is today as Panama, Colombia, and Ecuador. To the west are the Guaymies, or as they prefer to be known today, the Ngäbe-Buglé, and the smaller groups of Teribes and Bokotas.

Traditionally in Panama the Indigenous have been at the bottom of the totem pole, looked down on by the white

European conquerors and their ancestors even to this day. Military strongman Omar Torrijos empowered the Indigenous, and today the Indigenous control their traditional lands as autonomous territories and are a political force with which to be reckoned. The Embera and Wounaan by nature more spread out, living in small communities stretched out over immense rainforests stretching today over three countries. There is a movement amongst the Embera and Wounaan to achieve more autonomy and political clout.

Fortunately today the Indigenous in Panama have been discovered by tourists, with the result is that the country as a whole is learning to appreciate Indigenous people and their contributions, and have become more aware of the need to encourage the Indigenous communities to preserve their lifestyles.

The Kuna

The Kuna people live primarily along the Caribbean coast of Panama, east of the Canal, and on the low-lying San Blas Islands. Many live and work in Panama City and the women are easily recognizable because of their unique costumes and the rows of beads they wear on their forearms and legs.

Kuna Yala has its own political organization and the flag of Kuna Yala, with its swastika-like symbol of good luck, was around long before Hitler was born. The Kuna are monogamous. Their traditional beliefs have been mixed into religions like Christianity that were brought in by various missionary groups

Few cruise ships actually call in the San Blas Islands due to the fact that the powerful Kuna General Congress feared that their traditional society and culture was being negatively influenced by all of the cruise ships and, maybe more importantly, the Kuna chiefs felt they weren't getting a fair share of the pie.

[56]A Kuna woman displays her molas.

Zueleka, Katerina, and Erito, our Embera friends from Embera Puru in front of their house – Erito has a lot fewer problems with his house than I do with mine!

Subsistence agriculture and fishing has traditionally been the base of the Kuna economy. Today many are involved in producing the beautiful and colorful molas for tourists. "Mola" in Kuna means "cloth," so a mola can be any piece of cloth. Traditionally the Kuna have made brightly colored and complex designs out of cloth. The cloth is not cut with scissors, but ripped, and then turned under and sewn into the pattern. You will find Kuna molas for sale all over Panama City and maybe even by the shops on board. Like any piece of artwork, prices vary wildly according to the beauty, complexity and quality of the work. When shopping for a mola you want to turn it over and look at the quality of the hand stitchery on the back side of the piece.

The Embera

The other groups you are likely to meet around Panama City are the Embera and Wounaan, particularly if you opt to take the authentic Embera Village shore excursion.

Both the Embera and Wounaan come from the same genetic stock, but have developed different languages and slightly different cultural traditions over the centuries. Most of the Choco people you meet will be Embera.

Embera villages are small, generally under 150 people, and are usually grouped around one or two main families. If there is discord in a village the odd man out simply leaves and goes off to form another village.

Traditionally the Embera are hunters and gatherers, hunting in the jungle using blow guns, fishing underwater with spears, and growing basic crops such as corn, rice, and yucca. Typically villages are located near rivers and the *piragua* or *cayuco* boats made from hollowed out logs provide transportation. Embera are monogamous with young people traditionally finding mates from other nearby villages. Many are nominally Catholic with heavy intermixing of native beliefs.

Houses are raised for protection from jungle animals and flooding rivers and are made of palm and natural fibers. The sides are usually wide open except during the windy season.

Traditionally Embera women wore only a bright colored skirt that originally was made from tree bark. Today the Embera tribe sends traditional designs to Japan to be made into special fabric for dresses. These are, in effect, limited editions, so when you visit a village and you see a woman with a rack of brightly colored cloth in her house, she is showing off her collection of limited editions.

Traditionally men wore loin cloths, but today, except when there are visitors with whom they want to share their traditions, the guys just wear shorts. Believe me, loin cloths are highly overrated as a fashion statement. Older women dress in the accepted, traditional Embera way, i.e. "topless." Young, rebellious women may dress more Western wearing tops, much to the dismay of their elders. It's all cultural folks!

People always ask me how I came to live in Panama and "Why Panama?" If you want the complete answer you'll have to go to Amazon and get my book *The New Escape to Paradise: Our Experience Living and Retiring in Panama.*

The short version is that I was on a cruise ten years ago that stopped in Gatun Lake. My wife wanted to take the Embera Village tour but I opted just to go ashore at the "Gatun Lake Yacht Club," which as long as I've been doing the Canal has never had any kind of boat, let alone a "yacht." I met these Embera guys whose wives were selling baskets. One of these guys, Erito, and I got talking, so I started buying beer ... four hours of beer drinking later, when my wife returned from the village tour, Erito, his brothers and I were old friends. They kept telling me they wanted me to visit their village and so, when I went back to California, I scoured the Web for information on the Embera. In the process I discovered all of the benefits of retiring in Panama ... and here we are!

What does this all have to do about "topless" Embera women?

During our beer drinking, Erito's younger brother gave me the gift of a bead necklace. With nothing else to give him, I gave him the T-shirt off my back, whereupon he said, "I can't wait to get back to the village so I can put my girlfriend (a beautiful, bare-breasted 16-year-old standing nearby) in the T-shirt so she will look sexy like American girls." Pity me: I had to explain that in America we try to get the T-shirt *off* the girl! Like I said, it's all cultural!

The Embera are fantastic artisans fashioning beautiful baskets using all natural palm fibers and natural dies. The women make the baskets and the men are the carvers. Beautiful carvings are made out of the super hard *cocobolo* wood. The *tagua* nut, known as vegetable ivory, is carved into forms of frogs, birds, fish and animals.

The Embera are warm and wonderful people and if you have the opportunity to pay them a visit, you will want to buy some craft work. At the request of the village elders, please do not give anything (money, pencils, candy, etc.) to the children. The Embera chiefs want the children to learn to be gracious hosts and not beggars.

The Ngäbe-Buglé

The largest Indigenous group is the Guaymies or, as they prefer to be called, Ngäbe-Buglé. They are the only group in Panama who were never conquered by the Spanish explorers and settlers.

Today the Ngäbe-Buglé are most heavily concentrated in Chiriqui, Veraguas, and Bocas. They are an agricultural people growing rice, corn, bananas, yucca, fruits, and breeding domestic animals like cattle, pigs, and poultry. They are the backbone of Panama's agricultural economy.

Traditionally the Ngäbe-Buglé were polygamous with the man as the very strong head of the household, but increasingly many of the men I talk to assure me that one wife is "more than enough." In some traditional Ngäbe-Buglé families, although the husband spoke both the native language and Spanish, the women were not allowed to learn Spanish. The influence of Latino culture and very fluid family structure is leading more to a kind of serial monogamy of sorts, like in North America and Europe. The Ngäbe-Buglé children are looked upon almost as the children of "the village."

In the past two men might get drunk on payday and fight over a woman, with the winner of the fight taking the loser's woman by the hair and making her his woman. Increasingly Ngäbe-Buglé women are becoming more empowered, speaking Spanish, and demanding more say, not just at home but also in the community. One of the big Ngäbe-Buglé chiefs is a woman and has led the fight against the government selling off rivers in the Ngäbe-Buglé comarca to the highest bidder for hydro dams.

The Ngäbe-Buglé have been heavily influenced by Christianity in this officially Roman Catholic country, but their Christianity is often an interesting mix of Indigenous tradition, Christianity, and spiritualism.

The Ngäbe-Buglé women dress in traditional, bright-colored, hand sewn dresses. They use various plant fibers died with vegetable dies to create *chacaras* or bags which are used for everything from purses to baby bags. The *chaquira* is an elaborate wide bead necklace with multicolored geometric designs that is made by the women, traditionally for the men to wear on ceremonial occasions.

The Bokatas, Bibi and Teribes are very small Indigenous tribal groups living mostly in the area around Bocas del Toro on the westernmost end of Panama.

Panama's greatest treasure is her people. Panama historically has been the "crossroads of the world" and so people have come and settled in Panama from all over, resulting in an interesting mix of cultures, races, and traditions and widespread tolerance and acceptance.

Our Ngäbe-Buglé neighbors and their home when we moved to our coffee farm. Melida has picked coffee for us as long as we've had our coffee farm.

Melida's family and house today, with my wife, Nikki, and me as Santa on Christmas Day.

14. Booking Passage

If you are just in the planning stages for cruising to Panama and the Panama Canal, you should be aware that there are basically five different types of cruises to Panama.

Types of Cruises

1. There are Cruises that only call at a Panamanian port. These cruises make a port call either on the Pacific side at Amador [a/k/a "Fuerte Amador"], or on the Atlantic/Caribbean side at Colon. There are options for a variety of shore excursions that will allow you to get off the ship and experience some of Panama, including taking a small ferry through the Canal.

2. *Southern Caribbean Cruises* enter the Canal, go through Gatun Locks, disembark guests going on ship-sponsored tours, turn around and return through Gatun locks to Colon to await the return of guests on ship tours. There are a variety of excursions which, due to Canal regulations, can only be booked through the ship since you are disembarked in a secure area of the Canal. Guests remaining on board have a brief stop in Colon, with really only enough time to visit the super market and a few tourist shops at the pier. Colon is not a city to wander around on your own, even around the piers.

3. ***Ships that homeport in Panama,*** that is, you embark and disembark the ship in Panama. Guests on this type of cruise can book pre or post cruise stays in Panama or stay independently in order to experience the Canal and some of what Panama has to offer.

4. ***Ships transiting the Panama Canal*** go through the Canal from one ocean to the other, but do not actually stop in Panama or allow guests to get off and experience Panama. In the spring and fall repositioning cruises between Alaska and the Caribbean generally just transit the Canal, without stopping in Panama.

5. ***Ships transiting the Canal that stop in Panama.*** Happily more and more itineraries are including the chance to actually see something of Panama. There are a lot of itineraries offering a full day in Panama either before or after the Canal transit day.

Now the dreaded question: "Which is best?" Generally there is no "best" … it all depends on you, and what you want out of your experience. My personal preference is for an itinerary that allows you to experience some of Panama in addition to just seeing the Canal. You are coming all of this way to what is likely a new country, so why not see at least some of Panama?

I wouldn't make the decision on cruise line loyalty alone. Carefully study the itineraries to see what itinerary really matches your interests. Almost all cruise ships transit the Canal during the day, so "daylight transit" is exactly what you'd expect from everyone. Look carefully at the kind support that is offered on board to provide you with background information that's more than just talking about tours and preferred shops, i.e. qualified people who present interesting lectures about the Canal and Panama.

Don't make your decision based on price alone. A transit of the Panama Canal is the "trip of a lifetime" for most people, different from a week-long Caribbean get-away for sun and fun. Although price is obviously a factor, it shouldn't be the determining factor. On some ships the bow of the ship, if it is not filled with winches and equipment, is a crew-only area. Other ships open the forward deck on the bow so guests, and not just crew, have the best vantage point entering the locks. On other ships, because accessing this area may involve guests going through other crew areas, the best viewing area is closed to guests. I've sailed through the Panama Canal, even sailed out of New York City at sunset, with guests all crowded to the rails, while the crew enjoyed the million dollar view.

There is no one "best" vantage point on the ship for the transit. If you want to get the most out of your day in the Canal, move around the ship. Coming into the locks the forward part of the ship is the best place to be.

When the ship is in the locks move around! The view from the aft end is totally different.

Sometime when you are in the locks go down to the promenade deck and you will really appreciate just how little room there is to spare! It is so close that you feel as if you can almost reach out and touch the sides of the Canal. If you have a balcony the best time to enjoy that vantage point is when you are sailing through Gatun Lake.

If you have an outside cabin without a balcony on lower deck, sometime while you are in the locks, run down to your cabin and look out the window. Outside you will see the massive wall of the lock, just inches away!

The Panama Ports

There are a number of places where guests are embarked and/or disembarked in Panama. The two main ports are in Colon on the Atlantic side. In addition guests are sometimes disembarked in Gatun Lake to go on ship-sponsored

On this ship the foredeck was opened so guests could enjoy the view entering the locks.

Same locks, different ship. On this ship the foredeck is totally taken up by winches and Panama Canal linesmen.

excursions. Only guests with ship-sponsored excursions are allowed by the Panama Canal to disembark in Gatun Lake, since it is a secure area.

Amador is the causeway created at the Pacific entrance to the Panama Canal, a long strip of land created by joining together a number of small islands. The Pacific port is frequently called Fuerte Amador, which is part of the Amador peninsula, part of Panama City. There are continuing discussions about building a real cruise ship port in the Panama City area, but to date neither the government nor the cruise lines have committed to such development. So the Pacific side is a tender port, involving about a forty-five minute tender ride from the ship to the marina at Fuerte Amador. If it is a clear day, or a clear night, you will have fantastic skyline views of Panama City during the tender ride.

The causeway divides the Bay of Panama from the Canal and offers fantastic views of the new Panama City across the Bay. A military installation during the U. S. Canal Zone days, today the Amador Causeway is a favorite place for locals to jog, ride bikes, walk dogs, or just sit and enjoy the views. There are shops, restaurants, discos, a big new convention center, marinas, an outpost of the Smithsonian Tropical Research Institute, and the new Bridge of Life Museum of Biodiversity designed by Frank Gehry. It is about a thirty minute cab ride, depending on traffic, from Amador to downtown Panama City or the old French part of the city, Casco Viejo. There are usually taxis available and the giant red Hop On Hop Off Bus picks up at the port.

There are two piers used by cruise ships in Colon, Colon 2000 and Home Port. Colon 2000 is favored by cruise lines owned by Carnival Corporation. It offers some local shops and souvenir stores. In the same complex is a very nice Radisson hotel and Super 99, a big Panamanian grocery store chain. Home Port is a very new, functional terminal favored by Royal Caribbean and designed to embark and disembark several thousand people at once. Royal Caribbean homeports one Royal Caribbean ship and a vessel from its Spanish subsidiary in Colon.

During the days of the U. S. Canal Zone, Colon [Columbus] was the Panamanian section and Cristobal [Christopher] was the U. S. Canal Zone section. For many years cruise ships stopped at Pier 6, known as "Cristobal." Pier 6 was an old, traditional pier, like ones you used to find in New York, and San Francisco built in 1919. It was a great port with lots of shops and Indigenous stalls selling beautiful craft items. Unfortunately, since containerized shipping is more profitable for a port than cruise traffic, Pier 6 was demolished in 2010. Colon 2000 and Home Port will not allow Indigenous vendors unless they rent traditional retail space which is totally unaffordable for Indigenous vendors.

Colon is not a city to walk around in and explore on your own. There is a lot of poverty and the accompanying problem of street crime. And there isn't anything to see in Colon. All the interesting stuff in Panama is an hour to two hour ride away from Colon. The easiest, safest, and most efficient way is to take a ship's tour.

Colon is a commercial city, home to the world's second largest free port, the Colon Free Zone which does $21 billion a year in trade and exchanging wholesale goods. The Colon Free Zone is not a "duty free" shopping area for tourists, but a gigantic distribution point for container loads of goods to be shipped across the Americas.

Colon is not designed for cruise tourism and even Panamanians don't consider it a safe city in which to wander about. Ships advise that you remain within the confines of the terminal facilities and even there you need to be cautious.

Hopefully the Panamanian government will get its tourist act together, get more jobs into Colon, and use the locals to clean up the place and at the same time raise the standard of living in Colon. With remnants of French architecture from the French Canal era, Colon could be a charming tourist attraction

Colon 2000 Pier.

Passing underneath Centennial Bridge.

if it were cleaned up. As it is, the James Bond movie "*Quantum of Solace*" used it as a Haitian look-a-like. What kind of "recommendation" is that?

It is about an hour taxi ride to Panama City and the Tocumen International Airport, located outside of Panama City. There are sometimes cabs and vans available to assist you, but be prepared to pay. Frequently the cab will have to dead-head back to Colon, so that gets factored into the cost.

Inside, Outside, or Verandah

In terms of your day in the Canal, the stateroom you have really doesn't make much difference. While you are in the Canal, and particularly while you are in the locks, it is best to be out and about, viewing the Canal and the transit from as many different perspectives as possible.

There is nothing like having a verandah on a cruise in general, if not specifically for your time in the Canal. If you have a verandah cabin the time to enjoy it is while you are cruising Gatun Lake. Many cruise lines offer special champagne breakfast or lunch served on your verandah. This is a great treat for your day in the Canal.

As a former travel agent, and crew member, let me give you some advice about selecting your stateroom: you get what you pay for. Sometimes people see a string of cabins in a certain category, and right in the middle, is what looks like the same type cabin but in a different color and at a lower price. There is a reason for the lower price! Maybe there is noise from a crew stairway, behind an elevator, or next to a pantry which doesn't appear on the deck plan, but where cabin stewards will hang out and talk loudly, or it is underneath a piece of equipment that makes some noise. Unfortunately for guests, most cruise lines have streamlined deck plans so as not to show any white spaces, because they know people will avoid staterooms next to white spaces on the deck plan.

You won't feel any motion when you are in the Canal, but if

you are concerned about the motion of the ocean on the rest of your voyage, book a stateroom as close to the center of gravity as possible. This is usually a point not only midships, but also midway between the top deck and the lowest deck, including the decks below the water line. At certain times of the year the Caribbean may get rough due to tropical storms, or you may be going against the current in the Pacific along the western coast of Central America. If you have motion sensitivity, or, in more descriptive terms, tend to puke your guts out when it gets rough, pay attention to the location of your stateroom. Yes, ships have stabilizers, but because they create drag, stabilizers are less efficient for fuel consumption, and since the captain wants his fuel efficiency bonus, stabilizers frequently are not used, particularly at night.

I have had fleet officer cabins on the navigation deck, between the bridge and most expensive passenger suites, so you'd think it would be a great location, but I rocked and rolled continually. And I've had cabins down below in the crew areas where there was virtually no motion, because the cabins down in the crew area were closer to the center of gravity. If motion is a concern, get as close to the center of gravity as possible which is generally midships on lower decks.

Price Point

For the most part, you get what you pay for. The oversupply of cruise berths and the high cost of fuel have made pricing very competitive. Cruise lines have been cutting anything that can be cut in order to eke out a profit, while at the same time hiring advertising and public relations people to convince you otherwise. When we were in the travel agency business twenty years ago and cruise lines were moving away from the "all inclusive" concept, we used to think of it in terms of peeling an onion. We thought there is only so much you could peel off before nothing was left. We were wrong! They are still peeling! The difference between profit and loss for a cruise line is often determined by on board revenue. Filling the ship means you keep it operational and keep the crew employed. It is on board revenue that makes a modest profit, and so you have restrictions on bringing your own alcohol on board and the ship is pushing weddings, teeth whitening, unimaginable spa treatments, art sales, sidewalk sales, Botox, etc. It makes you wonder what's next. Plastic surgery? "Mildred, the world cruise must have agreed with you! You look years younger?" Weddings on board are big business, so can funerals be far behind?

I'd recommend against just picking the least expensive stateroom on the cheapest cruise line. Cruise lines have become just like hotels. Both Four Seasons and Days Inn both give you a clean, comfortable place to sleep and a bathroom, but there is a huge difference in price, service, and quality. If you don't want to feel like you are being "nickel and dimed," book an all-inclusive cruise. You'll pay a whole lot more, but you get what you pay for.

Once you've picked a good, quality cruise line, I'd look for specials ... everyone has them, including the more expensive cruise lines. Often the best deals go to the folks who book early and have the best choice of accommodations and those who book late, and have no choice but get a "good deal."

Booking direct or with a travel agent? As a former travel agency owner I can tell you that if people booked with us, and the cruise line came along with a lower price, we would proactively fight for our clients to either get the new lower price or an upgrade. Generally that does not happen automatically, unless you or your travel agent keeps after the cruise line. Believe me, a travel agency that's producing a lot of business for a particular cruise line, has a lot more clout than you do. The other side of that coin is that a travel agency is naturally going to steer you to the cruise line that gives them the highest commission override, is the easiest to work with, and is their preferential partner.

If you are just looking to do a transit of the Canal, without necessarily spending any time ashore, the best rates can often be found on repositioning cruises. In the spring the major cruise lines are repositioning ships from the Caribbean to the more profitable Alaska routes, and in the fall they are bringing ships back to the Caribbean.

The cruise lines who send the most people through the Panama Canal are Princess, Holland America, and Celebrity. Many times I've encountered guests on board ships transiting the Canal who just assumed the Canal was largely dependent on their business. Actually the passenger transit segment accounts for only 8.9 percent of Canal revenue. In 2013 there were 206 passenger ship transits carrying 225,367 passengers.

15. Seeing Panama

"Get off the Dam ship!"

That line worked well when I worked on Holland America since all of their ships are named dam-something … EURODAM, WESTERDAM, ZUIDERDAM, etc. I even wanted Holland America to print up T-shirts reading, "Get off the Dam ship!"

Yes, Panama is world famous for its Canal … but there is so much more to see and do, throughout Panama and in Panama City.

You've come all this way, so why not see some of Panama?

Unfortunately a lot of cruises, including many billed as offering "a complete transit of the Panama Canal," offer *only* a Canal transit, without stopping, and without any opportunity to actually see some of Panama.

Ships that do a "turn around" itinerary, usually 10 or 11 days, roundtrip from Florida, enter the Canal through Gatun Locks. Once they get into Gatun Lake they disembark guests by tender to go on various ship-sponsored tours. Because they are disembarking guests in the Canal in a secure area of the Canal with nothing but a parking lot, independent tour operators and taxis are not allowed. So if you are doing a turn around itinerary you must book your shore excursion through the ship.

There are about three major tour companies and a few smaller ones that serve the cruise industry in Panama, as well as a lot of smaller independent tour operators.

Ship Tour or Independent

There are advantages and disadvantages to booking your tour with the ship. The off-touted advantage is, "the ship is not going to leave without you." True! And, given that traffic in Panama can sometime be horrendous, worth considering. But most of the independent tour operators know where and when traffic is bad, keep abreast of current conditions, and understand that their future success depends on getting passengers back to the ship with time to spare.

The ship tours have done all the research and work so you just sit back and go with the flow. A big plus, since a cruise is a vacation, unless you are the type of person who likes to be in control.

On a ship tour you generally will be in a bus with thirty to forty other people. On an independent tour you will likely be in a minivan with eight to fourteen others, depending on the size of the van, or a small "coaster" bus. Just leaving the port with a smaller group doesn't mean that when you get to where you are going, you won't be surrounded with hordes of folks from your ship and other ships.

The larger companies that the cruise lines utilize are accountable to the ship for the safety and security of their operations, the knowledge and language skills of their guides, the safety of any food involved, and required to have insurance. When I've worked with cruise lines, I've often been assigned to go along on tours and make spot safety checks … things like does the driver have a license, what is the tread depth on the tires, do the driver and guide have working cell phones, are exits properly marked, are the brakes working, is there emergency equipment, and, if it involves a boat, are their life jackets and are guests instructed on their use. Sometimes, when there has been food involved in the tour, I've gone along with the ship's executive chef, who checks out the sanitation of the kitchen and temperatures of food and refrigeration.

When we did a 20-hour Copper Canyon tour in Mexico, the cruise line sent a crew of our room stewards to clean and sanitize the train before our guests boarded. In Egypt we traveled in a caravan of buses, with spare buses if needed, a police escort and an undercover policeman on each bus. In both cases the ship tour provided a level of sanitation and security that no independent tour could have offered. Although it may not be as important in Panama as in Egypt or Mexico, a ship tour does provide a level of safety and security. A lot of the choice between going with a ship tour, or independently, depends on your personal comfort with adventure.

Independent tour operators may or may not be cheaper than booking a ship tour. It depends. How do you find reliable independent operators? If you do enough online research you will find some of the same names coming up again and again. If you check out sites like CruiseCritic.com you will find some of the same independent operators who always get good reviews.

Most tourist buses in Panama do not have restrooms. Knowing that it may be a while until the first rest stop, I do not have a second cup of coffee for breakfast. And, just before the tour group is called to the gangway, or en route to the gangway, I make a quick rest room stop on board ship. If you don't dawdle, you'll still have time to get to the bus. In an emergency, given a little lead time, most drivers will find a place to stop. In Panama it's easy, and culturally acceptable, for men to find the nearest tree. It's a little more difficult for women. Know that in Panama, as in most places in the world, toilet paper is not necessarily provided, so bring some along. Also, like everywhere in the world, public facilities are not as spotless as those at home or on the ship.

Tour names vary from cruise line to cruise line, but since most of the cruise lines are buying tours from the same big operators, although the names of the tours may vary, the tours themselves are quite similar.

Unfortunately few ships remain in Panama overnight, so generally you've got one day with a lot of fantastic tour opportunities. Folks always ask, "What is the best tour?" I generally answer that it depends on you and your interests; unfortunately you can't do them all.

The tours offered in Panama will generally focus on three interests …

- Culture
- History
- Nature

Obviously, there will be overlaps.

Tours Focusing On Culture

Authentic Embera Indian Village Tour [Cultural - available Fuerte Amador, Gatun Lake … ship tour only, Colon]

Hands-down, this is my favorite tour. If I had to pick the "best" tour, it would be this one! Why? The Embera village experience is so different, so unique and special to Panama.

The Embera people inhabited a wide swath of what is today Panama, Colombia, and Ecuador long before Europeans arrived. Visiting the authentic Embera Village at Rio San Juan de Pequini has been accurately been described as "something right out of *National Geographic.*"

Tour companies use about six different villages. This helps spread the "wealth" around while not overwhelming any one village. River levels vary depending on the season, so some villages up river are only available during the wet season. Each village has developed its own traditions and while some may be more "authentic" than others, this is not a "show." These are real Embera people who live and work in the villages and are committed to preserving their culture.

These are warm, friendly, intelligent people who are committed to preserving a traditional lifestyle in a "second world" country that is rapidly moving toward "first world" status. After the Canal turnover much of the area that had been Canal Zone was turned into a National Park in order to preserve the rain forest, which is essential to providing the water supply necessary to keep the Canal operating. Suddenly the Embera people living in this area were no longer able to practice their traditional subsistence way of life since, as a National Park, hunting … even with traditional blow darts using poison from tree frogs … and agriculture were outlawed. Today they make their living by sharing their culture with visitors and selling crafts.

Usually, the chief of the village will give a welcome, translated by your guide, and explain about Embera history and culture. There will be traditional dances and music and the opportunity to sample traditional food such as delicious, freshly caught, fried tilapia fish, fried plantains, and incredibly fresh fruit. This is not a full meal, but a chance to sample the native cuisine. People always ask if it is "safe" to eat the food and drink the water. Bring your own bottled water from the ship, but the food is delicious and safe. The Embera are as concerned as you would be with guests in your home, and are knowledgeable about hygienic and safe food handling. They know if they send a bus load of sick people back to the ship the tour business is over.

You can wander around the village and view each family's selection of crafts for sale. The men carve a very hard tropical wood called *cocobolo*, and make beautiful animal carvings

Dug out canoe ride to the "best" authentic village, Embera Puru.

Natural, totally non-erotic, and forgotten in about ten minutes.

from a nut called a *tagua*, sometimes known as vegetable ivory. When *tagua* dries it is very hard and so is used to make buttons for high-end clothes. The women make beautiful baskets from palm fibers with all natural dies.

When I lecture on ships I always hesitate to oversell this tour, but I can tell you that, again and again, people come back from this tour, sometimes wet and muddy, and say things like, "that was the best shore excursion ever" and "it was the best experience of my life."

There are a couple of things to remember if you take this tour.

- The most authentic tour that visits the real villages, not touristy "demonstration" villages, takes all day.

- Take along enough money. You will see spectacular baskets and carvings at reasonable prices. Indians don't cash traveler's checks and they don't take credit cards.

- By request of the Embera village chiefs, do not take anything for the children. No pens, pencils, notebooks, no quarters or dollar bills. If you want to help the family, purchase some craft items. The Embera want their children to know the Embera tradition of hospitality, not become little beggars.

- If you'd like to take some educational supplies, which *are* needed and appreciated, ask the chief if you should give them to him, the village school teacher, or directly to the children.

- If you buy a craft item from the artisan, I suggest having your picture taken with the artist. It will make the souvenir of your visit even more meaningful.

This tour can also be booked independently from Colon and Fuerte Amador/Panama City. Anne Gordon is a former

Embera baskets are made out of totally natural palm fiber and dyes, and make a special souvenir of Panama.

Having your picture taken with the artisan makes your souvenir even more special.

Hollywood animal wrangler who came to Panama to film a movie that was in part filmed at Embera Puru. She fell in love with one of the Embera men, married, and they live in Panama City and do private tours to visit their families at Embera Puru. [EmberaVillageTours.com]

You should know that regardless of the price you pay for the tour, the host village receives around $15 per person. So if you want to "help out," and take home a unique souvenir of Panama, check out the craft items for sale.

History

The Shaping of Panama … or similarly named tour [History - available Fuerte Amador, Gatun Lake … ship tour only, Colon]

One of the challenges for cruise ship tourists in Panama coming from Colon is that it requires about an hour to drive across the Isthmus.

The post-European history starts when Columbus arrived in 1503, stopping near the Bay of Limon and later up in the area of Bocas del Toro to repair his ships. In 1510 Balboa founded the first settlement on the mainland of the Americas at Darien in Panama. At the site of the original city of Panama, "Old Panama" or "Panama Viejo," there is a bridge called "The Bridge of The King" that dates back to 1619.

Coming from the Atlantic side, typically this tour travels across the Isthmus to the Amador Peninsula, the peninsula joining several little islands that was created with earth from the Canal excavations. On the one side of Amador Peninsula is the Canal and on the other side is the Bay of Panama with incredible views of the towering skyline of the current, modern Panama City. There is usually a nice lunch at a restaurant in Amador before venturing to "Casco Viejo," the old French quarter of Panama City dating back to the French Canal days. Generally there is a forty minute walking tour around Casco Viejo led by your tour guide. The tour moves on to Balboa, the heart of the old U. S. Canal Zone, and usually stops at an Indian craft market behind the old Balboa YMCA, before returning back to the ship in Colon. If you aren't up to walking forty minutes, this is not the tour for you.

Portobelo … or similarly described tour [History: Fuerte Amador, Gatun Lake … ship tour only, Colon]

Portobelo was founded in 1597, was an important port for exporting silver and gold, and one of the important ports on the route of the Spanish treasure fleets. In spite of all the fortifications, many still standing, in 1668 the pirate Henry Morgan captured and plundered Portobelo.

Portobelo is also home to the statue of the Black Christ. There are several traditions as to how the life-size figure of Christ arrived in Portobello, all of which have three parts … the miraculous arrival of the statue, the statue's refusal to leave the village, and the miracles attributed to the statue. At the time of the arrival of the Black Christ statue, a plague was devastating the area, but when people began to venerate the statue the plague ended.

For three centuries, on October 21st, the Feast Day of Cristo Negro de Portobelo, as many as sixty thousand people make a pilgrimage to Portobelo to visit the statue.

The area around Portobelo is dominated by a West Indian culture and there is a lot of poverty. Sometimes cruise passengers complain when they see poverty or "trash in the streets." The reality is that not everyone in the world can live the same way folks do who take luxury cruises, and not everyone in the world is so compulsive about trash as North Americans and Europeans.

The Fort at San Lorenzo [History: Fuerte Amador, Gatun Lake … ship tour only, Colon]

Here's another great tour for history buffs! Now a UNESCO World Heritage site, Fort San Lorenzo, guarding the mouth of the Chagres River, is an outstanding example of Spanish

Looking from Casco Viejo across the Bay of Panama to the modern city. [57]

The heart of the old U. S. Canal Zone: Balboa Union Church, the only church founded by act of Congress; building donated by John D. Rockefeller.

colonial military architecture. Fort San Lorenzo was abandoned by Spain in 1821 when Panama became independent. During the California Gold Rush in 1849 it served as a camping ground for adventurers, particularly on the old town of Chagres below the fort and on the west bank of the Chagres River.

Unfortunately, the fortifications at Portobelo and San Lorenzo are in poor repair, but it is hoped with the patronage of UNESCO, eventually they will be restored.

Old Canal Zone [History: Fuerte Amador, Gatun Lake … ship tour only, Colon]

Generally refers to Balboa and surrounds, which was the "downtown" of the old U. S. Canal Zone. The tour generally visits Ancon Hill, where the officers lived, and some of the housing areas around what used to be Fort Clayton. Most of these places are now private residences or offices, but it does give you the idea of what life was like in the U. S. Canal Zone.

On this tour you usually drive by the Panama Canal Headquarters building, the residence of the head of the Panama Canal Authority that was once de Lesseps' mansion, and the Gorgas Institute of Tropical Medicine. This tour will usually stop at the craft market behind the old YMCA, a very good place to buy Embera baskets and carvings and Kuna molas at pretty good prices.

The Panama Canal Experience … or similarly named tour [History - available Fuerte Amador, Gatun Lake … ship tour only, Colon]

This is particularly valuable for people on a ship just calling at Panama, but not making a Canal transit. It is also good for folks on a cruise that is going to enter the Canal and turn around without making a complete transit. You board a small ferry boat at the midway point of the Canal and continue through Gaillard Cut, under the Centennial Bridge, through Pedro Miguel and Miraflores locks, under the Bridge of the

Americas, and out to Amador Peninsula, where a bus picks you up to take you back to your ship.

Going through the locks in a small boat is very different than on a giant cruise ship! You get a whole different perspective and really sense the immensity of the locks. You can actually reach out and touch the sides of the Canal from the ferry boat. The ferry is a ferry, a simple small boat and not a luxury cruise ship by any means. They have narration, free soft drinks and water, local beer for purchase … Atlas, Soberana, Balboa, and my favorite, Panamá … and a simple Panamanian lunch, definitely not like the buffet on board, but good.

Although this tour is available independently of the ship, departure and return times do not work well with the length of time that most ships are in Panama, so has to be booked through the ship.

The independent tour is aimed at tourists staying in Panama City.

Lock Tours & Observation Centers … or similarly named tour [History - available Fuerte Amador, Gatun Lake … ship tour only, Colon]

If you are transiting the Canal you, and not the folks at the two observation centers, will have the best view. There is no "behind the scenes" tour at the Canal; what you see is what you get.

The Miraflores Visitor Center has restaurants, a gift shop and a small museum and a new 3D movie about the history of the Canal. Admission is $15 and the Miraflores Visitor Center is open daily from 9:00 a.m. to 4:30 p.m.

What I consider to be the better museum is the Panama Canal Museum in the Casco Viejo or the "Colonial" area of Panama City. The Panama Canal Museum is located in what was a luxury hotel built during the French canal effort, and served as headquarters for both the French and U. S. construction

On the Panama Canal Experience tour you can reach out and touch the Canal walls.

View from Gatun Locks observation platform.

companies. Unfortunately, few tours seem to visit that museum.

The observation center at Gatun is just a raised platform. Frankly, if you are on a cruise that is actually transiting the Canal, you are paying top dollar for the best seat in the house, so I don't see the reason to pay more to go on a lock and observation center tour where the view won't compare.

There is a new observation center near Gatun where you can watch the construction of the new Atlantic Lock complex. When the present Canal was being built, people came from all over the world to see the construction underway. The new locks are a massive construction project and well worth seeing. A cab can take you to the Center for Observation of The Canal Expansion. It is open daily 8:00 a.m. to 4:00 p.m. Admission is $15.

Old Canal Zone, Old Panama, Colonial Panama [History: Fuerte Amador, Gatun Lake … ship tour only, Colon]

There are three different Panama Cities … "Old Panama," the ruins of the original city from the 1500's, "Colonial Panama" or "Casco Viejo" dating back to the colonial period and time of the Canal construction, and the modern-day Panama City. The Balboa area of Panama City was the heart of the U. S. Canal Zone.

Different tours combine different areas of the city. You want to read the tour descriptions carefully so you understand exactly what you are going to see. Given traffic in Panama City, it would be very ambitious to try and see all of this in one day.

Hop On Hop Off Bus Independent Sightseeing [History: Fuerte Amador]

Across Europe these big red Hop On Hop Off buses are everywhere. Now, thankfully, the operation is in Panama City as well. If an organized tour is not for you, this is an

The Canal from the Panama Canal Railway.

Regular car on the Panama Canal Railway.

excellent way to sightsee at your own pace.

There are two routes, one of which picks up passengers at the tender pier in Fuerte Amador. A single ticket, about $29, lets you enjoy both tours. You can purchase the ticket when you get on the bus. Buses run continually, so you just hop on and hop off. The entire tour, without getting off, is two hours. Recorded commentary is provided in six different languages.

You need to be aware that traffic in Panama City can be horrendous. If you are on a big ship or there is more than one big ship and everyone is trying to get back to the ship at the same time. your return can be delayed, so, allow plenty of time to get back to the ship. It is "independent" so only you are responsible to watch the clock. It's better to get back to the ship a little early, kick back and have a drink, rather than stress over possibly missing the boat. [citysightseeingpty.com]

The Panama Canal Railway [History: Fuerte Amador, Gatun Lake … ship tour only, Colon]

When the Chagres was dammed to create Gatun Lake much of the original route of the Panama Railroad ended up under water. The Panama Canal Railway is the lineal descendant of the original Panama Railroad. Today's railway exists solely to move cargo containers from one side of Panama to the other and is a joint venture between the Kansas City Southern Railroad and privately held Lanigan Holdings. Old Amtrak engines provide the power.

There is one passenger train that makes one run a day for locals and when cruise ships are in port provides tours for the ships. Cars are restored '60s Pullman cars and there is one dome car from 1938.

The run between Colon and Balboa takes about an hour, unless the tourist train has to pull over to allow freight trains priority. Although the track runs through stretches of rain forest, forget seeing wildlife at forty miles an hour! You will catch glimpses of the Panama Canal and some of the old

Canal Zone buildings. If you are a railroad buff, or just want a relaxing glimpse of some of Panama this may be a good choice.

Some cruise lines offer you the opportunity to ride in the glass-domed observation car. There is only one of these cars and it is usually sold out online long before the cruise departs.

The dome car is usually a lot more expensive. Is it worth it? It depends. In my opinion the view is the same from the dome car as from the regular cars. And it is a glass dome car in the tropics so it is often hotter in the dome car. Funny thing, people pay a whole lot extra to sit in the dome car and then complain that there are no shades to pull down to keep the sun from shining in!

So, unless you are looking for bragging rights or the other components of the dome car tour version are significantly different, I wouldn't worry if you are unable to book a seat in the dome car.

There, I just saved you a whole lot more than the price of this book!

Be aware that this trip is usually sold as one way on the train and one way by bus. Since there only is one passenger train offering trips only in one direction allows more cruise visitors the opportunity of riding the rails in Panama.

I should mention that the coffee sold on board the train is actually produced by my neighbor in Boquete, is the real deal, and is excellent.

Nature

Wildlife abounds in the area around the Panama Canal, but that doesn't mean that you are likely to see it. When the ship is actually in the Canal, it is far enough from the shore that you aren't going to see wildlife. It is "wild" life, and a Canal passage isn't a Disney-imagineered ride where animals pop up on cue. Most self-respecting wild animals are sleeping during the day and active at night.

When you cross Gatun Lake you will see many islands which are the tops of mountains that became islands after Gatun Dam was built and the lake was created. Many of these islands have been pretty much undisturbed. For over a hundred years, both during the U. S. Canal days and today with Panama running the show, the watershed around the Canal has been preserved and protected, not just to protect the environment but to provide the fresh water necessary to operate the Canal.

One of the most interesting islands, Barro Colorado, is home to a research center of the Smithsonian Tropical Research Institute, locally called "STRI." STRI provides a unique opportunity for long-term ecological studies in the tropics, and every year is used by visiting scientists from academic and research institutions in the United States and around the world. Thirty eight staff scientists reside at STRI and are encouraged to pursue their own research priorities without geographic limitations.

Scientists set up remote cameras that would automatically be tripped at night to record the habits of jaguars that still live on the islands. And these huge cats … a full grown male can reach 350 pounds [160 kilograms] … actually swim from island to island. So all the animals you would imagine are still here, it's just very unlikely that you will see them … except perhaps, monkeys.

Gatun Lake Safari [Nature: Fuerte Amador]

This tour is operated by a "gringo" [not an offensive term in Panama, just descriptive of expats] who actually lives on a houseboat on Gatun Lake. This tour used to be offered through the cruise lines. Now you have to book it independently and directly with Captain Carl. [JungleLandPanama.com]

Monkeys come right down onto the boat and eat out of your hand.

Gamboa aerial tram ride.

About twenty guests ride in small boats across Gatun Lake into some of the many little eddies and bays. This guy knows where the troops of monkeys hang out. When I did the tour we saw five of the six different types of monkeys and in several places the monkeys came right on the boat to eat grapes out of our hands. We saw caiman, iguana, and sloths as well as monkeys. It is the one tour where I can almost guarantee you will actually see some of the abundance of wildlife living in the protected area that surrounds Gatun Lake. Lunch is served on Captain Carl's houseboat and if you like, you can view and hold some of his pet animals.

Monkey Island Tour or similar [Nature: Fuerte Amador, Gatun Lake ... ship tour only, Colon].

When Captain Carl decided to no longer offer the highly popular "Gatun Lake Safari" through the cruise line shore excursion program, the cruise lines developed the "Monkey Island Tour." The small boat trip along the shores of Gatun Lake and stop at an island in the lake gives guests the opportunity to explore the rain forest and, hopefully, experience a little of Panama's wildlife.

Gamboa Aerial Tram [Nature: Fuerte Amador, Gatun Lake ... ship tour only, Colon]

The area along the Canal where Gamboa Resort is located is part of the 55,000 acre [222.6 square kilometer] Soberania National Park. The Gamboa Resort bills itself as an ecological experience and has a butterfly exhibit and even a little demonstration Embera village, created for tourists.

The Aerial Tram takes you through the treetops up a hill to a viewing platform from which you get a spectacular view of the Panama Canal snaking its way through the jungle. You need to climb stairs to get to the viewing platform ... think taking the stairs from Deck Five to Deck Twelve ... so if you aren't prepared for the climb, you might pass on this tour. I've seen monkeys, agouti, coati, parakeets, Amazon parrots and toucans, but of course wildlife is wild and there are no guarantees.

Fishing for Peacock Bass on Gatun Lake [Nature: Fuerte Amador, Gatun Lake ... ship tour only, Colon].

Peacock Bass are not native to Panama but came from South America where they are found on the Orinoco, Amazon, and Rio Negro Rivers. A Panamanian brought the fish to raise in a pond near Gatun Lake. In 1958 a flood wiped out his pond and the Peacock Bass accidentally got into Gatun Lake. The Peacock Bass have flourished and have become the dominant fresh water game fish in the Panama Canal. The tour departs from Gamboa Resort. I've done the fishing tour and I've caught fish. Nothing like the thirty-two pound record, but it was fun. If you are a serious fisherman you won't like this tour, but if you just want some time in a little boat along the shores of a beautiful lake, it's great.

Kayaking on Gatun Lake [Nature: Fuerte Amador, Gatun Lake ... ship tour only, Colon]

This is another tour that generally departs from Gamboa Resort. If you enjoy sit-on-top kayaking and just want a day enjoying the beauty of Gatun Lake and are looking for some exercise, this may be the thing. It is a group tour, so you will be with a group, and most cruise lines require operators to make you to wear a life jacket.

If your tour is departing from Gamboa Resort, there usually are some vendors selling various crafts including Embera baskets and carvings and Kuna molas in the lobby area of the Gamboa reception building.

Rainforest Hikes [Nature: Fuerte Amador, Gatun Lake ... ship tour only, Colon]

There are a number of variations offered but generally these are relatively easy walks on relatively open pathways through the rain forest with a knowledgeable guide who will introduce you to the rain forest and point out various plants, including

Peacock bass fishing in Gatun Lake.

This is your chance to explore the rain forest. Rope bridge to Anton's waterfall.

plants that are used for medicinal purposes.

The tour brochure narrative will read something like this, "Look for coati iguanas, sloth's, monkeys, and other birds and animal life." The operative word here is "look" ... not "see." You can look all you want, and you will probably see birds and you may see some wildlife. However, because most ship tours are going to be in the middle of the day, most self-respecting wild animals are curled up taking naps and not prowling around the jungle looking for tourists.

That being said, the tropical rain forest is an amazing ecosystem and Panama is one of the best places in the world to experience the rain forest first hand. Frequently you will spot a line of leaf-cutter ants, a sight which always amazes tourists who don't have to watch the leaf-cutter ants denude a bush in their garden overnight.

I know I really shouldn't tell you this story, and not to in any way discourage you from taking a guided walk through the rain forest, because this really is an aberration, but ... the story is just too good to pass up!

When I talk about Panama on ships, and take questions, someone inevitably asks about snakes. And, yes, we do have a lot of snakes, 127 varieties to be exact. But, not to worry, only 20 are poisonous. However, those 20 include some of the most venomous snakes in the world, including the fer de lance. Most of the really dangerous snakes stay away from populated areas, except, unfortunately, the fer de lance. The fer de lance can outrun a horse on an open beach and is an aggressive snake, known to even lie in wait in an area frequented by warm blooded animals.

When people ask about snakes I always tell them that you will be very lucky to even see a snake in Panama and your chances of getting bitten by a poisonous snake are less than your chances of getting struck by lightening. In most of Panama you are within an hour of a government hospital that has antivenin, so your chances of actually dying are nil. The people who do die from snakebite in Panama are either young children, elderly people in poor health, or agricultural workers in very remote areas.

After one talk a lady from Milwaukee came up to me and said, "Richard, I was bitten by fer de lance in Panama and lived to tell about it." I was dumbfounded!

"Really! How?"

You didn't hear this from me, but, the lady from Milwaukee took one of these rain forest walks. She was at the end of the line of guests when they stopped to hear the guide explain a particular plant. She felt something snap at her ankle, looked down, and didn't see anything but two tiny marks, which she assumed might have been insect bites. She mentioned it to the guide who told her she probably had just stepped on a twig.

By the time she got back to the ship her ankle was feeling sore and a little discolored so she went to the medical center. The ship's doctor told her she probably had stepped on a twig, gave her some aspirin and charged her account for an office visit. By the next morning she was feeling worse and went back to the doctor, who charged her for another visit, gave her some more aspirin and told her she would feel better the next day. That evening, feeling worse and with the discoloration spreading, she went back to the ship's doctor for yet another office call and another charge. By this time she says, "He was looking at me like I was some kind of hypochondriac, gave me some more aspirin and said I'd feel better in the morning."

By the next morning her leg was discolored, the discoloration was spreading to her arms, and she had blood in her urine. She went back to the ship's doctor, insistent that something *was* wrong and she was not leaving until he took notice. Finally, they did some blood tests, which they should have done in the first place, set up a video conference with their medical people in the United States and with the Centers For Disease Control, and it was determined that she had been bitten by a fer de lance. At this point the ship diverted to a port where they had a medical jet standing by to evacuate the lady to Miami, where she was in the hospital for two months recovering.

Wow! The woman was young, athletic in good physical shape, in her 30s, all of which contributed to her successful recovery. So it is possible to get struck by lightening, get bitten by a fer de lance, or even win the lottery! All very unlikely, but possible.

Sorry! It's still a great tour if you've never had opportunity to walk through a rain forest! I know some of you would love to see any snake in the wild, but that is very unlikely. Even herpetologists who visit Panama looking for snakes have a hard time finding them.

El Valle de Anton [Nature: Fuerte Amador, Gatun Lake ... ship tour only, Colon]

El Valle is a mountain town about two hours from Panama City that is actually nestled in the second largest volcano crater in the world. Unlike the humid, hot climate of Panama City, El Valle has a spring-like climate year round with jagged mountains, lush forest, and lots of flowers. Although I don't think it's as nice as Boquete, which is where I live, it does have the advantage of being closer to Panama City, so a lot of expats and retirees from North America have settled in El Valle. If you want to get a glimpse of another side of Panama, a trip to El Valle is a good choice. There is a market in El Valle where you can shop for craft items and sample local tropical fruits. There is a thirty-minute hike through the rain forest to a beautiful waterfall which gives you a chance to experience a bit of the rain forest.

Looking For Adventure

Most of the more adventurous tours are outside of the Panama City area. Where I live, in the province of Chiriqui, about a seven hour drive or fifty minute flight from Panama City, we have mountain climbing, ATV tours, birding, white water rafting, zip line canopy tours, deep sea fishing, hiking to the top of Volcan Baru, the highest point in Panama.

About an hour boat ride from Panama City are the Pearl Islands which is where some of the early "Survivor" reality TV shows were filmed. If you are embarking or disembarking in Panama City and want action, you can stay at Nitro City in Punta Chame which achieved some fame when teen-heartthrob Justin Beiber decided it was the perfect R&R spot. A little further up the coast is the Coronado beach area and even further the Azuero Peninsula with some of the best surfing in Central America.

Quickie Stops

Some ships stop and only spend an evening in Panama. Frankly, it really doesn't give you much opportunity to do much of anything.

If your port call is just at night in Colon, good luck. Colon is not a city in which to wander around at night! Panama City is too far away. The highlight of a night in Colon at Colon 2000 Pier is a visit to a Super 99 supermarket, a chain incidentally owned by the former President of Panama, Ricardo Martinelli.

Fuerte Amador is a tender port and the tender ride at night can give you a beautiful view of downtown Panama City with all of its high-rise buildings. Amador, or Fuerte Amador as some cruise lines like to call it, is an area of Panama City, but the main part of downtown Panama or Albrook Mall are about a thirty minute cab ride. Casco Viejo, the old French area, is also about a thirty minute cab ride away, but can be an "iffy" area at night, despite the of clubs and restaurants that are springing up.

The Amador Peninsula itself can be a happening area at night particularly on weekends, but most of the clubs open late and run until the early morning hours. There are some restaurants with great nighttime views of the city. A favorite activity in Panama City is to stroll along the Peninsula at dusk and watch the city lights come on. The view of Panama City from Amador Peninsula is fantastic. The "Panama City by Night" tours typically give you a bus tour of a big, busy bustling city at night which, I suppose, is better than nothing, and you do get a chance to see some of Panama City.

Colonial Panama by Night or the Casco Viejo [Fuerte Amador]

What is called "Casco Viejo" today was the Panama City of the French Canal era and the areas that weren't damaged in the U. S. Invasion still have a French architectural feel, almost like old New Orleans. The area is being preserved and restored and there are boutique hotels, craft stores, boutiques, and trendy restaurants and bars. It's a wonderful place to visit and while it may not be an area for the uninitiated to walk around alone at night, if you are going with a tour you will be fine.

Miraflores Locks by Night [Fuerte Amador]

Here is an opportunity to see the locks in operation at night. There aren't always ships actually in the locks, so it may just be the locks and Canal lit up. There is a lot of work going on at the new lock complex at Miraflores and this work generally goes on around the clock with the construction areas lit up by huge lights. If you are actually transiting the Canal, you will get the best view from your ship.

Advance Booking Online

More and more cruise lines encourage you to book your shore excursions online in advance of your cruise. This makes a lot of sense since you don't have to stand in long lines while on your cruise. However, sometimes tour information has changed between the time you booked online and when you are actually on the ship. Sometimes the folks writing the Internet copy haven't a clue what the trip is really like. A lot of cruise lines now include video clips of the actual tour which is a big help and some offer a way for guests to rate the tour, assuming the legitimacy of the rating game.

Go ahead and book your tours online, but before the final closing date, the date after which there is no refund, attend the port talks … which hopefully are more than just shopping talks pushing "preferred" stores … and the shore excursion lectures and find out the latest information.

Most lines allow you to cancel or change up until the final closing date with no penalty. Some cruise lines even allow you to book more than one tour for the same time period. I think it's a flaw in some systems and often I've seen guests book three or four tours with the idea that they will wait until they get on board and then decide which reservations to keep and which to let go. So even if the tour you really want is showing "sold out," go ahead and ask to be put on a waiting list.

Some of the most popular tours … the "Authentic Embera Village Tour"(not just any Embera tour), "Panama Railway Dome Car," and "Panama Canal Experience" can often be sold out before you board the vessel. This is a reason for booking these tours online in advance, but should this happen, go ahead and wait list for these tours.

Independent

Yes, you can do your own thing, hire a taxi for $25-30 an hour, and be independent. It works well for some people and in some ports. But Panama being Panama, I think most people will do best booking one of the shore excursions from the ship. There are a lot of adventures available and a limited time. The tour operators are vetted by the cruise lines, quality controlled, are required to have insurance and operate safely, and important in an area like Panama City with tons of unpredictable traffic, the ship isn't going to leave until the last ship tour bus has returned.

If you do wish to book your own tours in advance work the Internet. There are several bulletin board sites for frequent cruisers, like CruiseCritic.com and sites like TripAdvisor.com, where people share their experiences and recommend independent tour operators that they have used. There are lots of independent adventure tour operators who may be able to provide you with a more unique experience.

There are actually three "Panama Cities." Old Panama was the first Panama City. It was the richest city in the Americas until it was looted by the privateer Henry Morgan. In the fighting the old city burned and the citizens decided they would relocate and build a new city. Old Panama is a UNESCO World Heritage site and a very interesting place to visit. Unfortunately I don't know of a ship tour that visits Old Panama.

The ship tours do visit the second Panama City, known as Casco Viejo or sometimes "Colonial Panama." This is the picturesque city of the French Canal era, home of the president's residence known as the House of the Herons, the old opera house, and the Ministry of the Exterior which houses the actual little house where Simón Bolivar called the Congress of Latin American presidents in 1826. The Church of St. Joseph is located here where Panama's famous altar of solid gold is located. Most ship tours just drive past the church and I don't know of any who give you time to actually go inside and see the gold altar.

The Panama Canal Museum is located in Casco Viejo. Great museum and again, a visit inside isn't usually on the ship tours

The third "Panama City" is the contemporary city with its Singapore-like skyline of high rise towers and notably the new Trump Ocean Plaza with its sail-like profile reminiscent of Dubai's Al Arab Hotel and the Revolution Tower, derisively named "Screw Tower," which looks like a giant pile of CD jewel cases twisted askew and ready to fall

Briant Dominici is a trained botanist, fluent in English, who does a variety of nature tours around Panama City. Briant

Preparing to board dug out canoes to Authentic Embera Village.

Boarding the Panama Canal Experience ferry boat.

does full and half day tours, and if you are embarking or disembarking your cruise in Panama, even offers a nine-hour does full and half day tours, and if you are embarking or disembarking your cruise in Panama, even offers a nine-hour tour to the San Blas Islands which would only work if your cruise is beginning or ending in Panama City. We have several friends, including groups, that have used Briant. And Briant responds to emails. [PanamaTravelTours.com]

I've already mentioned Anne Gordon, who in addition to independent tours of her husband's Embera Village, also offers Whale Watching tours in season. [WhaleWatchingPanama.com and EmberaVillageTours.com]

We've talked about the Hop On Hop Off bus in Panama City which is a great independent choice. If you are really twisted you could always just do your own shopping tour of Panama City's giant shopping malls, each trying to outdo the other.

Independent is fine ... just be sure your driver or operator gets you back to the ship on time.

Just Be Aware

Accessibility - Please note outside of the United States, Canada and the European Union the concept of "accessibility" is virtually unknown. If you have specific mobility issues you will need to discuss those with the shore excursion folks on your ship. Most tours are not going to be suitable for wheelchairs or scooters.

Activity levels - For your own enjoyment and in consideration of your fellow guests pay particular attention to the tour descriptions and the amounts of walking and climbing involved. *Every tour is not for every body.* Know and respect your body and limitations. While others may admire your "can do" attitude, even when you suspect you can't, no one likes to have a tour held up or compromised by people who shouldn't have booked the tour in the first place. If you have physical challenges you may do best to book an independent

Making a new friend at on Captain Carl's "Gatun Lake Safari."

Boarding the Panama Canal Railway.

tour; just be sure to inform the operator *in advance* of your situation.

Buses – The buses used by tour operators are good and usually air conditioned, but may not be up to the standard you might expect in Europe or North America. Don't expect rest rooms on buses and don't always expect toilet paper in public rest rooms.

Roads – Can be bumpy, particularly on the road out to where you board the canoes for the Authentic Embera Village Tour.

Guides - Panamanians often speak English like they speak Spanish ... fast. So if your guide's rapid-fire Spanish-accented English is difficult to understand, just ask him or her to speak more slowly.

Rain – Panama is in the rain forest. It will usually rain sometime, so go prepared. It will be warm rain and it probably won't last all day, but it's a good idea to take along a plastic poncho. Incredibly the gift shops on most ships don't sell plastic ponchos even although the ship is visiting rain forest ports, so it's a good idea to pack an inexpensive poncho. If it rains your footwear may get muddy.

Mosquitoes and pests – The rain forest has more bugs than anyplace else on earth. Keep your eyes open and you will be amazed at the variety of insects. Sometimes there are mosquitoes although not nearly what you would expect. Yellow fever was eradicated in Panama during the U. S. era of Canal construction and malaria isn't a problem except in some remote areas like the Darien and Bocas which you won't be visiting. What is a problem in the Caribbean, Central and South America is dengue fever. I recommend bringing bug repellant along but using it only as needed. Again, incredibly, the shops on ships generally either don't sell bug repellant or are sold out. Go figure!

Safety – Generally Panama is a very safe country. Like any city of more than a million people, there are a few places in

Panama City where you need to be careful. Colon is, in my opinion, not a city where tourists should walk around. As in any place in the world there are a few *maleantes* (good Spanish word for crooks) who prey on tourists. You can help by dressing down, leaving the crown jewels and Rolex watches (including the fake Rolexes since a potential thief may not note the difference at first glance) in your stateroom safe, and not flashing excessive amounts of money.

Sometimes tour buses will have police escorts. This is primarily to get tour buses through traffic and back to the ship on time. And sometimes a tourist police officer will ride along with the group on the Authentic Embera village tour, usually to talk with the girls. Panama's special tourist police officers generally speak only Spanish … go figure!

Taxis - By law official licensed taxis must be painted yellow with a horizontal checkered stripe. Lots of folks with cars will make extra money carting folks around and may be even offering tours, but only the yellow taxis are licensed. Panama is experimenting with metering taxis, but most are not metered and operate on a zone fare system. Like anywhere else in the world there are "local" rates and tourist rates. A local may take a taxi within the same zone for $2 and you may pay $5 to $10 for the same trip. Taxi drivers are the same the world over. Keep in mind that the hourly rate for a taxi in Panama City is about $25-30 per hour.

Trash - What amazes me all over the world is that North American and European cruise passengers may take tours to some of the most exciting and famous places in the world, and when they come back to the ship … they talk trash!

Culturally people's attitudes about trash differ. I have been in villages along the Amazon where our guests are focused on trash along the trail while the people who live there are focused on finding food for that night's dinner. Not everyone has the luxury of worrying about trash in the streets.

Cleanliness, neatness, and order are very important cultural values in Europe and North America. What makes traveling the world interesting is that not everyone has the same cultural values. The reason why you visit far off places is to experience different cultures with at times different values.

You will see trash in some areas of Panama. Panama is aware of it and working on it, but it takes time to alter attitudes and traditions.

Unfinished houses – People often comment on all the little houses that are in various stages of construction. Most Panamanians build what they can afford and finish the project as they can afford it, rather than building what they can't afford, taking out a loan, and spending a lifetime paying off the bank.

Bars on windows - Yes, the bars are there to keep out burglars, just as you may have a more expensive security system in your home, or pay more for a private security service. In Panama people use bars and dogs instead, both of which are just as effective, if not more so. Bars on windows are actually an aspect of traditional Spanish architecture. If you visit any of the old Spanish colonial cities in Latin America you will find ornate bars on the windows. In Panama the bars are, yes, designed to keep out robbers, but they also send a message to your neighbors that you are so successful that your home is filled and you must put up window bars to keep out the thieves, whether you actually have anything worth stealing or not. Panamanians only invite close relatives inside the house, so bars on the windows are a good way to keep up the appearance of success.

16. Your Voyage

Canal Day! This is what you've been waiting for, the reason why you booked a Panama Canal cruise.

Along with most everyone else on board, you set an early morning wake-up call so you wouldn't miss a thing. Now you are standing on the foredeck of our ship along with many of your fellow passengers, staring into the darkness, waiting for the first glimpse of the Canal lights in the distance, and the first rays of dawn.

Some helpful hints

It will be a long day, so stay hydrated, wear a hat and sunscreen, and pace yourself.

The average time to pass from ocean to ocean is about ten hours, down from the over twelve hours just a few years ago. Panamax ships, like most of the large cruise ships, generally take ten to twelve hours. Often cargo ships have to tie up for periods at several spots along the Canal or anchor for a while in Gatun Lake in order to maximize traffic flow. Cruise ships generally get a priority transit.

Entering the first lock, everyone wants to be upfront, vying for the "best spot." By the end of the day the rails won't be nearly as crowded. People will be playing cards, working out in the gym, lying about on deck.

To prove the point, I actually took a picture of a couple for whom the trip through the Canal was a bucket-list trip of a lifetime. We were actually in the locks and these folks were on the promenade deck sound asleep! To each his own, but I hope you don't miss a thing.

There is no one "best" vantage point on the ship. If you want to get the most out of your day in the Canal, move around the ship. Coming into the locks, the forward part of the ship is the best place to be. When the ship is in the locks move around! The view from the aft end is totally different.

Sometime when you are in the locks go down to the promenade deck and you will really appreciate just how little room there is to spare! It is so close that you feel as if you can almost reach out and touch the sides of the Canal. If you have a balcony the best time to enjoy that vantage point is when you sailing through Gatun Lake.

One of the things people always worry about are mosquitoes. Panama does have some mosquitoes, but this is not like summer in North America. The problems of yellow fever and malaria were eliminated by the United States in order to construct the Canal. The biggest fear today in Panama, as throughout the Southern United States, Caribbean, and Latin America is dengue fever, so Panama has a very aggressive program of controlling mosquitoes. Should you be planning on going on a shore excursion into the rain forest, you probably should take along some bug repellant just in case you encounter mosquitoes. But on the ship … no way! First, the ship is quite a distance from the shore, and second there is likely to be a breeze and mosquitoes avoid any breeze. If you make your passage in the "summer," which for us is the months of January through April, you will often experience winds from the north that keep any bugs away and make it very pleasant out on deck. Your biggest enemy is going to be the sun, not mosquitoes. Panama is around nine degrees

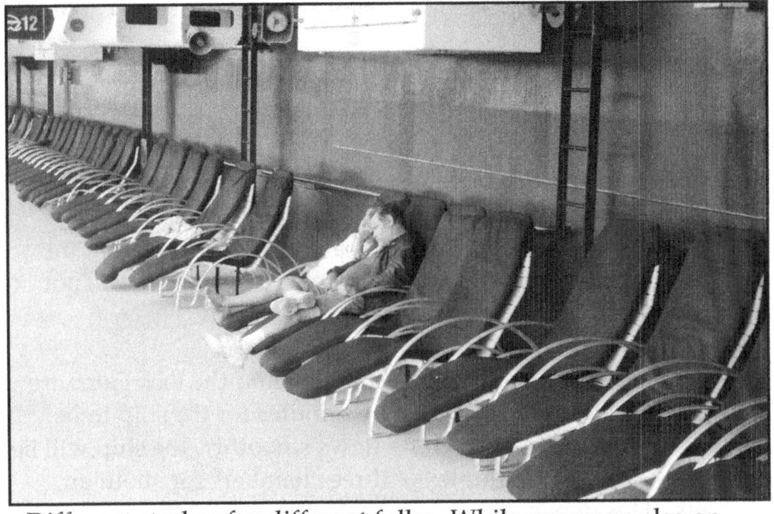

Different strokes for different folks. While everyone else on the ship was crowded onto the foredeck to watch our progress through the locks, this couple was sound asleep!

This picture, taken from the Canal ferry shore excursion, is the same view as you get from an outside stateroom on the lower deck.

north of the Equator so the sun is strong and can be very dangerous. Sun screen, head covering, and common sense are your best defenses.

You can cross the Isthmus southbound, that is Atlantic to Pacific, or northbound, Pacific to Atlantic.

To give you an idea of what to expect time-wise, here are two typical crossings, the first southbound and the second northbound. The time notations are actual entries from the ship's logbook and are, of course, for the existing locks, not the new locks under construction.

Once the ship is inside a lock chamber and the lock gates are closed, it takes only about thirty minutes for the ship to be raised. Assuming everything flows smoothly, the ship will be in the Gatun lock complex of three chambers for about an hour. This depends not only on the lockage of your ship, but also the ship ahead of you. Sometimes the process gets delayed and everything does not move on schedule. With some of the larger, boxy ships, like bulk carriers and tankers, it takes longer for the water to flow around the hull.

Southbound [Atlantic to Pacific]

- <u>Atlantic Ocean (Caribbean Sea)</u>

- Manzanillo Bay Breakwater entrance to Canal
  5:04 a.m. -- The first set of pilots were boarded

- Port of Colon, Cristobal
  6:00 a.m. approaching Gatun Locks

- Site of Proposed Third Bridge

- <u>Atlantic Lockage</u>
  <u>Gatun Locks</u> – 3 chambers – 85 feet [25.9 meter] lift
  6:20 a.m. connecting to the mules
  6:46 a.m. inside the first lock chamber at Gatun and gates closed

7:25 a.m. medical evacuation complete – passing to the second chamber
8:00 a.m. moving into the third chamber – line handlers and first pilot disembark, second pilot on board
8:55 a.m. exiting the third chamber of Gatun Locks and cruising into Gatun Lake
OR
New Atlantic Locks - 3 chambers, water saving basins – 85 feet [25.9 meter] lift

- Gatun Dam Chagres River – hydroelectric plant, spillway

- Gatun Lake

- Gatun River causeway, Monte Lirio bridge

- Gamboa

- Chagres River – upstream is Madden Dam and Lake Alajuela – hydroelectric plant, backup water supply for Canal

- Gold Hill and Contractor's Hill

- Culebra or Gaillard Cut

- Centennial Bridge

- Pacific Lockage
  Pedro Miguel Lock – 1 chamber – 31 foot [9.3 meter] drop
  12:10 p.m. another team of linesmen and another pilot is boarded
  12:32 p.m. vessel enters Pedro Miguel Lock
  1:10 p.m. gates are opened, mules disconnected and vessel moves into Miraflores Lake
  Miraflores Lake
  Miraflores Locks – 2 chambers – 54 feet [16.5 meters] drop

2:02 p.m. gates to Miraflores opened and mules connected
2:39 p.m. entering Miraflores locks
2:50 p.m. entering first lock chamber
3:29 p.m. inside the second lock chamber
4:00 p.m. gates opened and we left Miraflores
OR
New Pacific Locks - 3 chambers, water saving basins - 85 feet [25.9 meter] drop

- Port of Balboa

- Bridge of The Americas

- Pacific Entrance to Canal
  5:15 p.m. pilot disembarked and ship headed out to sea

- Pacific Ocean (Gulf of Panama)

Northbound - [Pacific to Atlantic]

- Pacific Ocean (Gulf of Panama)

- Pacific Entrance to Canal
  5:20 a.m. -- The first set of pilots were boarded.

- Bridge of the Americas

- Port of Balboa

- Pacific Lockage
  6:15 a.m. approaching Miraflores Locks
  6:30 a.m. lines connected to the engines
  6:51 a.m. inside the first lock chamber and gate closed
  7:29 a.m. passing to the second chamber
  Miraflores Locks - 2 chambers - 54 feet [16.5 meter] lift
  8:10 a.m. gates opened and left Miraflores Locks, passing into Miraflores Lake

Entering the locks.

Entering the locks the best vantage point is on the bow.
Notice the tiny row boat bringing the lines out to the ship.

Miraflores Lake
9:00 a.m. connected to mules and entering Pedro Miguel Locks
Pedro Miguel Lock - 1 chamber - 31 foot [9.3 meter] lift
9:00 vessel exits Pedro Miguel – line handlers and first pilot disembark, second pilot on board
OR
New Pacific Locks - 3 chambers, water saving basins - 85 feet [25.9 meter] lift

- Culebra or Gaillard Cut
  9:55 a.m. cruising Gaillard Cut and Gatun Lake

- Centennial Bridge

- Gold Hill and Contractor's Hill

- Chagres River - upstream is Madden Dam and Lake Alajuela - hydroelectric plant, backup water supply for Canal

- Gamboa

- Gatun River Causeway, Monte Lirio Bridge

- Gatun Lake
  1:10 p.m. standing by in Gatun Lake for clearance to enter locks

- Gatun Dam Chagres River

- Atlantic Lockage
  Gatun Locks - 3 chambers - 85 feet [25.9 meter] drop
  2:00 p.m. approaching Gatun Locks
  2:40 p.m. another team of lines men and another pilot is boarded
  2:50 p.m. connecting to the mules
  3:15 p.m. inside first lock chamber and gate closed
  3:55 p.m. passing to second lock chamber

4:35 p.m. passing to the third lock chamber
5:20 p.m. exiting Gatun Locks, line handlers disembarked
OR
New Atlantic Locks - 3 chambers, water saving basins - 85 feet [25.9 meter] lift

- Third Bridge

- Port of Colon, Cristobal
  6:00 p.m. pilot disembarked and ship headed out to sea

- Manaznillo Breakwater

- Atlantic Ocean (Caribbean Sea)

What to Look For

Here are some of the things to watch for as you make your way between the seas. For convenience we will list these in order of a southbound voyage.

Bay of Limon

The Pacific entrance to the Canal is from the Pacific Ocean and Caribbean Sea into the Bay of Limon. The Bay of Limon is the huge natural bay, 4.5 miles [7 kilometers] long and 2.5 miles [4 kilometers] wide, that provides anchorage for ships awaiting transit.

The bay is protected by breakwaters that extend from the west and east sides of the entrance to the approach to the Canal. The breakwaters are themselves a great engineering achievement - 6 miles [9.6 kilometers] long, and 425 feet [130 meters] wide at the base.

The breakwaters were originally built to protect the Canal from torpedoes. As the ship passes through the breakwater it is headed due south, and if you happen to be making a southbound passage and it is still dark and the skies are clear, at certain times of the year you can see the Southern Cross just above the horizon dead ahead. Once the vessel is inside the breakwater it turns southeast to the entrance of Gatun Locks. The reason for the turn is that during World War II torpedoes went straight ahead, so if one was fired from outside the breakwater it would miss the Canal entrance.

Today the breakwaters serve a useful function of protecting the inner harbor against storms and protecting the Canal channel from silting and surf.

The mast lights marking the entrance to the breakwater are among the tallest in the world.

If you are making a southbound transit, way off on the starboard side [port side for northbound transit], you will see a navigational light where the former U. S. Fort Sherman was located. The light is called Toro Point Light and was actually erected by the French sometime in the 1890s. It is a steel structure surrounding a masonry light house.

Off to the port side [southbound] or starboard side [northbound] was another U. S. military installation called Coco Solo.

During the U. S. Canal period there were twenty military forts and operations in the Canal Zone, including a jungle survival school where Indigenous Embera Indians were used to train troops, including the first U. S. astronauts.

Port of Colon, Cristobal

Colon was a very important area during the U. S. Canal occupation and home to several major U. S. military operations that provided a lot of local revenue and employment. Today Colon is the third largest city in Panama and home to the Colon Free Zone, the second largest free port in the world, second only to Hong Kong. It's not "duty free shopping" in the cruise port sense, but a port where goods can be assembled, purchased wholesale and distributed by

Pilot boat approaches.

Here two giant cruise ships are side by side in the locks.

container loads around the world. Location at the "crossroads of the Americas" is one of the main keys to the enormous success of the Colon Free Zone.

Other than the Free Zone, and a few new hotel and shopping complexes, the center of Colon is a pretty depressed area. It was actually used in the James Bond film "*Quantum of Solace*" to represent Haiti ... it's that bad. Although much of the city was burned during a Colombian civil war in 1885, and again in a massive fire in 1915, many of the surviving buildings still reflect the French style architecture of the Canal construction days. With some government investment and employment projects for locals, downtown Colon could be developed into a real tourist center.

There are two places cruise ships dock in Colon. Colon 2000 is a terminal used by a lot of Carnival Corporation companies. Home Port is used mostly by Royal Caribbean companies. Royal Caribbean homeports a ship in Panama during the North American winter cruise season.

For many years there was an old pier built in 1919 as a coaling station that was known as Pier 6 or Cristobal. In 2010 the old historic pier was demolished to allow more space for containerized port operations.

The huge port here is operated by the Panama Ports Company, part of Hutchinson Port Holdings, which operates 355 berths in forty-four ports around the world. Hutchinson is owned by Cheung Kong Group, one of Hong Kong's leading multi-national conglomerates. This company also operates a port on the other end of the Canal at Balboa. This has led to one of those crazy rumors, rampant in some places, including the United States, that the People's Republic of China owns or is running the Canal. Panama, not China, owns and runs the Canal. The People's Republic recognizes what hopefully are good investments, things like investing in U. S. Treasury Bonds ... and investing in Panama's port infrastructure.

As the ship makes its way to the entrance of Gatun Locks you will see the large channel, now under construction, that will be the entrance to the new, larger Atlantic Lock complex. Before it was enlarged for the Canal expansion this was called U. S. channel. The Canal opened in 1914, but rather quickly, folks began to realize that it wasn't large enough to handle all the demand, and with larger and larger military ships the Canal needed to be enlarged. So in 1939 the United States began an ambitious program to expand the Canal, enlarging it and building a "third lane" of larger locks … very similar in concept to the huge expansion project now being undertaken by Panama. The U. S. project began in 1939 but the effort was abandoned when the United States entered World War II. The idea was revisited periodically but with price tags in the billions of dollars nothing happened. The old U. S. channel has been greatly expanded for the new Atlantic Lock access.

If you look carefully on the other side of the ship you will see a tiny little passage known as the French passage. This inlet is all that is left from the original French attempt to dig the Panama Canal, an attempt that cost over 20 thousand lives.

Wildlife

The image and expectation that many people have is that they will see wildlife and birds along the shoreline as they transit the Canal. Although Panama is one of the most bio-diverse areas in the world, and the rainforests you will see along the sides of the Canal have an amazing diversity of birds and animals, don't expect to see much. Unless you have really good eyes and a great pair of binoculars the Canal channels are too far from shore to see much more than spectacular foliage. And we are transiting during the middle of the day when most respectable animals are napping. But they are there! Anteaters, jaguars, cougars, monkeys, deer, agouti, parrots, toucans, sloths, snakes, hundreds of butterflies including the iridescent blue morpho butterfly … they're all there. All of this giving you a great reason to come back and visit Panama and stay a while!

What you can look for are crocs! The Canal has American crocodile as well as caiman. Although often locally called "alligators," they are in fact crocodiles. How I remember: "canal" and "crocodile" both start with "C." Crocodiles like to hang out near Gatun Locks. Some of these guys have been here since before the Canal was built and some are huge! These big suckers can be very aggressive so Canal workers have to be very cautious when doing maintenance work in this area. Look on the banks ... or watch in the water. The tip off is what looks like a log ... moving in the wrong direction or against the current. And yes, both the crocodiles and caiman have attacked and killed people.

Caiman grow as large as 12 to 15 feet [3.7 to 4.6 meters], and crocodiles can get as large as 18 feet [5.5 meters] and weigh as much as a ton. People have been killed in this area, in Gatun Lake and in Miraflores Lake and since it is common for the animal to take its victim and hide the body underwater, the bodies of those attacked are usually never found. So keep your hands and feet inside the ship!

People always ask about the large birds with the forked tails. These are frigates, and you see lots of them around the Canal. Panama has 940 bird species, but unfortunately you aren't going to see a lot from the middle of the Canal. You may hear first, then see, some flocks of the little green parrots we have ... noisy buggers. You'll probably see them in the tops of the trees along the Canal.

Navigation Lights

As you make your way through the Canal you will see a number of navigational lights, as well as nineteen different lighthouses in the Canal designed originally as navigational lights.

Gatun Locks

Gatun lock complex consists of three chambers. The ship will be lowered 85 feet [25.9 meters] back down to sea level. By

One of the nineteen lighthouses originally used for navigation.

now you are an expert and know to watch for the row boat, the "bumpers," and understand the role of the locomotives and how water flows through the lock system and eventually out to sea.

When it was built the concrete construction of the Panama Canal was the largest ever undertaken and the record remained until the construction of the Hoover Dam in the 1930s. Pedro Miguel was the first lock complex, completed in 1911, and Miraflores was finished in 1913.

Since much of the concrete in the Canal is now over a hundred years old, the Canal Authority spends a great deal of money to repair and replace deteriorating concrete. It is believed that within the Canal walls there are pockets of concrete which still have not completely dried.

The main culverts are 18 feet [5.5 meters] in diameter, the same size of the tunnels that carried the railroad lines under the Hudson River into New York City.

By now you also understand why there are two sets of lock gates for the chambers that connect directly into Gatun Lake. In some catastrophic event where a ship's engines failed and the locomotives were unable to stop the forward motion, the second set of locks would prevent Gatun Lake from emptying.

As you approach Gatun Locks you will catch glimpses of the massive construction project building the new Atlantic lock complex and approach channel.

People are always curious about the bulls-eye targets on the center wall of the third chamber. These are used by the line handlers to practice throwing hawser lines, the object being to put the "monkey fist" at the end of the line through the center hole. Line handlers have competition events to determine who wins the prize for accuracy and height.

Another competitive event that has been around the Canal since 1954 is the annual Cayuco Race. A *cayuco* is the

Entering Gatun Locks.

Gatun Locks Observation Center.

traditional Indigenous canoe made by hollowing out a giant log. The race started when a Panama Canal worker had the great idea to take a group of Boy Scouts to meet a native Embera Indian community on the Chagres. The boys learned how to paddle the traditional Indian *cayuco* which eventuated in an annual race through the Panama Canal, from one side to the other covering a 41 mile [66 kilometer] long route over three days. Over seventy-five boats make the trek each year.

Just below the steps that lead up to the observation platform you can see one of the early General Electric locomotives or "mules" used on the Canal. Originally a fifty horsepower motor operated gears to open and close lock leaves. Now a fifteen horsepower motor operates hydraulic arms that open and close the leaves. Near to the old locomotive you can see one of the original giant gears used to open and close the locks.

Looking to the Starboard or right-hand side of the ship on a southbound transit, or to the Port or left-hand side of the ship on a northbound transit, you will see the crest of the Gatun Lake Dam and the top of the spillway.

Gatun Lake

At the time it was built, Gatun Lake was the largest man-made lake in the world. Today, Gatun Lake doesn't even make the top-thirty list of man-made bodies of water. Gatun Lake has an area of 164 square miles [425 square kilometers] at its normal level. The lake stores 4,200,000 acre feet of water [5.2 cubic kilometers] which is about as much water as comes down the Chagres River during an average year. Which means if you emptied Gatun Lake, it would only take an average year's rainfall to refill the lake, which gives you some idea of the enormous amount of rain that falls in this area of Panama. So my usual weather forecast for the Panama Canal is that sometime it's going to rain, even if just a few sprinkles. But when it really decides to rain in Panama, it rains! Sometimes, when it really decides to rain in Panama, it's like someone in the heavens is dumping out oil barrels full of

One of the old gears used to open and close lock gates.

One of the early General Electric "mules."

water.

Gatun Lake has a 1,100 mile [1,770 kilometer] shoreline. The lake is about 85 feet [25.9 meters] deep, but, as part of the Canal expansion program with the new locks, the Canal will require more water, so Gatun Lake needs to be increased. One way, raise the dam, but ... oops ... the existing locks are then eight feet [2.4 meters] under water ... so they are increasing the water in Gatun Lake by deepening the lake. And you will see as we go through the Canal work in progress as they are dynamiting the bottom of the lake and dredging to increase the depth. That will increase the volume of water as well as enable ships with deeper draft to get through the Canal.

What you see as islands in Gatun Lake today are actually the tops of mountains that used to be here before the lake was flooded.

One of the tours offered on cruises that stop in Panama is peacock bass fishing on Gatun Lake. Peacock Bass are not native to Panama but originate in the Rio Negro river basin in the Amazon. In 1958 a flood wiped out a shore side pond where a man was raising peacock bass and some of the fish were washed into Gatun Lake. The peacock bass have flourished and have become the dominant game fish in the Panama Canal and fish as big as thirty-two pounds have been caught.

Another tour offered on cruises that stop in Panama is a tour where you take a small motor boat and explore some of the little islands and many coves along the shoreline. In some of these coves the monkeys jump on the boat for grapes.

Many of these islands have been pretty much undisturbed for almost 100 years because of the Canal's policy, both during the U. S. Canal days and today with Panama running the show, that all of the area around the Canal needs to been preserved as protected area to protect the rain forest and watershed that provide the fresh water necessary to operate the Canal.

From the bridge, cruising Gatun Lake.

U. S. Army Corps of Engineers aerial photo of Gatun Dam spillway.

One of the most interesting islands is Barro Colorado, home to the Smithsonian Tropical Research Institute [STRI], a bureau of the Smithsonian Institution founded in 1923. Barro Colorado provides a unique opportunity for long-term ecological studies in the tropics. Every year the island is used by visiting scientists from academic and research institutions in the United States and around the world. Additionally thirty eight resident staff scientists are encouraged to pursue their own research priorities.

The little old Canal Zone town of Gamboa is home to the Panama Canal Dredging Division. Dredging is a continuing operation in the Canal with routine dredging maintenance before the expansion program running about $150 million annually. Now, with the expansion, there is major additional dredging going on as part of the Canal expansion. There is also a dock here for Barro Colorado. A boat leaves here each morning to take workers to the Smithsonian Tropical Research Institution. It's a forty-minute ride to work, and the boat returns each afternoon for the commute home.

The lock leaves or gates for the Canal are made of steel and each weighs from 390 to 730 tons. The gates are hollow so that they can be floated out for repair. Nice, but ... how do you pick up a 390-730 ton steel gate to be able to float it out?

Enter the cranes. The Panama Canal has had two giant floating cranes; the largest is named "Titan," and the smaller one, "Hercules." Titan was originally built by Hitler's Germany and claimed by the United States as war booty. Titan spent fifty years in Long Beach, California before being moved to Panama in 1999. The crane can be floated into the locks of the Panama Canal and is used for the heavy lifting required to maintain the lock leaves of the canal. It can lift 350 metric tons and is one of the strongest cranes in the world. If the cranes are not in use elsewhere in the Canal they are docked at the Dredging Division.

Gamboa is a stretch of the Canal where you will usually get to see the Panama Canal Railway in operation.

A tiny part of the railroad operation is the one passenger train that runs in the morning from Panama City to Colon and in the evening from Colon to Panama City, mainly to transport business men who are doing business at the Colon Free Zone. When cruise ships are in port, the passenger train operates during the day as a shore excursion for cruise ship visitors. All of the rolling stock of the present railroad is refurbished old engines and cars brought in from the United States.

Many cruise passengers opting for a shore excursion riding the rails of the Panama Canal Railway assume that they are following the route of the original Panama Railroad and will wind their way along the Panama Canal. One cruise line even hyped this excursion on their Internet site by saying that as you rode along you could "watch for monkeys and toucans."

First, the original route of the Panama Railroad is different than the route of the current Panama Canal Railway.

Second, the current Panama Canal Railway exists primarily to move shipping containers across the Isthmus and, although it occasionally provides glimpses of the Canal, runs mostly through jungle and not next to the Canal.

Third, about that rain forest and those "monkeys and toucans" ... Yes, the animals are there, but being self-respectable animals they are not hanging around next to the railroad tracks and, even if they were, the train is whizzing along at forty miles an hour. You can "watch for monkeys and toucans" all you want, but don't expect to see any from the train.

When the Carter-Torrijos Treaty turned what remained of the Panama Railroad over to Panama, the railroad was in poor repair and losing $4 million a year. Panama's aggressive process of privatizing many of the assets it acquired with the Canal turnover included the railroad.

Today the Panama Canal Railway is a very profitable operation moving containers across the Isthmus. Panama is the only place in the world where it is possible to transship containers in-bond from the Atlantic to the Pacific in under four hours. Often container ships have containers stacked too high to meet Canal restrictions, and so they can offload extra containers at one end of the Canal and by the time they reach the other end the containers are waiting to be reloaded. Because containers can be transshipped in bond, they can be sent from the Pacific port to the gigantic Colon Free Zone on the other side of the Isthmus.

Just outside the town of Gamboa is the entrance to the Gamboa Rainforest Resort, a sprawling megaresort located on the shores of the Panama Canal. Gamboa is the jumping off point for a number of tours including peacock bass fishing, kayaking, and the Gamboa Aerial Tram.

Chagres River

You will see a small bridge crossing the Chagres River. It really doesn't look like much, certainly not like a river mighty enough to support the Panama Canal. The small bridge carries the Panama Canal Railway and one lane of traffic at a time. It's fun to drive across, especially when you're sharing the bridge with a train.

The Chagres River with all its many tributaries upstream is the source of the water in Gatun Lake and provides the fresh water necessary to run the Panama Canal.

Upstream is another dam called Madden Dam that created Alajuela Lake. The lake is an important part of the Canal water system and is 250 feet [76.2 meters] above sea level. It can store one-third of the Canal's annual water need. Madden Dam controls the possible torrential flow of the Chagres river into the navigational route of Lake Gatun. The water is also used to generate hydroelectric power, and to supply Panama City's freshwater. Its upper basin is covered by dense tropical forests and to protect it, Panama created Chagres National

Titan, the giant floating crane built by Hitler's Germany.

Dredging is a continual operation in the Canal.

Park in 1985.

One of the fantastic opportunities when you visit Panama is the chance to actually go up into Chagres National Park and visit the Indigenous group of Embera Indians who live in the Chagres. To visit my Embera Indian friends who live in a tiny village on Rio San Juan de Pequini that feeds into Alajuela Lake, you first go to Alajuela Lake where the Embera will meet you with a dug out canoe. You travel across the lake, then up the river through dense jungle for another forty-five minutes to visit their village. It's a fantastic, once-in-a-lifetime experience.

Two fairly recent events significant to the Canal occurred at this spot.

In November 2012 a bulk carrier, nearly slammed into the bridge when a problem with the ship's control mechanism caused the pilot to lose control. The incident was caught on a scary video that shows the ship coming within one meter of the bridge. By ordering full reverse and dropping anchor the pilot was able to avert disaster.

In December 2010 heavy rains forced the Panama Canal to be closed for only the third time in history. In 2010 so much water was pouring uncontrolled down the Chagres River and into the Canal that whole islands of land were breaking loose and floating into the Canal channel. An incredible YouTube video shows these floating islands being washed into the bridge with huge trees snapping off as the islands were forced under the bridge. The Canal was closed by landslide shortly after it opened from late 1915 to mid 1916, and in 1989 when the United States invaded Panama.

When you drive from Panama City to Chagres you drive through Soberanía National Park, just 15 miles [24 kilometers] from Downtown Panama City. The park was established in 1980 and is a strip bordering much of the eastern side of the Canal. In the protected area there are 105 species of mammals,

Bridge where the Chagres River flows into Gatun Lake.

Entering Culebra or Gaillard Cut with a storm brewing. What's left of Gold Hill is on the left and Centennial Bridge is dead ahead.

525 species of birds, 79 reptiles, 55 amphibious and 36 species of fresh water fish, so the park is an important wildlife refuge.

Among the mammals you can find jaguar, the white-tailed deer, neques, raccoons, ant eaters, sloths, herds of wild pigs, and various species of monkeys.

On the Panama City side of the Chagres, near the banks of the Panama Canal, is El Ranacer Prison, where the former dictator Manuel Noriega is in prison. It doesn't look like much like a U. S. super-max prison, and it isn't. It's an old, Panamanian prison where Noriega lives in simple cell with some accommodation made for his age and security.

Culebra or Gaillard Cut

Gaillard Cut, originally known as Culebra Cut, passes through what was once nine miles of solid rock including what was known as Culebra Mountain. The mountain was cut in half to allow the Canal to pass through. The two remaining parts of Culebra Mountain are now called Gold Hill, the higher one, and the lower one, Contractor Hill. Through the years these hills, formerly part of a mountain and the continental divide, have been sculpted down to prevent landslides.

What is left of Gold Hill rises 662 feet [201.8 meters] above sea level atop a sheer cliff, its side blasted away for the Canal. Gradually over the years to control erosion and slides the hill has been whittled away.

Why "Gold Hill?" Remember that overeager copy writer of the French Canal Company who promised, "This mountain is full of gold and it is believed that the ore from this place alone will be worth more than will be the total cost of the canal construction?" All these years and gold was never found, but the name stuck.

During the U. S. Canal construction the worst slide happened on the east side of Gold Hill when the mountain slid covering a 75 acre [30.4 hectare] area, destroying buildings in Culebra village and requiring the removal of some 10 million cubic yards [7,645,540 cubic meters] of material. Another Gold Hill slide required removal of some 7 million cubic yards [5,351,884 cubic meters] of material.

The cut was the most difficult part of the construction taking nine years to excavate, during which 100 million tons of rock were removed and the mountain was cut down from 210 feet [64 meters] to 40 feet [12.2 meters].

More than 100 million cubic yards [about 76.5 million cubic meters] of spoil had to be hauled away from the excavation site and dumped. Part of the spoil was used to link four small islands on the Pacific side to create a breakwater which is today known as the Amador Peninsula running over 3 miles [4.8 kilometers] out into the Pacific. Spoil was also used as fill to create the town of Balboa and what became the Fort Amador military reservation.

The time spent cruising through Culebra or Gaillard Cut is a good time to reflect on the achievement of cutting through the continental divide, linking the oceans, and accomplishing a herculean feat. It is also a good time to reflect on the high cost of human life to create the Canal, The conservative death toll to construct the Canal, including both the French and American efforts, is 25 thousand … that's 500 lives for every mile of the Canal. These were ordinary people, struggling to make a living and striving to do the impossible.

Centennial Bridge

Centennial Bridge, built to celebrate the 100th anniversary of the Republic of Panama, was dedicated in 2004. It is the second bridge across the Panama Canal joining the continents. The bridge crosses Gaillard Cut just before the Pedro Miguel locks. The Bridge didn't actually open to traffic until 2005 while the United States and Panama argued about who was responsible to clean up the cache of poisonous gas canisters and other weapons that the United States had left buried near the bridge site.

Centennial is a cable-stayed bridge with a total span of 3,451 feet [1,052 meters]. The main span is 1,051 feet [320 meters]. The supporting towers are 604 feet [184 meters] high. The bridge clears the Canal by 262 feet [80 meters], allowing large vessels and even "Titan," Hitler's giant floating crane, to pass under the bridge.

The west tower of the bridge is set back about 164 feet [50 meters] to allow for future widening of the Canal.

Pedro Miguel Lock

The first lock on the Pacific side is Pedro Miguel, again named after one of the little towns that were flooded during the construction of the Canal. Because of the large tidal variance on the Pacific side, it was thought better to separate the locks. Pedro Miguel has only one chamber which will raises or lowers the vessel 29 feet [8.9 meters] from or into a small man-made transit lake Miraflores Lake. It is 1.3 miles [2 kilometers] between Pedro Miguel Lock and Miraflores Locks.

On the Gatun Lake side of Pedro Miguel you will see a parking area where folks who live in Panama City like to bring visitors to see ships in the Canal. There aren't always ships actually in the locks, so sometimes you have to try a couple of spots if you want your friends to see more than an empty lock.

Miraflores Lake

Miraflores Lake is a small, man-made lake that serves only as a connection between the single lock at Pedro Miguel and the double locks at Miraflores, and is 54 feet [16.5 meters] above sea level.

The drop from Miraflores Lake to the Pacific approach varies due to the tidal differences on the Pacific, between 43 feet [13.1 meters] at extreme high tide and 64.5 feet [19.7 meters] at extreme low tide.

Centennial Bridge.

Captain and pilot on wing bridge.

There is a spillway at Miraflores with eight gates similar to those at Gatun Dam. The spillway controls the flow of water from the Rio Grande and Coccoli Rivers and to control the level of Miraflores Lake. There still are crocodile in this area. Several years ago a guide was taking tourists around Miraflores Lake when one of the tourists dropped a camera into the lake. The helpful guide hoped overboard to retrieve the camera, was grabbed by a croc and never seen again.

Miraflores Locks

The Panama Canal Authority has three Web cams and one is midway up the red and white communications tower next to the Miraflores Visitors Center. On one ship they convinced guests to prepare signs for the folks back home and to wave flags as we passed by the final Canal Web cam. [PanCanal.com]

People had a lot of fun getting ready for the grand event, and the ship's photographers and videographers had a field day, but the folks back home ... Well, if they looked very closely they might have seen a few pixels that were their friends with their carefully crafted signs. But it did look good on the videos and pictures taken by the ship photographers.

If you are making a Northbound transit the Miraflores Visitor Center will likely be closed early in the morning. The Visitor Center is very popular with tourists and is on the Hop On Hop Off bus route. The center provides observation decks, restaurant, areas for meetings and events, a small museum, and a new 3D film about the Panama Canal. When the Visitor Center is open it is always a big event for the people ashore to see a cruise ship passing through the locks. There is lots of waving, shouting, and picture taking.

Below Visitor Center, next to the Canal, you can see one of the early locomotives or "mules" used on the Canal that was built by General Electric.

From the bridge, entering Miraflores.

The Visitor Center at Miraflores.

At the entrance to the Miraflores Visitor's Center, which unfortunately you can't see from the ship, stands one of the trains that was used by the French found buried in the mud while the Canal was being dredged.

From the start of the Canal effort there was recognition that the Canal would split Panama in two. This was a challenge even during the U. S. construction when barges had to be used to ferry construction workers back and forth.

The old swing bridge at Miraflores, no longer used, was built in 1942, but could be used only when ships weren't passing. In 1942 ferry service was added as well, known as the Thatcher Ferry after a former member of the Canal Commission who introduced the legislation that created the ferry.

Until the Bridge of the Americas was built in 1962, there was no other way to cross. I suggest going up to the top deck of your ship at some point while you are in Miraflores because there are several things to look for.

Looking toward the Pacific you will see Ancon Hill, a 654 foot [199.2 meter] hill overlooking Panama City on the other side of the hill. During the U. S. Canal Zone days it always irked Panamanians that because of military installations on Ancon Hill access was limited. Ancon Hill historically had served as a kind of emotional heart of the city and during the Canal Zone days was off limits to Panamanians. On the stroke of the new millennium, when all of the Canal Zone officially became once again part of Panama, a huge Panamanian flag was raised on Ancon Hill which flies day and night.

On top of the hill, where the flag flies, is an overlook where you get a fantastic view of the city. I've sometimes stayed at a little bed and breakfast up on Ancon Hill. Because the hill was never developed in the U. S. Canal Zone days, monkeys still come to eat bananas off your balcony and you see brightly colored toucans. When I've stayed there I've gotten up early to hike to the top of Ancon Hill and watch the sun rise over

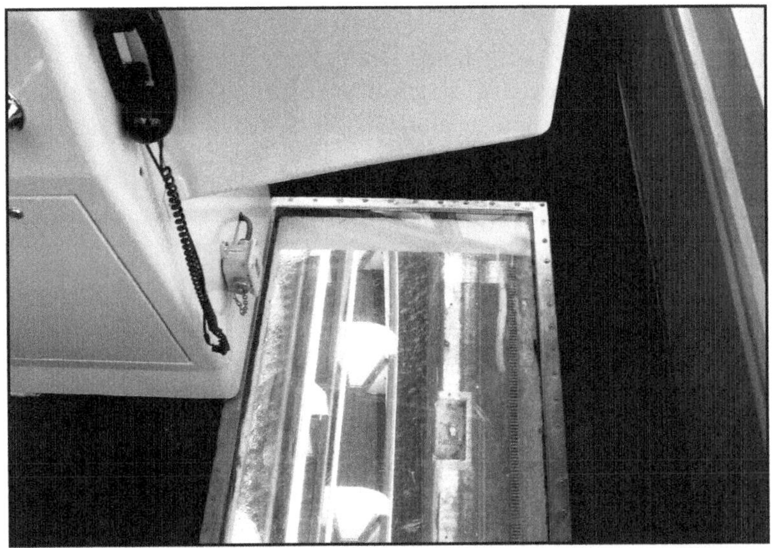

To give you an idea of how tight the squeeze is in the locks: the captain's view of the lock wall (right) and the ship railing (left).

When the winds blow the ship can act as a giant sail, so the tugs assist.

the Pacific. The view of Panama City and the Bay of Panama is breathtaking.

If you let your eye travel down Ancon Hill you may be able to make out the Panama Canal Headquarters building that was completed in 1914.

One of the reasons Ancon Hill was never developed was that inside the United States had created an underground headquarters for U. S. command and control had Panama ever been overrun and captured. The Joint Command Post facility was constructed of reinforced concrete beneath 200 feet [60 meters] of native porphyry rock. A 302 by 7.5 foot [90 by 2.3 meter] tunnel led from the entrance, cut into the solid rock at Quarry Hill, just above my favorite bed and breakfast, led to a 14,000 square foot [13,000 square meter] building carved into the mountain that included a hospital, chapel, offices, barracks, cafeteria, generators, water supply and giant shredding machines. The structure cost $400 thousand in 1942, about $5.7 million today. The facility was used as a command post center by the United States until 1997.

Looking south east you will see a large complex of buildings that was Fort Clayton during the days of the U. S. Canal Zone. Today it is known as the "City of Knowledge" and is home to a number of large high tech and computer operations, call centers, and university buildings. There are hotels, housing developments, and the gigantic U. S. Embassy.

On the Pacific side of Miraflores Locks you will see a lot of construction taking place creating the access channel for the new Pacific Lock complex, as well as construction of the new locks.

Balboa

During the U. S. days the lower slopes of Ancon Hill contained residences for officers and Gorgas Hospital. Higher up was the residence of the Governor of the Canal Zone. Originally the Governor's residence was the mansion de

Lesseps had built for himself. It was later moved to Ancon Hill and has expanded over the years. Today it is the home of the Administrator of the Panama Canal Authority. On up was the headquarters of the U. S. Southern Army Command.

The most pretentious old public building in Panama is the Panama Canal Headquarters Building on Ancon Hill. If you look over to Ancon Hill while you are still in the locks you can see the Panama Canal Headquarters about halfway up the hill. The building opened in 1914.

Inside are remarkable murals depicting the history and construction of the Canal that were created by William B. Van Ingen. Van Ingen, who had achieved considerable fame for his murals in the Library of Congress, agreed to produce the murals at $25 a square foot. The artist visited Panama twice during the Canal construction and made charcoal sketches. The murals were painted in his New York studio and eventually moved to Panama.

The Balboa area is mostly reclaimed land created with spoils from Culebra Cut. During the days of the U. S. Canal Zone Balboa was the central downtown for the U. S. Canal Zone with civic buildings, hospitals, movie theaters, a huge YMCA, and the major church in the Canal Zone.

Another U. S. installation, Albrook Air Force Station, was located just to the east of Balboa. Today it is Albrook or Gelabert Airport which is the national airport for flights within Panama. There is also a huge bus terminal with buses departing to all parts of Panama and Costa Rica as well as the gigantic Albrook Mall.

The Balboa container port is another massive port owned by the same Chinese company that owns the port on the Atlantic side.

The Chinese have been here since before there was a country named Panama. In 1852, "The Chinamen, one thousand in number, had been brought to the Isthmus by the [Panama

Until the Bridge of The Americas this old swing bridge was the only way to cross the Canal.

The entrance to the formerly secret U. S. Southern Command underground headquarters dug into Ancon Hill.

Railroad] Company, and every possible care taken which could conduce to their heath and comfort. Their hill-rice, their tea, and opium, in sufficient quantity to last for several months, had been imported with them - they were carefully housed and attended to - and it was expected that they would prove efficient and valuable men. But they had been engaged upon the work scarcely a month before almost the entire body became affected with a melancholic, suicidal tendency, and scores of them ended their unhappy existence by their own hands."[58]

The Chinese were involved in both the French and American efforts to build the Panama Canal. When you go under the Bridge of the Americas, on the west side of the Bridge, which you can't see, is a Chinese pagoda and a monument to the Chinese presence in and contributions to Panama for the past hundred years. Outside of Panama City most of the little "corner" stores are run by Chinese. We have tons of Chinese restaurants. Unfortunately for me, since I'm used to Chinese food in San Francisco and New York, Chinese food in Panama has been somewhat corrupted by a hundred years in Panama. (No Chinese restaurant in San Francisco or New York considers *patacones* or fried green plantain slices a staple of Chinese cuisine!)

Panama is one of the few countries in the world to recognize Taiwan. And since you can't recognize both, Panama doesn't officially recognize the People's Republic of China. To help preserve that relationship Taiwan has given Panama enormous amounts of aid. Of course the People's Republic of China, second largest customer of the Panama Canal, would dearly like to be the ones with official recognition, so it also gives enormous amounts of aid to Panama. Panama sits in the catbird seat, collecting cash from both sides.

Bridge of the Americas

The Bridge of the Americas was built by the United States in 1962 at a cost of $20 million and became the first permanent,

The mansion Ferdinand de Lesseps built for himself was moved to Ancon Hill by the United States and today serves as the residence of the Administrator of the Canal de Panama.

Van Ingen mural in the rotunda of the Panama Canal Headquarters.

non-swinging bridge to link together not just the country of Panama but also the continents of North and South America. Originally the bridge was called the Thatcher Ferry Bridge after the ferry service it replaced, but quickly became known as the Bridge of the Americas. When it was built it was the only permanent connection between the continents. Today there is also the Centennial Bridge and new proposed bridges at both ends of the Canal. A new road and bridge is proposed on the Atlantic side that will link Colon to the rest of the country and really open up development along the beautiful Caribbean coast of Panama and there are tentative plans for an additional bridge on the Pacific side to connect to new development around the old Howard Air Force Base.

The Bridge of the Americas has a total length of 5,425 feet [1,654 meters] in 14 spans, abutment to abutment. The main span measures 1,128 feet [344 meters] and the tied arch (the center part of the main span) is 850 feet [259 meters]. The highest point of the bridge is 385 feet [117 meters] above mean sea level; the clearance under the main span is 201 feet [61.3 meters] at high tide.

On May 18, 2010, the bulk cargo ship ATLANTIC HERO struck one of the protective bases of the bridge after losing engine power partially blocking this section of the Canal to shipping traffic.

The Bridge of the Americas and Centennial Bridge not only link the country together, but are jammed daily with commuters. They also carry the Pan American Highway traffic. The Pan-American Highway is a road network running from Prudhoe Bay, Alaska to the southern tip of Chile and Argentina. Except for a 54 mile [87 kilometer] break in the Darien jungle of Panama, the road links together the Americas for 29,800 miles [47,958 kilometers]. Although the road is quite good and safe through Panama, in some countries it is passable only in the dry season and in many places unsafe, particularly at night.

The Bridge of the Americas as seen from the top of Ancon Hill.

The bulk of Canal traffic is freight – only 8.9% of Canal revenue is from passenger ships.

Colombia would like to complete the section through the Darien jungle and connect with Panama, but that is unlikely. The Darien is a dense, impenetrable jungle that separates Colombia and Panama. Panama has enough problems with FARC Rebels, drug runners and clandestine drug laboratories set up by the Colombians along the border. Panama has begun working with the U. S. military to help with the problems along the Colombia border in the Darien.

Sometimes when listening to Panamanians, it sounds like all of the problems in Panama are caused by the Colombians. Drugs, en route to the United States, are an enormous problem. Panama has this huge coastline, much of it lined with jungle, and is right next door to Colombia. The drug problem will continue to worsen until the United States decriminalizes drug use, regulates and taxes distribution, and removes the profit incentive.

Once I have fought my way through Panama City traffic and I am up on the Bridge of The Americas, it is a seven-hour drive to my house in Boquete, not very far from the Costa Rican border.

Amador

During the construction of the Canal, waste material from the Culebra Cut was used to create the breakwater. Later the breakwater was expanded to create the Amador Peninsula linking together the mainland with the nearest offshore island of Naos.

During the U. S. days three forts protected the Pacific side of the Canal. On the Panama City side was Fort Amador, named for Manuel Amador Guerrero, the first president of Panama. Fort Grant consisted of the islands just offshore, some connected to Amador by the causeway. Fort Grant was named after the future U. S. president, then Captain Ulysses S. Grant, who marched across Panama in 1852. Fort Sherman was located on the other side of the Canal.

On the northern side of the Canal, opposite the Amador Peninsula, set back where you cannot see it, is what used to be Howard Air Force Base.

Since the United States pulled out of Panama, turning over all U. S. facilities to the Panamanians, Howard has sat virtually untouched. Panama wisely chose to wait on developing many of the former U. S. facilities. Recently the giant former USAF airstrip has been opened to charter flights. Copa Airlines, Panama's private flag carrier, has its maintenance center at Howard, and also maintains the aircraft of other major airlines. Copa flies out of Panama's Tocumen International Airport, operating 310 daily scheduled flights to destinations in twenty-nine countries in North, South, and Central America and the Caribbean. The airline has ninety planes and forty-three new Boeing aircraft currently on order. Tocumen is growing so rapidly that Copa and the airport facilities can hardly keep up with the demand. Much of the demand is from folks who don't want to put up with the intrusive hassle of connecting through the United States, so they choose Panama instead.

There are ambitious plans to develop Howard into a brand new city and free zone to be called Panama Pacifico, which will be one of the largest planned master developments in the hemisphere. The first stage of the project is a 58 acre [23.5 hectare] International Business Park that will offer industrial and commercial office space. Panama is working on plans for either a new underground subway system which may eventually go under the Canal to this new city, or another bridge across the Canal.

On the Southern, Panama City side, is the Country Inn & Suites hotel, complete with a T.G.I. Friday's restaurant. It costs about $130 a night for a room facing the Panama Canal. Frequently when I'm getting off a ship either with the pilot in the Canal or if the ship docks in Amador, I like to use this hotel. If I'm flying home, only about fifteen minutes from Albrook Airport, or if I'm driving its easy to get on the Pan American Highway.

During the U. S. Canal Zone years the area was closed to all but military personnel. After it was turned over to Panama, Amador was opened up and became a favorite place to stroll, bike, skate, walk, or just enjoy the fantastic view of Panama City. There is a major Convention Center which, among other things, has hosted the Miss Universe Contest. There are shops, hotels, condos, marinas, restaurants and clubs. The Smithsonian Tropical Research Institute [STRI] has a marine research station and a small museum area on one of the islands.

On the starboard side is the new Bridge of Life Museum of Biodiversity, designed by Frank Gehry who designed the Walt Disney Concert Hall in Los Angeles and the Experience Music project in Seattle. Panama's secret to getting this world-renowned architect to design this museum: his wife is Panamanian. The brightly colored jagged roofs are intended to represent the forces of nature that shape our world and created the Isthmus of Panama, the "bridge of life" connecting the continents.

If you look back over Amador you will catch a glimpse of modern day Panama City. Panama's population is around 3.7 million, and about fifty-five percent live in and around Panama City. Panama has one of the strongest economies in the region and is rapidly developing. The modern Panama City is crowded with high rise towers and I like to think of it as "Miami on steroids."

One of the iconic towers of Panama City is the Trump Ocean Club, a sail shaped building similar to the Al Arab hotel in Dubai. If you have good eyes, or binoculars, you may be able to catch a glimpse of the Trump Ocean Club on the port or left side, off in the distance over Amador peninsula.

Pacific pilot Station, where we bid farewell to our pilot, is located on Amador and this is the point where we officially leave the Panama Canal.

Fuerte Amador

The final islands at the end of Amador are called "Fuerte Amador" by the cruise lines, a fancy-sounding name for Naos Island, Perico Island, and Flamenco Island. At one time these islands were home to Fort Grant and provided major protection to the U. S. Panama Canal Zone. There were gun emplacements, defensive tunnels, and even a Hawk missile installation. Today the island hosts very expensive yachts of the rich and famous, has little boutiques and restaurants and those caves ... at night are discos where folks can crank up the music as loud as they wish.

The islands were favorites of the English pirates and privateers who raided the Spanish ships visiting Panama City. Sir Francis Drake, Captain Henry Morgan, and Captain James Cook all hid out in these islands.

At present there is no pier to handle cruise ships, so ships calling at "Fuerte Amador" anchor out and guests are tendered to a landing dock at the yacht club. If you are looking over Amador you are looking east. If you are taking a northbound cruise, you may actually get to see the sun *rising* over the Bay of Panama and the Pacific Ocean.

To the west, going up the Panama coast toward Costa Rica, is where a lot of the Pacific beachfront development is taking place. Farther up the coast there are a lot of resort communities and there is a lot of development going on the Azuero Peninsula that juts out into the Pacific.

Panama City skyline as seen from Amador.

Last look back at Panama City.

17. Questions & Answers

What I really look forward to when I lecture on ships transiting the Canal are the Q&A sessions. If you are in the planning stages for a Panama trip, you obviously have many questions. Based on questions I've answered in the past, maybe I can anticipate some of your concerns.

When is the best time to cruise the Panama Canal?

There is no one "best" time to cruise the Panama Canal or to visit Panama. Since we are about nine degrees off the Equator the weather is pretty much the same all year round. In the Canal area it is always hot and humid, just like you would expect in the Tropics. There is almost no variance in the daytime temperatures and very little in the nighttime temperature.

The Canal is surrounded by Rain Forest and so ... it rains! No matter when you visit it is likely that sometime during your transit of the Canal you will get some rain, even if it is just a sprinkle.

Usually in Panama there is more rain from May through November, the "green" season, and less rain from December to April, the so-called "dry" season, which in the Canal area just means the "less wet" season.

In Colon the driest months are January, February, and March and the wettest are September, October, and November.

The rain is warm and usually comes in a rather brief downpour and really doesn't interfere with our enjoyment of the Canal. Stick a cheap plastic poncho in your luggage and you'll do fine.

Most of the Canal cruises you find will be in the September to May period, not because the weather is better, but because during June to September the cruise lines make more money by having their ships positioned in Europe and Alaska.

Month	Mean Temperature °F		Mean Total Rainfall (mm)	Mean Number of Rain Days
	Daily Minimum	Daily Maximum		
Jan	65.3	92.1	29.3	2.9
Feb	65.1	93.6	10.1	1.3
Mar	65.1	94.6	13.1	1.4
Apr	67.1	95.7	64.7	4.9
May	70.0	94.1	225.1	15
Jun	70.3	92.8	235.0	16
Jul	69.8	93.0	168.5	14
Aug	69.6	93.0	219.9	15
Sep	69.8	91.2	253.9	17
Oct	69.4	90.7	330.7	20
Nov	68.5	91.2	252.3	16
Dec	66.6	91.9	104.6	7.5

Temperatures in °F – rain in millimeters – 25 mm is about 1 inch

What is the weather like?

As I said, it's pretty much the same the year round. January to March is a time when we get northerly winds which can make maneuvering the ship into the locks a little more tricky, since the ship acts as a giant sail. But, with a nice northerly breeze blowing across the decks, it makes it feel less hot and humid.

Panama is outside the hurricane zone, although we do

sometimes catch the edge of a tropical depression which can make for more rain than usual. While Panama is outside the hurricane zone, you may have to deal with tropical storms as you cruise in the Caribbean. Usually the ship can avoid the storm itself, but sometimes weather can delay airport traffic in and out of South Florida.

We are getting a balcony, which side of the ship is best?

There is nothing like a balcony stateroom I suppose, since if you are a crew member you are lucky and privileged if you can snag an old fashioned porthole! But from my days as a top-producing travel agency owner, I know that there is nothing like sitting on your own balcony in your Jockey shorts, or less, sipping wine and watching the sun set.

A balcony is ideal when you are cruising through Gatun Lake, but you don't want to spend the entire transit on your balcony! You want to move around the ship so you get to see different perspectives of the action.

In the locks it is a crap shoot. There is absolutely no way of knowing whether your ship will be assigned the port or left-hand chamber or the right or starboard side chamber. There is no way to psych this out, so either side is great!

Is it safe to do an independent tour in Panama?

The safest way to take a tour is always going to be with the ship. If the tour is late, stuck in traffic, or there is an accident along the way, the ship is going to wait until all the tours are back. If you have booked independently and are delayed you may miss the "boat" and have to find your own way to the next port to catch up with the ship. The tour operators the cruise lines use are vetted; they must have insurance, and are checked for basic safety. They are dependable, and the ship shore excursion office sends along ship escorts who report back on the quality of the tour. Additionally all guest comments are continually reviewed. If an operator doesn't perform, they are out.

In most ports it is easiest, most hassle free, and often most cost effective to use a ship's tour.

In some ports, like Panama, there is limited availability on things like the Panama Canal Railway and the Canal Ferry Excursion, and guess what? Right! The cruise lines and their big operators book all the space they can get which is generally all the space available.

I work cruises all over the world, including round the world cruises. There are some places in the world where you just want to go ashore and soak up the ambience or where there is convenient public transportation and it is easy to do your own thing. Panama is not that kind of place!

However, all that being said, there are people who just don't like hanging out in the lounge to be "stickered" and then marched ashore like a group of first-graders on a field trip, or delayed by one or two people who shouldn't have booked the tour in the first place. There are folks who just don't want to be with a giant group of "tourists," but in places like Ephesus, Athens, Rome, Paris, and London, or even exotic places like the Taj Mahal, Angkor Wat and Machu Picchu ... you may go independently, but you are going to end up at the "sights" surrounded by the same hordes of people and ship tours you sought to avoid.

There are a number of very reliable and excellent smaller tour operators in Panama who work out of both the Pacific and Atlantic ports. If you do your homework, you should end up with a good tour operator and have a fantastic day. Just be sure they allow for traffic and get you back to the ship on time!

How can I find independent tour operators I can trust?

Start your research online doing a Google search. Then try places like CruiseCritic.com, looking under the ports of call bulletin board. Another good source of information is

TripAdvisor.com. These sites and others will give you not only names of tour operators but evaluations of their services.

Naturally these independent tour operators are going to expect full or at least partial payment up front. Would you expect anything different? Would you hire and assign guides, and reserve buses just hoping that people might show up as promised? Of course not! Sometimes these independent tour operators will take credit card payments, but because they are small players, many times they will want you to use PayPal or similar. If you're not comfortable paying in advance, book with the ship.

There is also a Hop On Hop Off bus tour available of Panama City [City-Sightseeing.com] which you can book online in advance or just pay when you hop on the bus. Their big red buses are usually sitting near where the ship docks, or in the case of Fuerte Amador, where the tender drops you off.

Are there taxis available at the pier that will do tours?

But of course! Regular licensed taxis in Panama must be painted yellow with checkered stripe along the side. There are no meters. Taxis around town are relatively inexpensive, which is why everyone uses them. Traditionally there have been set zones and fares within those zones or if you cross over to another zone, although Panama City is experimenting with taxi meters. All the locals know these rates and of course you don't. Bingo, or as it's known locally, "Gringo Bingo!" Just accept that world-over many taxi drivers are out to take advantage of tourists. If you just accept that, and go with the flow, you will enjoy travelling the world a whole lot more with less frustration. Of course, sometimes you are going to get "ripped off"; it's just a part of travel.

There may also be "unofficial" drivers and vans eager to take you on tour. Many of these are just working guys with families eager to make a few extra bucks. They may even take you home to meet their families.

Generally the rate for a licensed taxi is going to run around $25 to $30 an hour.

Are they "safe"? Generally, yes. You pay your money and take your choice. If safety is your primary concern, stick with the ship.

What kind of vaccines do we need?

If you're from the United States, Canada, or Europe, generally vaccinations are unnecessary. If you are coming from a country that has yellow fever, you may be required to have a yellow fever vaccination.

Do I need to take malaria pills?

For the Canal and almost all of Panama, no! Your doctor may have a different opinion. Of course your doctor is in the business of ... well, you know. If you are just transiting the Canal ... no way!

Do we need a tourist visa?

If you are on a cruise ship transiting the Canal generally not, but the cruise line can advise you of any particular requirement given your citizenship. For North Americans no visa is necessary on a cruise. If you are flying in from North America to pick up a ship in Panama the cost of a tourist visa is included in the cost of your flight.

Are there lots of mosquitoes?

Sure, we have some mosquitoes, but nothing like Alaska or the mid-western United States in the summer. Since the days of the Canal construction controlling the mosquito population has been a priority. Transiting the Canal you are far enough from shore and the breezes are strong enough that you aren't going to find many mosquitoes. If you are taking a shore excursion into the jungle or on Gatun Lake you might want to

Watching the Canal go by from the Promenade Deck.

At work: Canal commentary from the Bridge.

take along bug spray to use if needed, but do so carefully without spraying everyone else or bathing in DEET.

Dengue is a problem throughout Latin America, the Caribbean, and the Southern United States, so it is best to be prepared. Interestingly, many ships don't sell insect repellant or cheap pocket plastic ponchos in the shops on board. Go figure!

Where can we find good coffee to take home?

Panama is known the world over for superb coffee, yet the good stuff is incredibly hard to find if you are on a cruise. Sometimes ships will sell "Coffee of The Type Used in The Panama Canal." That tells you nothing! The packages I've seen don't even tell you if it is Panamanian coffee or how old it is. At the grocery stores, like Super 99 in Colon, you will find the good local brands that people drink in Panama, like Cafe Ruiz, Palo Alto, Sitton and Duran. On the Panama Canal Railway they sell coffee from Boquete, where I live.

People always ask about my coffee. Our coffee is sold to a Panama Canal Pilot who has a number of coffee farms in our area. His coffee, containing our beans, is sold under the name Pilot's Coffee, which is very popular with the container crews transiting the Canal, and Eco Green Mountain Farm Café Arauz, which is sometimes available in stores in and around the Canal.

How can I get from the airport to the pier in Colon?

The best, easiest, most stress-free, and possibly cheapest way, is to use the cruise line transfer. There are cabs at the airport who will take you but it can be very expensive. It takes over an hour and the cab driver isn't going to have a return fare so is probably going to charge you close to double. A lot of Panama City cabs are using propane with a tank that may take up most of the trunk space so you may end up in a tiny Toyota in the back seat holding your suitcases.

If you are staying overnight at a hotel in Panama City you can ask the front desk to arrange something. You'll end up with someone's brother-in-law giving you a ride.

It is easiest and best to use the cruise line transfers. A car or van will run about $70 to $150 depending on the number of people, size of the vehicle, and where you are staying in Panama City.

I'm confused. Which Canal itinerary is best?

This is a frequent question, and, as I've said, there is no one "best" itinerary. It all depends on you, your time frame, your budget, your interests and the cruises you've taken before. Do you want to focus on the Panama Canal or do you want it to be just another experience of many?

The nice thing is that with the 100th Anniversary of the Canal and the completion of the new locks, there is a lot of interest in the Canal so cruise lines have developed a lot of great itineraries. I particularly like the ones that give you time to get off the ship and experience a full day exploring Panama before or after the Canal transit.

Repositioning cruises are generally offered in spring and fall and are longer and generally attractively priced. However, most repositioning cruises simple transit the Canal without allowing you opportunity to see Panama. You just need to choose what you want to do and what works out best for you.

There appear to be so many excellent tour choices in Panama. How do I decide?

Most cruise lines, when they list available tours, will list the most general, most popular tours that give you the best "overview" of a place first. As you move down the listing you'll find tours that concentrate on a particular aspect of a port, and near the end you generally find tours that are designed to appeal to more "active" people, or people who have visited that port previously. Which tour is best for you will depend on your interests and your physical abilities. Unfortunately most people only have a single day, so you've got to choose a single tour that is most in line with your interests. There is no one tour that is "best" for everyone.

You'll discover that Panama has so much to offer that you'll want to come back and visit again!

I've tried to include enough information in the "Seeing Panama" chapter to help you make an informed decision.

Our itinerary says we will do a daylight transit but also that we enter the Canal at 500 a.m. What time does sun rise? Won't it be dark?

Cruise ships almost always make a daylight transit of the Canal. The pilot comes on board around 5:00 a.m. The sun is up by 6:30 a.m. which is when you should be entering the first lock.

Why do we have to get up so early?

You don't! It's your cruise; you can sleep all day if you want. But if you came to experience the Panama Canal, you will want to experience the entire transit. Early morning on Canal day as the sun is coming up is absolutely magical! The pilot will generally come on board at 5 00 a.m. By 6:30 a.m. you are generally moving into the locks. It's your choice, but I'd suggest an early wake up call.

Where can I find Indian crafts, Kuna molas and Embera baskets?

You will find some of this craft work in gift shops all over Panama and maybe the shops on board will even bring some on board to sell the day you are in the Canal. Although what is sold on board may be hand made, it is lesser quality than you will find ashore. The best place to buy Embera crafts is on the Authentic Embera Village tour, since there all of the money is going directly to the Indian family who made the craft. There used to be a big Indian craft market at Pier 6 Cristobal, when that was still in existence. The operators of the new piers will only allow the Indians to sell their crafts if they pay exorbitant prices to rent retail spaces just like the same big stores you see in every cruise port. There is a great selection of craft items behind the YMCA in Balboa, a regular stop on some of the Panama City tours. If you are going independently and visit the Old City (the original city which is different than Casco Viejo) there is also a big Indian craft market right next to the famed Old Panama Tower. There are several stores in Casco Viejo that have a great selection of Indian crafts as well.

Our ship is going to be in the Canal over the Holidays; will that make a difference?

No, the Panama Canal operates twenty-four hours a day 365 days a year. I was actually in the Canal doing a turn around cruise on Christmas Day. Santa managed to locate the ship and arrived on the fore deck while we were in Gatun Lake! All of the tours operated as scheduled.

Spending the holidays at sea is a fantastic idea ... all the celebration and fuss ... without any work! What could be better?

Which cruise line is best?

You think I'm crazy? For fifteen years I ran successful "cruise only" agencies and frequently was asked this question. My answer has always been the same, "It depends." All of the cruise lines work hard to cultivate a particular niche of the market and aim their product at a particular type of guest. You need to find one that is a good fit for you and meets your expectations.

The Canal itself is the same regardless of the cruise line. I'd look at itineraries and I'd look at the type and amount of information and background they give you about the Canal transit. On Caribbean cruises, world cruises, and other

Christmas Day in the Canal.

Up close and personal with the Canal on the Promenade Deck

itineraries, people book to get away, to escape bad weather or to see "the world." On Canal cruises people book for one very specific reason: the Panama Canal. So you want to find a cruise that focuses on the Canal, and where it isn't just "another cruise" with bingo and line dancing as highlights.

Where is there duty free shopping? I've heard Colon has a huge free port?

There are duty free shops at the airport and at or near some of the cruise terminal areas. These are the same duty free shops you see at airports around the world, which may, or may not have better prices than Walmart.

Panama is not known for "duty free shopping" for cruise passengers, like in St. Maarten, the Virgin Islands, Aruba, etc. Colon does have the world's second largest Free Zone but that is not "duty free shopping" in the cruise ship sense of the phrase. A free zone allows manufacturers and companies to import huge containers of goods that can be assembled, or labeled, or just broken up and shipped off to other ports without paying any import or export duty. Buyers come from all over the world, and particularly this region, to buy container loads of goods. Major companies stockpile goods and parts to be able to conveniently ship them around the world from Panama, the "crossroads of the world."

Tourists from other Latin American countries do come to Panama to shop, but they are usually here with enough time to find the things they want, or they hire a local who knows the way around the giant, sprawling Colon Free Zone.

If you have your passport and cruise card or are a crew member sometimes you will be allowed into the Colon Free Zone, but you will be disappointed. It is a vast city set up for wholesale, not retail. And while you may find an occasional little store that will sell retail, you have to know where you are going and it can be very time consuming.

For many Latin American tourists, Panama City is a giant

shopping mall. There are several large malls, each trying to out do the other. Wealthy Latin Americans come to Panama just to shop and purchase goods they cannot get at home, including high end designer items.

What is the difference between an eastbound and a westbound transit? Is one any better than the other?

As you undoubtedly know by now, because the Canal runs north-south, going from the Pacific to the Atlantic is northbound and from the Atlantic to the Pacific is southbound.

I frankly can't think of any reason why one way is better than another. If you come up with a reason, please let me know.

The only one possible advantage of going southbound is that on most ships, because of changing time zones, they turn the clock back and you gain an extra hour of sleep so 5:00 a.m. doesn't seem quite so early.

We're cruising with a disabled family member. How accessible are the tours in Panama?

It really depends on the nature of the disability. Be sure to discuss this with the shore excursion desk on board. They are in touch with the tour operators and know what, if any, accommodation can be made. Although Panama is making great strides, we do not have anything to compare with the Americans With Disabilities Act and for the most part "accessibility" is a new concept.

We're traveling with our children, grade school through high school. The Authentic Embera Village tour looks very interesting but I am concerned about the nudity.

First, talk with your kids. I suspect they have been exposed to a whole lot more nudity than you've ever imagined, including a whole lot else! Attitudes toward nudity are pretty much cultural, and even within a culture attitudes vary at different times. An infant sees bare breasts and thinks, "lunch," and when he's a teenager he is off to his room locking the door. In the context of the Embera Village it is very natural, totally non erotic, and forgotten about in the first ten minutes.

It will be fantastic experience for your kids regardless of their age. I would encourage you to let your younger kids just run off and play with the Indian kids and make new friends. The Indian kids love this and so do the children of guests. Kids tend to cross cultural differences and barriers much more quickly than adults. Let your kids get painted with the black juice or *jagua* fruit tattoo ink. Don't worry, it only lasts for about three weeks and if your kids go back to school with Embera body decoration they will be the envy of all their classmates! And you might try it yourself! Just imagine going back to work with black decorations on your face!

Where can I find Panama Hats?

The real Panamanian "*campesino*" hats run $25 and up, but are rarely found in Panama City, and usually not in gift shops. They don't look like your stereotype of a "Panama Hat." The Panama Hats you are probably thinking of are the ones made in Ecuador. You'll find cheap made-in-China ones for $10 and up in most tourist shops, the good ones for $80 and up, and the really good Montecristi ones start at $500!

We are embarking and disembarking our cruise in Colon. Is it feasible to rent a car and see the country safely in two weeks time? I'm very interested in the non city experience, in seeing rural Panama, both coast lines, the mountains etc.

Absolutely. Driving in Panama City is a hassle and not for the faint of heart. But once you are outside of the city, driving is fine. Main roads are generally in good condition. Except for one small section of the Pan American Highway, now being rebuilt, the Pan American Highway is a good road and the seven hour trip from Panama City to Boquete is interesting and gives a good view of the lives of most Panamanians outside the city. All the major rental car companies have offices in Panama City as well as in David should you choose to fly to David and rent a car. Here's my suggestion for two weeks.

Days 1-4 – Panama City area. You can hire a cab for around $25 to $30 an hour. The front desk of your hotel can give you suggestions. See Old Panama, the old French area of Casco Viejo including the Interoceanic Canal Museum, Opera House, and Golden Altar. See the Canal itself including the Miraflores Locks visitor center. Your driver can call and check the schedule so you are actually at the visitor center when a ship is in the locks. Or you can try the Hop On Hop Off bus in Panama City. [City-Sightseeing.com] Arrange an all day tour to the Embera Puru, maybe through Anne Gordon, a *gringa* who married an Embera guy. [EmberaVillageTours.com]They will pick you up at your hotel and it will be a memorable day.

Days 5-6 – Stay at the beach. Decameron is an all-inclusive beach resort that's about an hour from Panama City. [Decameron.com] Most of these all-inclusive resorts have transfers available from Panama City.

Days 7-10 – Fly to David, rent a car, and drive forty minutes to the tiny town of Boquete, nestled in the mountains where the air is fresh and cool. We have hiking expeditions, river rafting, canopy zip line tours, coffee tours and more.

Days 11-12 – Drive to Bocas del Toro, a funky, laid back, somewhat noisy town in the Caribbean islands.

Days 13 – Drive back to David, and fly back to Panama City.

Day 14 – Fly home.

That will give you a whirlwind tour of Panama and you'll be anxious to return for more. Of course you can work out a much shorter itinerary as well.

Are there any beaches nearby to the ports in Panama?

Not really. Panama has fantastic beach areas and beach resorts, but they just aren't near to Panama City and Colon.

Why are there no shore excursions to the San Blas Islands?

There just isn't enough time for a shore excursion to visit the San Blas Islands, but it is one of the things that you want to arrange when you return to Panama. It's definitely at least an overnight trip even flying from Panama City.

Is it possible to just rent a car and do your own thing in Panama?

Anything is possible, but ... definitely not recommended. You have to be nuts to drive in Panama City or Colon. If you are planning to spend time in Panama outside the cities either before or after your cruise, renting a car may work well. All of the major car rental agencies are at Tocumen International Airport. If you are just spending a day or a few hours in Panama, it will take you that long to get anywhere, and you may well miss the boat and spend the rest of your life driving in circles!

Is it safe to just walk around town without a shore excursion? What could we see and what would we miss?

Short answer: no, and you'd miss everything.

There is nothing really to see in Colon and it is not an area where it is safe to wander around.

At Amador you are out on the end of the Amador Peninsula and except for some shops and restaurants there isn't much there. It's a twenty-minute ride into Panama City proper. At night I wouldn't just wander around in the city without knowing which areas are safe and which areas are sketchy. I wouldn't wander around alone Casco Viejo at night without knowing what I was doing. During the day if you take a cab into town you can wander around a mall, but the things you want to see are spread around town and you'd have to keep jumping in and out of cabs. What I'd suggest is the Hop On Hop Off bus which will pick you up at the port on the Panama City side. If you're not booking a tour in Colon, stay on the ship and have a massage.

Our tour leaves at 10:00 a.m. and doesn't return until 4:00 p.m., but there is only a snack included. My husband needs to eat regularly because of a medical condition.

You didn't hear this from me, because every ship in the world is going to tell you not to take any food off the ship. There are some places in the world (Australia, New Zealand, and the United States for example) where they are incredibly anal about this; Panama is not. I'm sure there must be signs, somewhere, but I have never seen any actual agricultural inspection, although I suspect this is going to change as Panama moves toward "first world" status.

For most cruise passengers missing a meal is not an ordeal but a needed privilege! But there are people who do need to have something to eat on a regular basis and, I agree, it isn't too smart to take people out over lunch time without giving them something to eat or at least the opportunity to purchase something.

Don't tell anyone, but my wife always sticks a box of Fruit Loops from the breakfast buffet in her purse or back pack. If you take a bagel sandwich, an apple, or some nuts and dried fruit from the noontime buffet, I doubt if you will get thrown in a Panamanian jail. Packaged items, like a little box of cereal, generally aren't problems, except of course in Australia and New Zealand.

Why are so many of the tours in Panama so long? Seven or eight hours are a long time!

Unfortunately the things that you really want to see aren't

right next to the pier. The "better" tours in Panama are all longer ones.

How can I find out if you are going to be lecturing on my cruise?

Heck, I'd like to be on them all! Obviously, that's not possible and there is a whole world out there to explore. You can ask the cruise line; in fact I'd like it if you do!

We're only going to be in Colon for a few hours. Is there anything to see or do?

Unfortunately the short evening calls are mainly "service calls" to pick up guests returning from shore excursions. There's really nothing to see or do in Colon, nor is it particularly a safe area. Get off and you'll end up spending most of your time in a long line waiting to get back on board. There are some gift shops at Colon 2000 and a Super 99 where you can pick up essentials.

Can you drink the water? What about mixed drinks?

In most parts of Panama water is pretty safe, but I think visitors are always advised to take along bottled water. It is hot, humid, and you need to keep hydrated, so take a big bottle from the ship.

Almost all ice in Panama is made commercially and is fine in drinks.

Are there bathrooms on the buses?

Generally, no. The buses in Panama may not be what you are used to in other parts of the world. Ease up on the coffee the morning of your tour. Go before you leave the ship. If you need to go en route, tell the driver and he will find a place to stop. Public restrooms, although they have western-style toilets (i.e. not squat toilets), generally aren't the cleanest (as is true everywhere in the world) and usually do not provide toilet paper, so stick a small roll in your backpack or take along a pack of tissue.

This is usually easier for men, since it is culturally appropriate, except in cities and built-up areas, to just go beside the road. On more than one excursion I've watched the tour bus driver pull over, walk to the back of the bus, and relieve himself while the ladies on the bus went into apoplectic shock because the driver, who'd already been sitting at the port for two hours waiting for the tour to board, was relieving himself.

I understand there are a lot of North Americans and Europeans moving to Panama - what's the deal?

Oh, bless you for asking! Panama has become a very attractive destination for expats from around the world. The lower cost of living, beautiful beaches and weather is attracting many Baby Boomer retirees. Others, maybe fed up with the direction their home governments are taking or looking for a "safe haven," are relocating to Panama. If you want the whole story order my book *The New Escape to Paradise: Our Experience Living and Retiring In Panama.*

Thank you for purchasing and reading *Panama Canal Day*. I know you will have a more enjoyable cruise knowing about Panama, the amazing history of the Canal, and what to expect on your Panama Canal Day!.

Please **do me a favor and write a review about the book on Amazon. If you're a CruiseCritic.com fan, mention it there as well. Thank you!**

Here's toasting your Panama Canal Day!

It is more fun if there is another ship in the next chamber.

Our Ship & Our Bill

We need a hypothetical ship for our journey since Canal tolls and procedures vary according to the size of the ship, so meet … our ship!

MV OUR SHIP

- Built 1999 at Fincantieri, Monfalcone, Italy
- Cost $350 million
- Gross Registered Tonnage 77,441 tons
- Net Registered Tonnage 44,193 tons
- Panama Net Registered Tonnage 63,441 tons
- Length 856 feet [260.9 meters]
- Breadth 105 feet [32 meters]
- Draft 26 feet [7.9 meters]

- Total Berths 3,070
- Propulsion 4 Diesel Electric Engines
- Thrusters 2 Bow, 2 Stern
- Cruising Speed 21 knots

Now comes the moment of reckoning … how much?

Total toll based on 3,070 berths at $134 per berth $411,380[59]

Estimated Additional Costs $76,802

Advance transit reservation fee $25,000
Daylight transit reservation fee $30,000
Regular pilotage included
Tug services $11.445
Line handlers $4.745
Wires to locomotives $3,600
Inspection fee $118
Sanitary Inspection Fee $173
Medical Disembarkation in Locks $632
Disembarkation & escort ship's photographers $590
Vessel Internet information charge (prorated) $135
Launch Services $364

TOTAL COST $488,182

Over a hundred years later, a salute to the men and women who did the impossible.

"It is not the critic who counts, not the man who points out how the strong man stumbled, or where the doer of deeds could have done them better. The credit belongs to the man who is actually in the arena; whose face is marred by dust and sweat and blood; who strives valiantly, who errs and comes short again and again; who knows the great enthusiasms, the great devotions, and spends himself in a worthy cause; who, at the best, knows in the end the triumph of high achievement; and who, at the worst, if he fails, at least fails while daring greatly, so that his place shall never be with those cold and timid souls who know neither victory nor defeat."
- Theodore Roosevelt

Concrete forms for locks.

Concrete mixing team.

Roughnecks.

Italian workers.

Goethals on site 1914.

American engineers pose for group photo.

Main culvert Pedro Miguel.

Workers from Barbados arriving on the SS ANCON.

Key Dates in Panama History

- 1501 -- Rodrigo de Bastidas, sailing west from Venezuela was the first European to sail along the coast of Panama
- December 1502 -- Christopher Columbus, on his fourth voyage to the New World, lands in Bocas del Toro
- January 1503 -- Christopher Columbus built a garrison at Rio Belen
- 1509 -- Spanish colonization began in what is today Colombia, Ecuador, Venezuela and Panama
- September 25, 1513 -- Balboa claimed the "Southern Ocean" (later renamed the Pacific) for Spain
- 1519 -- Panama City was founded
- 1538 -- Royal Audiencia of Panama, a judicial court with jurisdiction from Nicaragua to Cape Horn, established in Panama City

- 1572 -- Sir Frances Drake successfully captured Nombre de Dios on the Atlantic side
- 1573 -- Drake captures a mule train carrying silver across the Isthmus
- January 27, 1671 -- British privateer, Sir Henry Morgan, captured Panama City
- 1698 -- Creation of the ill-fated Scottish colony of New Caledonia in he Darien
- 1713 - Creation of the Vice Royalty of New Granada
- 1819 - Liberation of New Granada from Spin
- November 10, 1821 -- "The Cry of Freedom of The Village of Los Santos"
- November 28, 1821 -- Panama declares independence from Spain and joins New Granada and Venezuela in Bolivar's recently founded Republic of Colombia
- December 26, 1848 -- California-bound gold seekers began arriving in Panama
- 1850 -- Colon founded as the terminus of the Panama Railroad
- 1855 -- Panama Railroad opened
- 1880 --- Ferdinand de Lesseps began the French effort to build the canal
- May 3, 1881 -- Compagnie Universelle du Canal Interocéanique incorporated under French law
- February 4, 1889 -- The French effort was abandoned and Compagnie Universelle du Canal Interocéanique was declared bankrupt and dissolved

- 1894 -- Philippe Bunau-Varilla became stockholder and spokesman in the New Panama Canal Company, offering to sell the company's assets to the United States for $109 million, asking price later reduced to $40 million

- June 19, 1902 -- U. S. Senate voted in favor of Panama as the canal site

- June 28, 1902 -- The Spooner Bill authorized the United States to construct canal and purchased concession from France for $40 million

- September 17, 1902 -- U. S. troops sent to Panama to keep railroad open as local Panamanians struggled for independence from Colombia

- January 22, 1903 -- Hay-Harran Treaty with Colombia giving the United States right to build a canal was passed by Senate, but not ratified by Colombia

- October 10, 1903 -- Philippe Bunau-Varilla met with U. S. President Theodore Roosevelt warning him of imminent rebellion in Panama

- November 3, 1903 -- With USS NASHVILLE standing by in Panama and Bunau-Varilla standing by in Washington, Panama proclaimed independence from Colombia with the only casualties being a shopkeeper and a donkey

- November 6, 1903 -- Panama officially declared its separation from Colombia

- November 7, 1903 -- The United States officially recognized the Republic of Panama

- November 18, 1903 -- Claiming to represent the newly created Republic of Panama, the Frenchman Bunau-Varilla granted the United States a strip of land across

Panama and the rights to build a canal and in return the United States agreed to protect the new country

- February 3, 1904 -- U. S. Marines clashed with Colombian troops attempting to re-establish Colombian sovereignty in Panama

- February 23, 1904 -- The United States paid Panama $10 million for the Canal Zone

- May 4, 1904 -- The United States began Canal construction

- 1904 -- Panama adopted U. S. dollar as its currency calling it the "Balboa"

- 1904 -- Dr. William Gorgas took over as chief sanitary officer

- November 8, 1906 -- U. S. President Theodore Roosevelt visited Panama becoming the first U. S. president in history to leave the country while in office

- 1907 -- George Washington Goethals took control of the Canal Zone and construction

- August 24, 1909 -- The first concrete was poured in the locks

- 1912 -- The Chagres River was dammed

- October 10, 1913 -- U. S. President Woodrow Wilson pushed a button in Washington triggering an explosion in Panama, exploding the temporary Gamboa Dike and allowing water to fill Gatun Lake

- August 15, 1914 -- With the world occupied by a World War, the Panama Canal quietly opened with the ANCON making the first official crossing

Southbound from the Atlantic to the Pacific

- April 20, 1921 -- Thomson-Urrutia Treaty signed – United States paid Colombia $25 million in return for Colombia's recognition of Panama's independence

- October 2, 1941 -- El Banco Central de Emisión de la Republica de Panamá was established and authorized to issue 6 million balboas worth of paper notes, but only 2.7 million were issued

- October 9, 1941 -- Ricardo Adolfo de la Guardia Arango replaced Arias as president in a coup supported by the United States and the new government immediately closed the bank, withdrew and burned the so-called "Arias Seven Day" notes

- November 2 & 28, 1959 – Feelings of prejudicial and discriminatory policies against Panamanians in the Canal Zone led to pressure to fly the Panamanian flag within the Zone and when demands to fly the flag were refused, Anti-American riots broke out in Panama City

- September 1960 – U. S. President Dwight David Eisenhower authorized the Panamanian flag be flown alongside the U. S. flag in designated areas of the Canal Zone

- January 1963 -- U. S. President John F. Kennedy orders that wherever a U. S. flag is flown in the Canal Zone that is not on a U. S. military base, a Panamanian flag should be flown next to it. This was hated by the Zonians[60] and began what are called "The Flag Wars" exacerbating tensions between Panamanians and the United States (After Kennedy was assassinated, the Governor of the Canal Zone took it upon himself to rescind the Presidential order.)

- January 9, 1964 -- Anti-United States rioting broke out

United States Panama Canal construction.

Can you find the two little guys in the lower left hand corner?[61]

and twenty-one Panamanian civilians and four United States soldiers were killed including six Panamanian teenagers; now celebrated as a national holiday called "The Day of the Martyrs"

- January 10, 1964 -- Panama broke off relations with the United States and demanded a revision of the original Canal treaty

- October 11, 1968 -- Panamanian President Arnulfo Arias was ousted in a coup by General Omar Torrijos

- August 10, 1977 -- United States and Panama began negotiation for Panama Canal turnover

- September 7, 1977 -- U. S. President Jimmy Carter and General Omar Torrijos signed the Torrijos-Carter Treaties abrogating the Hay-Bunau-Varilla Treaty and setting 1999 for the turnover of the Canal

- April 18, 1978 -- U. S. Senate ratified the Torrijos-Carter Treaties by a vote of sixty-eight to thirty-two

- October 1, 1979 -- Under terms of the 1977 Panama Canal Treaties the United States returned the Canal Zone to Panama, excluding the Canal itself

- July 31, 1981 -- General Torrijos died in a plane crash

- August 12, 1983 -- General Manuel Noriega assumed command of the National Guard

- 1985 -- Dissident leader Hugo Spadafora was decapitated - Noriega later sentenced in Panama to 20 years in prison for the murder

- February 25, 1988 -- Panamanian President Eric Arturo Devalle removed Noriega as commander and was subsequently ousted as President and Noriega took control

- March 18, 1988 -- Noriega declared a "state of urgency"

- April 8, 1988 -- U. S. President Ronald Reagan issued an Executive Order blocking all Panamanian interests, property, and funds in the U. S.

- May 7, 1989 -- Voters rejected Noriega but Noriega refused to recognize election results

- May 9, 1989 -- U. S. President George H. W. Bush in the light of "massive irregularities" in Panamanian elections called for Noriega to step down

- May 10, 1989 -- Noriega nullified elections won by his opposition leader Guillermo Endara

- May 11, 1989 -- U. S. President George H. W. Bush recalled U. S. ambassador and beefed up U. S. troops stationed in Panama

- October 3, 1989 -- Noriega foiled attempted coup and had coup leaders executed

- December 20, 1989 -- United States military invaded Panama in "Operation Just Cause" – In the early morning hours on a U. S. Military base Guillermo Endara was sworn in as President. (Endara was the "presumed winner" in a scheduled presidential election cancelled by General Noriega.)

- December 24, 1989 -- Noriega took refuge at residence of Papal Nuncio in Panama City

- January 3, 1990 -- Noriega surrendered to U. S. forces, was flown to Miami and arraigned in U. S. Federal District Court in Miami on drug-trafficking charges

- January 18, 1991 -- United States acknowledged that

the CIA and U. S. Army paid Noriega $322,226 from 1955-1986 and that Noriega began receiving money from the CIA in 1976 giving credence to the claim of Noriega's lawyers that he was the "CIA's man in Panama"

- April 9, 1992 -- Noriega convicted of drug and racketeering charges, sentenced to serve forty years as a POW, entitling him to maintain his rank as a General ... of an army of one since Panama had abolished the military
- 1995 -- Noriega was convicted in Panama in absentia for the 1989 murder of officers involved in a failed coup
- October 1, 1996 -- Fort Amador was transferred to Panama
- November 1, 1999 -- United States turned over Howard Air Force Base, Fort Kobbe and other territories to Panama
- December 14, 1999 -- Former U. S. President Carter symbolically turned over Panama Canal to Panamanian President Mireya Moscoso
- December 31, 1999 -- United States officially turned over Panama Canal to Panama
- 2000 -- Panama was named the "#1 Retirement Destination" and North American and European retirees began relocating to Panama
- September 1, 2004 -- Panamanian President Martin Torrijos proposed an $8 billion expansion of the Panama Canal
- October 22, 2006 -- Voters approved $5.25 billion Panama Canal Expansion proposal by 78 percent

- September 3, 2007 -- Construction began on the Panama Canal Expansion adding a "third lane" of new locks

- April 26, 2010 -- Noriega completed his U. S. prison sentence and after a lengthy legal fight was extradited to France where he began serving sentence for money laundering, not as POW treated as a General, but as a common criminal

- September 4, 2010 -- The one millionth ship transited the Panama Canal, a Chinese vessel named FORTUNE PLUM, carrying steel and crossing from the Pacific to the Atlantic

- February 1, 2011 – First concrete poured for new locks in Panama Canal expansion project

- December 2011 -- United States and France agreed to let Noriega be extradited home to Panama where he faces a 67-year prison term. Noriega was incarcerated in El Renacer Prison in Gamboa, next to the Panama Canal

- February 2012 -- Panama introduces a one Balboa coin equal in value to $1 U. S. because of the short lifespan and high expense of U. S. paper $1 bills, called the "Martinelli" after Panama's President Ricardo Martinelli

- November 2013 -- Panama's Metro line 1 opens, the first subway in Central America

- August 14, 2014 --The 100th Anniversary of the Panama Canal

- June 2015 the expanded Panama Canal is scheduled to go into service but due to cost overruns, contractual disputes, date is pushed to January 2016

U. S. Military Installations in Panama 1904 to 1999

Many people who served in the U. S. Military in Panama, or had relatives who served, are curious as to what happened to some of the bases that were abandoned when the U. S. withdrew.[62]

Name	Unit	Abandoned	Current name	Current use
Galeta Island, USN - Atlantic	CDAA (Wullenweber) radio detection	2002		
Fort Randolph, USA – Atlantic, Margarita Island	coastal defense	1999		
Coco Solo, USN – Atlantic, near Colon	submarine base	1999	Manzanillo Internationa l Terminal	container terminal
Fort De Lesseps, USA – Atlantic, Colon	coastal defense	1955		
Fort Sherman, USA – Atlantic, opposite Colon	coastal defense, Jungle Operations Training Center	1999	harbor: Shelter Bay Marina	unused, marina

Name	Unit	Abandoned	Current name	Current use
France Field, USN & USAF – Atlantic, near Colon		1949	Enrique Adolfo Jiménez Airport	airfield
Gatun Tank Farm, USN – Atlantic, near Gatun Locks	underground fuel storage with oil terminal at Cristobal	1991		
Fort Gulick – Atlantic, Gatun Locks	School of the Americas	1984, 1999	Fuerte Espinar	hotel Melia
Fort William D. Davis, USA – Atlantic, Gatun Locks	infantry, jungle warfare training, special forces training		Jose Dominador Bazan	residential area
Semaphore Hill, USN – Inland, Culebra Summit	long-range radar and communications link	1979, 1995	Canopy Tower	nature observatory
Summit, USN – Inland, Culebra Summit	Naval Communications Station Balboa, VLF (sender)			
Fort Clayton, USA – Miraflores Locks	HQ US Southern Command, communications	1999	Ciudad del Saber	academic campus, residential housing, schools
Albrook AFS, USAF - Pacific, near Balboa		1999	Albrook "Marcos A. Gelabert" Internationa l Airport (PAC)	regional civil airport
Arraijan Tank Farm, USN – Pacific, opposite Balboa	underground fuel storage with oil terminal at Rodham	1997		civil usage (PATSA)

Name	Unit	Abandoned	Current name	Current use
Rodman Naval Station, USN – Pacific, opposite Balboa	harbor		Vasco Nuñez de Balboa, PSA Panama Internationa l Terminal	Panamania n National Maritime Service, container terminal
Fort Amador, USA – Pacific, near Balboa	coastal defense	1999		recreation, new hotel (2001)
Naval Communications Station Balboa, USN – Pacific, near Fort Amador	HQ radio communications			
Farfan, USN – Pacific, near Howard AFB	Naval Communications Station Balboa (receiver)		Radio Holland Panama	marine communica tions
Howard Air Force Base, USN – Pacific, opposite Balboa		1999	Panama Pacifico	real estate (developme nt)
Fort Grant, USA – Pacific, near Balboa	coastal defense	1948	Islas Naos, Perico, Flamenco	tourism
Fort Kobbe, USA – Pacific, near Howard AFB		2000		
Transisthmian Pipeline, USN – cross Isthmus				

By The Numbers

Republic of Panama

- Panama 28,702 square miles [74,338 square kilometers], a little smaller than South Carolina or the Czech Republic
- 1,547 miles [2,490 kilometers] of coastline
- Highest Point: Volcán Baru 11,398 feet [3,474 meters]

Transit

- New York to San Francisco via Canal 6,000 miles [9,656 kilometers] compared to 14,000 miles [22,531 kilometers] around Cape Horn
- From beginning to end the Canal is 50 miles [80.5 kilometers]
- 35-40 ships a day 365 days a year, 24 hours a day since 1963 for a potential maximum of 14,600 per year
- About 225 passenger ships per year
- Flags & Designation:
    - "Zulu" - Priority Transit
    - "Hotel" - Pilot on Board
    - Southbound - Even numbers
    - Northbound - Odd numbers
    - "Bravo" - Flammable cargo on board

        - "Tango" - Toxic or radioactive material on board
        - "Golf" – I need a pilot
- Average transit time 10 – 12 hours
- Passenger ships, over 50 passengers, get priority transit
- Top five customers: United States, People's Republic of China, Chile, Japan and South Korea
- 36 tug boats

Atlantic Side

- Bay of Limon 4.5 miles [7 kilometers] long and 2.5 miles [4 kilometers] wide
- Bay of Limon Breakwaters 6 miles [9.6 kilometers] long and 425 feet [130 meters] wide at the base
- From Limon Breakwater to Gatun Locks is 5.4 miles [7.2 kilometers]

Pacific Side

- Bridge of The Americas built 1962 by United States at cost of $20 million. Total length 5,425 feet [1,654 meters] in 14 spans. Main span 1,128 feet [344 meters]. Center part of main span is 850 feet [259 meters] and at highest point is 384 feet [117 meters] above mean sea level. Clearance under the main span is 201 feet [61 meters] at high tide.

Locks

- Gatun Locks – 3 stages – raises or lowers vessel 85 feet [25.9 meters]
- Gatun Lock chambers 110 feet [33.5 meters] wide, and 1,000 feet [304.8] meters long
- Lock gates throughout operated by 15 HP motor and hydraulic arms, originally 50 HP motor operated giant gears

- Culverts deep within the walls 18 feet [5.5 meters] in diameter
- 14 lateral side wall and 10 lateral center wall culverts
- 105 openings in chamber floor 4.5 feet [1.3 meters] wide
- The upper lock has an additional "T" culvert with 5 additional openings in the chamber floor
- Each steel lock leaf is 65 feet [19.8 meters] wide, 7 feet [2.1 meters] thick and from 47 to 82 feet [14.3 to 25 meters] high and weighs from 390 to 730 tons
- Tides on Atlantic 1-2 feet [.5 meter], Pacific tides can be as high as 23 feet [7 meters]
- Pedro Miguel is one chamber – raises or lowers ship 29 feet [8.8 meters] between level of Gatun Lake and Miraflores Lake
- Miraflores Lake is man-made transitional lake about 1.3 miles [2.1 kilometers] and is 54 feet [16.5 meters] above sea level
- Drop from Miraflores Lake to Pacific approach varies due to tidal differences on the Pacific between 43 feet [13.1 meters] at extreme high tide and 64.5 feet [19.7 meters] at extreme low tide

Locomotives

- $1.9 million each, electric powered by third rail, 50 tons, 2 winches
- 100 locomotives each weighing 50 tons
- Powered by 290 HP traction units
- Towing capacity 178 to 311.8 kilo depending on speed
- Maximum return speed 10 miles per hour [16 kilometers] per hour

Gatun Lake & Water

- Not unheard of to have rain falling at 3 to 4 inches [76 to 102 millimeters] an hour
- Can get up to 200 inches [5 meters] of rain a year, average 130 inches [3.3 meters]

- Each transit uses 53.4 million U. S. Gallons [202,000 cubic meters] during transit
- Gatun Lake has area of 164 square miles [425 square kilometers] at normal level
- 1,100 miles [1,770 kilometer] shoreline
- About 85 feet [25.9 meters] deep prior to current Canal expansion project

<u>Gatun Dam</u>

- 2100 feet [640 meters] thick at bottom
- 7,500 feet [2,286 meters] long at the top
- 98 feet [30 meters] thick at the top
- At normal level of Gatun Lake top of dam is 30 feet [9 meters] above lake level
- Crest of dam spillway is 16 feet [4.9 meters] below normal lake level
- Spillway dam has 14 electrically operated gates each 46 feet [14 meters] wide by 20 feet [6 meters] high
- Capacity of spillway is 140,000 cubic feet [4,100 cubic meters] of water per second more than the maximum flow of Chagres River
- If necessary lock culverts theoretically can release additional 49,000 cubic feet [1,400 cubic meters] of excess water per second
- Dam contains 22 million cubic yards [17 million cubic meters] of material and weighs some 30 million short tons [27 million long tons]
- Dam covers 290 acres [1.17 square kilometers] of ground
- Earth and rock in Gatun Dam could build a wall 5 feet [1.5 meters] high and1 foot [.3 meters] thick all around the earth at the Equator
- Lake stores 4,200,000 acre feet of water [5.2 cubic kilometers] which is about as much water as comes down the Chagres River in an average year

Excavations & Gaillard Cut

- Total 232 million cubic yards excavated by United States
- French excavated 78 million cubic yards, 30 million cubic yards of which were useful to the United States
- Added together about 262 million cubic yards more than four times the volume originally estimated by de Lesseps
- Gold Hill 662 feet [201.8 meters]
- Continental divide taken from 210 feet [64 meters] to 40 feet [12.2 meters] above sea level
- Centennial Bridge opened in 2004, built by Panama at a cost of $120 million. Total span 3,451 feet [1,052 meters], main span 1,051 feet [320 meters] clears canal by 262 feet [80 meters]. Supporting towers are 604 feet [184 meters] high. West tower set back 164 feet [50 meters] to allow for future widening of Canal.
- Average depth of Canal channel is 43 feet [13 meters] and the minimum depth is 41 feet [12.5 meters] although changing as Canal is deepened as part of expansion program
- Width varies from 500 to 1,000 feet [152 to 305 meters] and is increasing as Canal is enlarged as part of expansion program

Cost of Construction

- The cost of the Canal including French and American expenditures was $639 million, in today's dollars, with inflation, that $639 million is well over $16 billion
- The final U. S. cost was $23 million below the 1907 estimate
- Lives lost:
    - 20,000-25,000 lives lost during French effort
    - 5,609 lives lost during U. S. construction
    - Approximately 500 people died for every mile of the Canal

Revenue

- Preferential booking fee $25,000
- Daylight transit reservation $30,000
- No show forfeit
- Late 50-100 percent
- Passenger ships pay $134 per berth
- In 86 years U. S. operated Canal paid Panama the original $10 million, plus $250,000 per year after the first nine years, or a total of $29,250,000
- In the first year of Panama's operation the Canal made a direct transfer to the government of $252 million
- During first four years of Panama's operation Canal made direct transfers to the government of $1.1 billion
- Annually has been contributing around $400 million per year
- When expansion completed direct transfer to government estimated to be $1.2 billion per year
- Canal generates over $2 billion per year
- $5.25 billion is cost of expansion program

For Further Reading

Since this book only briefly hits the highlights of the history of the Canal and Panama, hopefully you will be intrigued and stimulated to do further reading.

Abbot, Willis J. *Panama and The Canal: In Picture and Prose.* New York, Syndicate Publishing, 1914.

Detrich, Richard. *The New Escape to Paradise: Our Experience Living and Retiring in Panama.* Amazon-Createspace, 2014.

Detrich, Richard. *A Gringo's History of Panama.* Amazon-Createspace, 2014.

Dinges, John. *Our Man in Panama: How General Noriega Used The US and Made Millions in Drugs and Arms.* New York, Random House, 1990.

DuTemple, Lesley A. *The Panama Canal: Great Building Feats.* Minneapolis, Lerner Publishing Group, 2003.

Frair, William. *Adventures in Nature: Panama.* Berkeley, Avalon Travel Publishing, 2001.

Galbraith, Douglas. *The Rising Sun.* New York, Atlantic Monthly Press, 2001.

Green, Julie. *The Canal Builders.* New York, Penguin Press, 2009.

Independent Commission of Inquiry on the US Invasion of Panama, *The US Invasion of Panama: The Truth Behind Operation Just Cause.* Cambridge, South End Press, 1999.

Jackson, Eric. *"The Martyrs of 1964'*, online article at czbrats.com.

Johnson, Willis Fletcher. *Four Centuries of The Panama Canal.* New York, Henry Holt and Company, 1906.

Keller, Urlich. *The Building of The Panama Canal in Historic Photographs.* New York, Dover Publications, 1984.

Kempe, Frederick. *Divorcing The Dictator: America's Bungled Affair with Noriega.* New York, Putnam, 1990.

Koster, R.M. & Sanchez, Guillermo. *In The Time of Tyrants: Panama 1968-1990.* New York, W W Norton & Co, 1990.

Lindsay-Poland, John. *Emperors in The Jungle: The Hidden History of The US in Panama.* Durham, Duke University Press, 2003.

Mc McCullough, David. *The Path Between The Seas: The Creation of The Panama Canal 1870-1914.* New York, Simon & Schuster, 2004.

Noriega, Manuel and Eisner, Peter. *The Memoirs of Manuel Noriega: America's Prisoner.* New York, Random House, 1997.

Parker, David. *Panama Fever.* New York, Doubleday, 2008.

Perkins, John. *Confessions of An Economic Hit Man.* San Francisco, Berrett-Koehler Publishers, 2004.

Ridgely, Robert S and Gwynne, John A. Jr. *A Guide to The Birds of Panama.* Princeton, Princeton University Press, 1992.

One of the best resources about the Canal is the official Canal de Panamá website *www.PanCanal.com.* It is well done and loaded with information.

More Panama from Richard Detrich

Ever wonder why so many people from all over the world are choosing to retire in Panama?

In ***The New Escape to Paradise: Our Experience Living and Retiring in Panama,*** I share why we choose Panama and how we discovered a lifestyle that enables us to live better for less.

Here's what you need to know if you've ever thought of "escaping" to paradise.

"Not only informative, but well-written, funny and keeps your attention."

"Escape from superficial 'blue sky' Panama travelogues ... Richard goes the extra mile to give you a realistic assessment."

"This book has honestly been more helpful to me than any other expat book I have picked up."

"Part memoir, part practical information, Richard's book is full of helpful information about what to consider when moving to another country. His writing style is friendly and I felt like I was listening to a friend sharing his experiences."

"The best information I have found anywhere about relocating to Panama."

"Like a good friend, he gives you honest answers."

Panama A to Z is the companion book to ***The New Escape to Paradise.***

Here's the A to Z of what we've learned about living in Panama ... important stuff, not so important but interesting stuff, and funny stuff. Included is an English Guide for The Panama Citizenship Test.

If you have thoughts about getting a Panamanian Passport you'll need to pass a multiple choice test in Spanish about the government, history and culture of Panama. The test is in Spanish, but it is easier to learn the information you need to know first in your native language.

Panama has a fascinating history and the more you know about the history of Panama, the better you will be able to appreciate living in Panama.

Sometimes I hear tourists and expats pontificating about the history of Panama and they have it all backwards, so I wrote ***A Gringo's History of Panama***. Interestingly a private university in Panama has decided to use this book as a textbook in a history course for Panamanians who are learning English!

Endnotes

---

[1] All Holland America ships are "dam" something or other! WESTERDAM, ZUIDERDAM, ROTTERDAM, etc.

[2] According to the Panama Canal Office of Admeasurement Billing Supervisor the per berth fee applies to all berths whether occupied or not and to all crew berths whether occupied or not.

[3] "Panamax" are the mid-sized cargo ships that are capable of passing through the lock chambers of the Canal. A Panamax vessel cannot exceed 294 meters [965 feet] in length, 32 meters [105 feet] width and 12 meters [39.5 feet] draught in order to fit in lock chambers and fit under the Bridge of the Americas. "Post Panamax" ships are those that were knowingly built too large to use the original Canal locks. "New Panamax" is the official Panama Canal term for ships that will be able to utilize the new locks. A New Panamax vessel cannot exceed 366 meters [1,200 feet] in length, 49 meters [160.7 feet] in width, and 15 meters [49.9 feet] draught.

---

[3] People always ask about my coffee. Our coffee is sold to a Panama Canal Pilot who has a number of coffee farms in our area. His coffee, containing our beans, is sold under the name Pilot's Coffee, which is very popular with the container crews transiting the Canal, and Eco Green Mountain Farm Café Arauz, which is sometimes available in stores in and around the Canal.

[5] Wikipedia, Creative Commons Attribution-Share Alike 3.0 Unported license.

[6] Wikipedia, Creative Commons Attribution-Share Alike 3.0 Unported

[7] Wikipedia, Creative Commons Attribution-Share Alike 3.0 Unported license
[8] F. N. Otis, *Illustrated History of the Panama Railroad, 1862*, p. 26.

[9] Ibid, pp. 26-27.

[10] Ibid, pp. 27.

[11] Gatun now lies under the Panama Canal, the Gatun Locks having been named to honor the city that was flooded to created Gatun Lake.

[12] Otis, p. 34..

[13] Ibid, p. 35.

.

[14] Ibid, pp-35-36.

[15] Ibid, p. 56.

[16] Otis p. 72.

[17] Ibid, p. 139.

[18] Ibid, p. 78.

[19] Ibid.

[20] Ibid., pp. 78-79.

[21] Ibid, pp. 46-49.

[22] Ibid, p. 103.

[23] Ibid, p. 104.

[24] Ibid, pp. 108-109.

[25] Although often locally often called alligators, the animals in Panama are actually the American crocodile.

[26] Ibid, pp. 109-110.

[27] Ibid., p. 121.

[28] Ibid.

[29] Ibid, p. 127.

[30] Mathew Parker, *Panama Fever*, P. 49.

[31] The "Monroe Doctrine" [1850] said that further efforts by European nations to colonize or interfere in countries in North and South America would be viewed as acts of aggression requiring U. S. intervention. Likewise, the United States would not interfere with existing European colonies nor meddle in international concerns of European countries. Obviously, this "doctrine" has been selectively applied through the years, always in what was thought to be the best interests of the United States.

[32] Willis Fletcher Johnson, Four *Centuries of The Panama Canal* [1906], P. 100.

---

[33] Ibid, P. 101.

[34] Matthew Parker, *Panama Fever*, p. xxi.

[35] David McCullough, *The Path Between The Seas: The Creation of The Panama Canal 1870-1914*, p. 323

[36] R.M. Koster and Guillermon Sanchez, *In The Time of The Tyrants: Panama 1968-1990* New York, W.W. Norton & Company, 1990. p 390

[37] pp. 390-391

[38] David McCullough, *The Path Between The Seas: The Creation of The Panama Canal 1870-1914*, P. 610

[39] Ibid, p. 611

[40] David McCullough, *The Path Between The Seas: The Creation of The Panama Canal 1870-1914.*

[41] Wikipedia, GNU Free Documentation License, Version 1.2. The diagram shows six outlets on the floor, there are actually only five.

[42] The Panama Canal Society [pancanalsociety.org], CZ Brats [czbrats.com], and the Panama Canal Museum in Florida [cms.uflib.ufl.edu/pcm/Home.aspx] which closed the actual museum in 2012 and transferred its collection to the George A. Smathers Libraries at the University of Florida, in Gainesville, FL, are all aspects of preserving the experience and history of the U. S. Zone. These organizations hold reunions and frequently sponsor trips and cruises back to Panama.

[43] I have been unable find the original source of this photograph.

[44] *Life Magazine*, January 24, 1964.

---

[45] Journalist Eric Jackson has written one of the best accounts of these events entitled, "*The Martyrs of 1964*" and is reproduced online at http://www.czbrats.com/Jackson/martyrs/martyrs.htm

[46] Frederick Kemp, *Divorcing The Dictator: America's Bungled Affair With Noriega.* New York, G.P. Putnam's Sons, 1990 p. 29

[47] An interesting story: on another cruise, working a ship doing the Canal on a regular basis, on the final formal night, I was working the crowd before the evening show, and volunteered to take a photo of two couples, with one of the men decked out in a formal military uniform. I took the shot, then stupidly asked what uniform it was. Turned out it was a U. S. Army dress uniform. That was when I noticed the stars. This retired U. S. Army General had been in charge of the Adjutant General's office of the Southern Army Command and had overseen the arrest of Noriega. He had sat in on all of my lectures. Unfortunately since it was the last night of the cruise we never had the opportunity to talk further.

[48] Peter Eisner in *The Memoirs of Manuel Noriega, America's Prisoner.* P. 249.

[49] Canal de Panama, *2013 Annual Report*

[50] Ibid.

[51] Ibid.

[52] PanCanal.com

[53] Ibid

[54] For what it's worth … If *I* were President of Panama I would nationalize the country's gold production, since by Panama law all mineral rights already belong to the government. I'd horde all the gold in the national treasury and operate the country with *two* currencies, the U. S. dollar *and* the Balboa. The currency of commerce would be the U. S. dollar. The Balboa currency would be gold coins in large denominations. I would say to the United States, "Fine, we've given you access to all our bank records for deposits of U.S. dollars, but when it comes to the Balboa … go pound sand." You would see a flood of money moving into Panama.

[55] And you can read all about it in my books *The New Escape to Paradise: Living and Retiring in Panama* and *Panama A to Z.*

[56] GNU Free Documentation License, Version 1.2

[57] Photo: Rodolfo Aragundi Wikipedia Creative Commons Attribution-Share Alike 2.0 Generic license.

[58] F. N. Otis, *Illustrated History of the Panama Railroad, 1862*, PP. 35-36

[59] According to the Panama Canal Office of Admeasurement Billing Supervisor the per berth fee applies to *all* berths whether occupied or not and to *all* crew berths whether occupied or not. [5-12-14]

[60] "Zonians" is a term still used to describe mostly U. S. citizens who worked and lived in the U. S. Canal Zone, some military and some civilians working for the Canal. Sometimes these were people whose families had lived in the Zone for several generations.

[61] Actually *four* guys: two holding the ladder at the bottom, one at the top, and one climbing.

[62] Wikipedia, based on William H. Ormsbee, Jr.

051414

CPSIA information can be obtained at www.ICGtesting.com
Printed in the USA
LVOW01s2131190914

404947LV00008B/189/P

9 781495 388361